English Vocabulary Elements

English Vocabulary Elements

A Course in the Structure of English Words

THIRD EDITION

WILLIAM R. LEBEN

BRETT KESSLER

AND

KEITH DENNING

Oxford University Press is a department of the University of Oxford. It furthers the University's objective of excellence in research, scholarship, and education by publishing worldwide. Oxford is a registered trade mark of Oxford University Press in the UK and certain other countries.

Published in the United States of America by Oxford University Press
198 Madison Avenue, New York, NY 10016, United States of America.

© Oxford University Press 2023

All rights reserved. No part of this publication may be reproduced, stored in a retrieval system, or transmitted, in any form or by any means, without the prior permission in writing of Oxford University Press, or as expressly permitted by law, by license, or under terms agreed with the appropriate reproduction rights organization. Inquiries concerning reproduction outside the scope of the above should be sent to the Rights Department, Oxford University Press, at the address above.

You must not circulate this work in any other form
and you must impose this same condition on any acquirer.

Library of Congress Cataloging-in-Publication Data
Names: Leben, William Ronald, 1943- author. | Kessler, Brett, 1956- author.
Title: English vocabulary elements : a course in the structure of English words / William R. Leben and Brett Kessler.
Description: 3rd edition. | New York, NY : Oxford University Press, [2023] | Includes bibliographical references and index. |
Identifiers: LCCN 2022041742 (print) | LCCN 2022041743 (ebook) | ISBN 9780190925475 (hardback) | ISBN 9780190925482 (paperback) | ISBN 9780190925505 (epub) | ISBN 9780197521083
Subjects: LCSH: Vocabulary. | English language—Grammar. | English language—Study and teaching (Higher)
Classification: LCC PE1449 .L329 2023 (print) | LCC PE1449 (ebook) | DDC 428.1—dc22/eng/20220902
LC record available at https://lccn.loc.gov/2022041742
LC ebook record available at https://lccn.loc.gov/2022041743

DOI: 10.1093/oso/9780190925475.001.0001

9 8 7 6 5 4 3 2 1

Paperback printed by Sheridan Books, Inc., United States of America
Hardback printed by Bridgeport National Bindery, Inc., United States of America

CONTENTS

Preface vii
List of Figures xiii
List of Tables xv
Symbols and Abbreviations xvii
About the Companion Website xxiii

1. The Wealth of English 1

2. The History of English and Sources of English Vocabulary 19

3. Morphology: The Structure of Complex Words 45

4. Allomorphy 91

5. Phonetics 115

6. Regular Allomorphy; Numeric Elements 137

7. Meaning Change 167

8. Usage and Variation 193

9. Latin and Greek Affixes in English 213

10. The Prehistory of English and the Other Indo-European Languages 235

11. Later Changes: From Latin to French to English 257

Appendix 1. Elements to Glosses 275
Appendix 2. Glosses to Elements 293
Glossary 311
Further Reading and Research Tools 327
Index 331

PREFACE

INTENDED AUDIENCE FOR THIS BOOK

This book is designed for college-level courses about English words and word structure. It explores how units of a language—sounds, word elements, words—function together and how a language functions in society over time. The ultimate aim is to acquaint native and nonnative English speakers with aspects of English vocabulary that may be new to them. This includes practice in analyzing complex words, tracing how English got to its present state, and outlining factors that influence people's attitudes toward English usage. We hope this book will serve students in any field of study looking for better comprehension of English vocabulary as well as anyone curious about the language, its development over time, and its growing importance as a world language.

As the primary language of the World Wide Web, English is a more widespread tool of communication than ever. We hope that this book will supply readers with knowledge that will help them use English more effectively and understand others better. Ideally, we hope to impart the curiosity about the language that has motivated us to write this book.

The book's first goal is to expand vocabulary skills by teaching the basic units of learned, specialized, and scientific English vocabulary. To make sense of current English word structure and to build word analysis skills that will continue to prove useful, the book presents basic principles of word formation and word use and shows how these have affected

English since its beginnings. This in turn leads to further topics, including phonetics and the relationship of English to other Indo-European languages. Along the way, we make a stab at the difficult question of what is considered good English. In covering such a broad range of material, the book provides an introduction to some of the most important concepts of modern linguistics.

USING THIS BOOK

Key concepts are shown in boldface when introduced (e.g., **gloss** and **doublet**). We stress, though, that as important as the definitions may be, a bigger goal is to gain an idea of the role of these concepts in the overall system of language.

Lists of word elements to be memorized accompany most chapters. Wherever possible, the elements are placed in a chapter where they will illustrate and round out some of the chapter's content. Following them are a variety of exercises. Some help build familiarity with word elements by putting them to use in words. Others apply principles from the chapters to new cases. We hope the book's organization encourages you to master material as you encounter it instead of saving memorization until the end.

VOCABULARY-BUILDING TECHNIQUES

Students may find flashcards useful for memorizing word elements. A simpler method is to cover one side of the list of elements and glosses and, going from top to bottom and then from bottom to top, to try to recall the element for each gloss and then the gloss for each element. Other approaches to the task of self-drilling for memorization include repeating word elements and glosses to yourself until you cannot internally hear one without the other, or finding a rhyme or mental picture that helps you associate elements with their glosses (e.g., *"tom* 'cut' is easy to remember as the root of *atom* or because it's the name of my friend Tom, who can be very **cut**ting").

USING A DICTIONARY

As a companion to this text, we strongly recommend a bound or online dictionary designed for college level or above. An excellent choice is *The American Heritage Dictionary of the English Language*, https://www.ahdictionary.com. A particularly useful feature of this dictionary is an appendix of Indo-European roots, tracing many everyday words back to their source. A more comprehensive version of that appendix was published separately as *The American Heritage Dictionary of Indo-European Roots* (3rd ed., 2011). Another good choice is *Merriam-Webster's Collegiate Dictionary* (11th ed., 2020, https://www.merriam-webster.com).

For a larger dictionary, consult the *Oxford English Dictionary* (*OED*, 2nd ed. in 20 vols. plus CD-ROM; Oxford: Oxford University Press, 2009). A more current version is available online through some libraries or by subscription: https://www.oed.com. The *OED* is an ideal resource for this course, offering detailed etymologies and tracing word meanings through their entire history in the language. Another standard resource is *Webster's Third New International Dictionary, Unabridged* (Springfield, MA: Merriam-Webster, 1961). It is undergoing constant revision under the name *Merriam-Webster Unabridged*, accessible by subscription at https://unabridged.merriam-webster.com.

Later in the book we refer you to specialized references for topics like medicine and botany.

Using a dictionary effectively is a skill that must be learned. The first step is to become comfortable with the basic layout of the dictionary. Most good ones make this task easier with explanations of entries, lists of abbreviations, and so forth, in the introductory pages. Taking the time to read this material can help avoid frustration later.

Nowadays most dictionaries are also accessible online. These are invaluable for many kinds of searches (e.g., finding all words that end in *-archy*, or words whose definition contains the word *government*). An additional advantage is that many online dictionaries are updated far more often than their hard-copy counterparts. Still, many readers find that going to the printed page permits a level of browsing that can't be duplicated on computer screens.

One of the best ways to attack the bewildering variety of English vocabulary is to check a dictionary when you confront unfamiliar, difficult, or interesting words. For the most recent additions to the language, the most useful tools may be Urban Dictionary at https://www.urbandictionary.com and the English version of Wiktionary at https://en.wiktionary.org. Each has its limitations. Many of Wiktionary's entries are compiled by bots, and Urban Dictionary is 100 percent crowdsourced. But for many purposes, the loss in authority is well balanced by access to very recent changes in the language.

When you come across an unfamiliar word or element, take a moment to look it up or at least make a note of it for later reference. In the end, learning to look for and recognize the elements and words you have already learned in the course (as well as those you acquire on your own) will keep you from having to check the same references again and again, thus maximizing the time available for exposing yourself to entirely new information.

MOVING BEYOND THE FINAL CHAPTER

This book doesn't contain 1 percent of what the authors find interesting about English vocabulary. We will judge the text successful if the groundwork laid here motivates readers to explore further and provides enough skills to undertake such explorations.

More comprehensive lists of Latin and Greek word elements than those in the appendices (compiled from the element lists at the ends of chapters) can be found in works listed at the end of this book. These works list elements according to a variety of principles, but a little searching can help you find and identify many new word elements.

The World Wide Web is a rich source of lists of words and word elements. By far the most comprehensive is https://www.english-corpora.org, a collection of very large English-language corpora representing many varieties of written and spoken English, accessible through a versatile set of search tools.

ACKNOWLEDGMENTS

We owe profound thanks to our students and teaching assistants over the years for many helpful and insightful suggestions. The course that led to this book owes its development to the textbook *Structure of English Words*, by Clarence Sloat and Sharon Taylor—now in its fifth edition (Dubuque, Iowa: Kendall/Hunt, 2011)—and to course materials prepared by Robert Stockwell, and we are indebted to these sources for first showing the way. We are also grateful to many colleagues for generous and helpful comments and corrections: to J. David Placek, Robert Vago, and R. M. R. Hall, and the late John J. Ohala, who offered extensive suggestions for the first edition. Special thanks to JoAn Chase, Ivan Chow, Bahram Darya-Bari, Sally Eberle, Tamiko Eto, Herant Katchadourian, Suzanne Kemmer, Joan Maling, Joe Meyers, Nasreen Sarwar, Beverly Benz Treuille, Rosette Weiss, and many students over the past few decades for corrections to the first and second editions. Thanks also to Daniel Leben-Wolf for doing the art.

Tragically, Keith Denning, coauthor of the first edition, passed away suddenly in 1998.

NEW TO THIS EDITION

Most chapters have been revised to bring out key principles of word analysis; illustrative examples have been updated and new ones added. One guiding principle was to make the book easier to follow for students—native and nonnative speakers alike—seeking to improve their English vocabulary skills. Analyses of individual words and word groups have been updated and corrected, and Chapter 3, the longest chapter, has been rewritten for greater clarity. Because it introduces the principles and tools of word analysis that are used in the rest of the book, and because we hope the book will be of use even in courses with no prerequisites, many definitions of technical terminology appear that may be new to students. To bring chapter 10 into closer conformity with updated Indo-Europeanist transcription practices, we now use the same system found in Wiktionary's etymologies rather than conjectural International Phonetic Alphabet. Some reconstructions have also been updated.

Most figures were redrawn for improved readability. New word study questions and exercises have been added to the end of each chapter, with more explicit instructions replacing some of the ones for existing questions and exercises. The more technical chapters now include self-tests to help students check their progress through the chapter. Bibliographical references have been revised extensively to replace older references with more up-to-date ones, and all now have current web links.

The glossary and appendices have been streamlined, the first by omitting terms too well known or too peripheral to require a definition, and the second by omitting word elements not in the element sets at the end of chapters. These element lists have added examples to better illustrate the range of variant forms the elements take. The index, too, was streamlined by dropping entries for specific words and word elements. In their place are entries and subentries on additional topics from the book.

Finally, we have added a companion website to the third edition to help students master the course material. The website has quizzes on vocabulary elements and supplementary interactive exercises and drills on essential points from the text. The companion website is available at https://oup.com/us/EnglishVocabularyElements.

FIGURES

2.1 Stages in the development of English and some of its relatives 23
2.2 Major paths of borrowing from Greek and Latinate sources into English 35
2.3 Developments involving word elements meaning 'wine' up to Modern English 36
3.1 Representing the ambiguity of *undoable* 52
5.1 The articulatory apparatus 118
7.1 Development of the meaning of *horse* 174
7.2 Development of the meanings of *hysterical* 174
7.3 A real horse 176
7.4 A metaphorical horse 177

TABLES

1.1 Changes in sound in Latin and French and their results in borrowings 9
2.1 The Great Vowel Shift 33
5.1 Places and manners of articulation of English consonants 124
5.2 Vowels of American English 126
6.1 Most common pronunciations of the Latin letters in Classical Latin and in Modern English 139
6.2 Classical numeric elements 153
6.3 Prefixes of the International System of Units 155
7.1 Meanings of the suffix *-ous* 168
7.2 Meanings of the suffix *-ic* 168
7.3 Stages in the history of the word *horse* 173
7.4 Metaphoric extensions of meaning of spatial prefixes 178
7.5 Building words with Latin spatial prefixes 186
7.6 Building words with Greek spatial prefixes 188
9.1 Nominative plural endings in Latin and Greek 216
9.2 Noun-forming suffixes 220
9.3 Adjective-forming suffixes 221
10.1 Cognate words in Latin, Greek, and Sanskrit 236
10.2 Some obstruent correspondences and reconstructed PIE 238
10.3 The consonants of Proto-Indo-European 241
10.4 Consonant correspondences for PIE, Greek, Latin, and English 247

SYMBOLS AND ABBREVIATIONS

INTERNATIONAL PHONETIC ALPHABET

The following symbols are used in the text when a pronunciation must be described precisely. The boldface parts of the words beside each symbol illustrate the sound; more precise definitions can be found in chapter 6, "Phonetics." Unless otherwise noted, the keywords are to be given current standard American pronunciations. The phonetic symbols used here are those of the International Phonetic Association (IPA). This is the standard transcription system for linguistic work as well as for popular reference sources such as Wiktionary, https://en.wiktionary.org/. Further information about this phonetic alphabet is available in the *Handbook of the International Phonetic Association* (Cambridge: Cambridge University Press, 2013, https://www.internationalphoneticassociation.org/content/handbook-ipa).

When these symbols are used, they are enclosed in square brackets. For example, "the word bathe is pronounced [beð]" or "the sound [ʒ] occurs at the end of the word *rouge*."

a	h*o*ck; also in *ride* [raɪd], ***ou**t* [aʊt]
ɒ	h*aw*k
æ	c*a*t
b	*b*oy
d	*d*og

dʒ	*badge*
ð	*they*
e	*made*
ə	*elephant, cut*
ɛ	*pet*
f	*fat*
g	*go*
h	*hot*
i	*machine*
ɪ	*pit*
j	*hallelujah, yell*
k	*kiss*
l	*left*
m	*mark*
n	*nice*
ŋ	*sing*
o	*rose*
ɔ	*horse*; also in *joy* [dʒɔɪ]
p	*pot*
r	*run, irk*
s	*sit*
ʃ	*ship*
t	*top*
tʃ	*catch*
u	*prune*
ʊ	*put*
v	*vote*
w	*worm*
x	German *Bach*, Scottish *loch*, Hebrew *Hanukkah* (a raspy [k])
y	French *tu*, German *Übermensch* ([i] with rounded lips)
z	*zoo*
ʒ	*pleasure*
θ	*thigh*

SYMBOLS AND ABBREVIATIONS   xix

Many North Americans do not distinguish [a] and [ɒ] in their speech, so that *hock* and *hawk* sound alike. In addition to these symbols based on letters, we also use the following characters:

'   Precedes a stressed syllable: "*record* is pronounced [ˈrɛkr̩d] when a noun and [rɪˈkɔrd] when a verb."
ː   Follows a long sound. For American English the mark is not necessary, but the contrast between short and long sounds is important for many other languages: "Latin [ˈakɛr] 'maple' vs. [ˈaːkɛr] 'sharp.'"
r̩   A vertical stroke under a consonant means that it forms the core of a syllable instead of a vowel: "*butter* [ˈbətr̩], *apple* [ˈæpl̩]."

MODIFIED ORTHOGRAPHY

When the precision of the IPA is not required, it is often more convenient to indicate certain aspects of the pronunciation of a word by adding diacritics to the standard spelling, or **orthography**, of the word. For example, if we wish to note that the first vowel in the Latin word for "sharp" is long, we can write "*ācer*" rather than "⟨acer⟩ [aːkɛr]." The diacritics used in orthography are as follows:

¯   Placed over a long vowel: "Latin *ācer* 'sharp'
˘   Placed over a short vowel: "Latin *ăcer* 'maple' "

ABBREVIATIONS

A	adjective
ADV	adverb
cf.	compare (Latin *confer*)
G	Greek
L	Latin

lit.	literally
ME	Middle English
ModE	Modern English
N	noun
OE	Old English
PREP	preposition
SI	International System of Units
V	verb

TYPOGRAPHICAL CONVENTIONS

Typefaces

italics	When words are cited (talked about rather than used functionally), they are set in italics. The same applies to word elements and phrases: "It depends on what the meaning of *is* is"; "The word *prefix* begins with the prefix *pre-*."
bold	Boldface is used to draw the reader's attention to a specific word or element: "*epi-* means 'additional' in words like ***epi**thet* 'nickname.'"
CAPS	Small capitals are used for words and abbreviations describing parts of speech: "*record*$_N$ has a different stress from *record*$_V$."

Punctuation and Other Symbols

In addition to regular double quotes—"..."—which have their everyday meaning, the book uses the following types of quote marks for specific linguistic purposes:

⟨...⟩   When the discussion deals specifically with spelling, letters are enclosed in angled brackets: "the letter ⟨s⟩."

SYMBOLS AND ABBREVIATIONS

[...]   Pronunciation may be indicated by placing phonetic symbols between square brackets: "[tɪr] and [tɛr] are both spelled ‹tear›."

' ... '   If meaning (rather than sound or spelling) is the focus, a word or phrase appears within single quotes: "Greek *cosmos* 'universe.'"

ˣ ...   The mark ˣ before a word means that it is ill-formed: "the past tense of *write* is not ˣ*writed*."

* ...   The mark * before a word or element means that it is unattested, but we have reason to believe it existed: "The word *chief* must come from a popular Latin word **capum*, not the classical Latin *caput*."

Other special symbols include the following:

X < Y	X descended from Y: "*oak* < OE *āc*."
Y > X	Y developed into X: "*āc* > *oak*."
Y → X	X developed from Y by some morphological or analogical process: "Irregular English plurals include *ox* → *oxen* and *goose* → *geese*."
X~Y	X and Y are variants: "The past tense of *dive* is *dived~dove*."
∅	Zero, the absence of a sound or letter: "The plural of *deer* is formed by adding ∅."
X-	More material must be added at the end of X to make a complete word. Prefixes and stems are cited with a trailing hyphen: "*pre-*," "*writt-*."
-X	X is a suffix: "*-ism*."
X-Y	A hyphen inside a word separates morphs: "There are three meaningful components in the word *black-bird-s*."
(...)	When part of a word or morph is in parentheses, that part doesn't always appear: "The morpheme *cur(r)* appears in *recur* and *recurrent*."
/	In a phonological rule, / separates the statement of the change from the description of the environment in which it takes place.
___	In the environment of a phonological rule, ___ stands for the sound under discussion: "n → m / ___ p" means that [n] becomes [m] before a [p].

ABOUT THE COMPANION WEBSITE

www.oup.com/us/EnglishVocabularyElements

Oxford has created a website to accompany *English Vocabulary Elements: A Course in the Structure of English Words*, Third Edition. The companion website includes supplementary materials that could not be published in the book. For instructors, there is a password-protected Instructor's Manual with an answer key and additional quizzes. For students and other readers, there are sets of flash cards for each chapter. These learning materials are intended to help the student master the content of each chapter.

One

The Wealth of English

WORD POWER AND A WORLD POWER

In the number of speakers who learn it as a first or second language, and in its range of uses and adaptability to general and specific tasks, English is the world's most important language today. It is the mother tongue of several hundred million people. Its rich verbal art, great works in science and scholarship, and major role in international commerce and culture have made English the most frequently taught second language in the world.

English is not the first language of as many individuals as Mandarin Chinese. But it is spoken over a much vaster area. In North America, Europe, Asia, Africa, and elsewhere, it is the official language of many nations, including some where English is not most people's first language. Native speakers of English number about 5 percent of the world's population, yet over 60 percent of websites are in English.

A history of political importance as well as a certain linguistic suppleness has endowed English with an enormous vocabulary. *Webster's Third New International Dictionary* contains 476,000 words, and these do not include the many technical terms that appear only in specialized dictionaries for particular fields or recent neologisms, not to mention all the regular plural forms of nouns, the different present and past tense forms of verbs, and other words derived from these words.

The size of the English vocabulary has some wonderful advantages. Although it may be true that any concept can be expressed in any language, a language can make the process easier or harder by providing or not providing appropriate words. Thanks to the well-developed word stock of English, English speakers have a head start over speakers of other languages in being able to express themselves clearly and concisely.

Whether one uses this head start or not is, of course, up to the individual, but speakers with a good command of vocabulary can say things in more subtly different (and, hence, often more effective) ways than others can, and this ability is noticed.

- We refer to friends and acquaintances as good speakers, fast talkers, or boring conversationalists.
- Vocabulary knowledge is a key to good academic performance.
- A job or school application or interview often turns on how adept at using language the interviewee is.
- We find that we can overcome individual and group handicaps once we're recognized as effective communicators.

In cases like these, success or failure hinges on our degree of skill in expressing ourselves and in understanding others in speech and in writing. The expressive power of language is enormous, and every time a word acquires a new shade of meaning—a common development, as we will see—the language is enriched. Still, novel uses of language are not always welcomed by everyone, and in a later topic we have a look at changes to language that are treated by some as signs of decline and by others as signs of growth.

The enormous size of the English vocabulary also has its disadvantages, as we are reminded each time we have to use a dictionary to look up a word we don't know or because a word we recognize is used in a way unfamiliar to us. A language as vocabulary-rich as English is full of surprises, and however wonderful it may be that this richness is always increasing, it places a potentially painful burden on us when we first learn words and their meanings.

To sum up, English is extraordinarily well endowed with words. As versatile as the language already is, the supply of words is ever on the rise, with their meanings shifting in time to reflect new uses. These are the facts that we deal with in this book.

ON THE ATTACK

A challenge of such large proportions calls for a well-organized attack. Although there are no real shortcuts to a better vocabulary, some of the work has already been done for us, since most of the complex words in the language have similar, fairly transparent, structures. Learning the rules that uncover the structure of a certain kind of word relieves some of the burden (and, perhaps, boredom) of learning all the words of that type individually.

We must divide to conquer. The study of word structure (known as **morphology**) will lead to a better understanding of the contribution of the individual parts to the meaning of the whole. It also creates a feel for how English came to be the way it is and a feel for the languages English has drawn on over the centuries.

PRECISION AND ADAPTABILITY

Thanks to a wealth of words that are nearly synonymous yet embody subtle differences in meaning, English vocabulary offers a wide range of choices for expressing exactly what we mean. A simple example is a choice between the words *paternal* and *fatherly* in the following sentences—a distinction few other languages make.

paternal or **fatherly?**
a. *The judge's decision restricted Tom's ___ rights.*
b. *George gave Kim a ___ smile and then went back to reading.*

You would likely choose *paternal* for the first sentence and *fatherly* for the second. Certainly, *fatherly* and *paternal* share the same basic meaning or **denotation**, and you could have used *fatherly* in the first sentence and *paternal* in the second, but the opposite choice is preferred because of **connotation**, the subtler secondary associations of a word. Connotation includes factors such as style, mood, and level of familiarity. *Paternal* is a more formal choice and therefore appropriate to a legal context like that in the first sentence, while *fatherly* is less formal in style. *Fatherly* connotes idealized qualities of fatherhood, like personal warmth and love, more strongly than *paternal*.

Another feature that increases the expressive power of the language is its adaptability. English provides many means for creating new words. If our dictionary does not list an appropriate word, we often create one. To fill the need for, say, a verb meaning 'falsify in advance', we may add the **word element** *pre-*, which means 'before', to the existing verb *falsify* and then use it in a sentence: *The author must **pre-falsify** the manuscript.*

Similarly, the element *-like* (as in *childlike* or *treelike*) will attach to an endless number of other nouns to create an adjective you've never heard before, such as *syzygy-like*. If we invent a device for examining wings and recognize that in many words *pter* means 'wing' (as in *pterodactyl*) and that *scope* means 'a viewing device' (as in *microscope* 'a device for examining very small things'), we may call the new device a *pteroscope*, a word never before recorded in the dictionary. It is hard to imagine a new idea that couldn't be expressed by combining English words or their parts in new ways.

Such adaptability means that even the largest dictionaries can't capture every possible word in the language. The number of possible combinations of word elements like *pre-*, *pter*, and *scope* and the immeasurable amount of speaking and writing done in English require that dictionary editors restrict themselves to listing only the most frequent words in a language, and even then, only those used over a substantial period of time. Dictionaries are therefore always at least slightly out of date and inaccurate in their descriptions of the language's stock of words. In addition, the use of many words is restricted to specific domains. For example, medical terminology involves a tremendous number of words unfamiliar to those outside the medical community. Many of these terms never enter general dictionaries of the language and can only be found in specialized medical dictionaries.

THE CONSTANTLY EVOLVING NATURE OF ENGLISH VOCABULARY

Change and innovation are integral to English, as they are to every living language. The productivity of the language has brought in new verbs using the element *-ize*, such as *conceptualize, operationalize,* and *collateralize*. While reviled as "corruptions" by some writers, teachers, and usage specialists, these examples are undeniably part of the current language, and experience tells us they are unlikely to be questioned by coming generations.

Taste and style are often matters of personal discretion and are also subject to change. In the course of this book, we hope to build a greater sense of security about how each of us chooses to use the language. Mastering vocabulary means not only learning new words and meanings but also knowing enough to make informed decisions about how and where to use a given word so that we can move freely between the informal, formal, and technical domains of spoken and written English.

WHY ENGLISH IS SO RICH

Modern English is the product of a long and complex process of historical development. English today, as always, is a composite of features retained from an earlier state and features that have changed. As a result, present-day English offers many clues to its past—a past as rich as its current vocabulary. The most important historical factor in the growth of the English vocabulary has been the ease with which it has **borrowed** words from other languages and adapted them to its own uses. The word *clique*, for example, came into English from French around the year 1700. As grammarian Otto Jespersen pointed out in 1905, *clique* has since become a familiar English word. As such, it has undergone processes that originally applied only to native vocabulary, forming the new words *cliquish, cliquishness, cliquey, cliqueless*, the verb *to clique*, and others. In fact, English now has many more words derived from *clique* than French does.

Underlying our plentiful and diverse stock of words is a long history of adapting words from foreign sources, as we see in the next chapter. Recognizing that the greater part of modern English vocabulary has either been borrowed or formed from borrowed elements gives us an invaluable aid in learning to master it. English has two words with such similar meanings as *fatherly* and *paternal* simply because it retained a native word (*fatherly*) while borrowing from Latin a near synonym (*paternal*). In a sense, this allowed *fatherly* to share its duties with *paternal*. This is the general pattern with native and borrowed synonyms: the native word is more familiar or more basic and usually shorter, while the borrowed word is more formal or more technical and longer. A few additional synonym pairs illustrate this point.

Native	**Borrowed**
tell	*inform*
spin	*rotate*
pretty	*attractive*

In each pair the first member is more appropriate for everyday use, more conversational, and less formal or technical than the second. But the choice between familiar and formal words is only one small part of the picture. With its wealth of native and foreign resources, English vocabulary has tremendous freedom to expand. Specialized and technical terminology, which generally involve the use of elements borrowed from Latin and Greek, are the most frequent sites of vocabulary innovation.

PNEUMONOULTRAMICROSCOPICSILICOVOLCANOCONIOSIS

The forty-five-letter word *pneumonoultramicroscopicsilicovolcanoconiosis* is often cited as the longest word in English. It names a lung disease caused by inhaling extremely fine particles of volcanic silicon dust. It is an invented word, developed by word puzzle fans expressly for the sake of creating the longest English word, yet it is accepted by many mainstream dictionaries. Even as a fake word, its structural resemblance to bona fide technical vocabulary helps make the point that scientific terms tend to be built on elements borrowed from foreign languages and stacked on top of one another, and the word is famous enough to merit its own Wikipedia entry. The word it replaced as the longest in English—*electrophotomicrographically*—drives home the same lesson, encouraging us not to be intimidated by monstrous word length, since such words can be broken down into simpler elements, many of them already familiar to you by themselves or as they appear as parts of other words, e.g. *electro*, *photo*, *micro*, and *graphically* for the second example. For the first example, we have *pneumon* (recognizable from the **lung** disease *pneumonia*), *ultra* 'extremely' (as in *ultraconservative*), *microscopic*, *silic* (as in the word *silicon*), *volcan*, and *-osis* (as in *tuberculosis* or *neurosis*) 'medical condition' or 'disease'. The most unfamiliar element of this word is *coni*, which means 'dust' in specialized terms such as *conidium*, a type of spore, and *coniology* 'study of the health effects of dust'. It is also related to the element *cin* 'ashes' in *incinerate*. So *pneumon-o-ultra-microscopic-silic-o-volcan-o-coni-osis* literally means 'lung-extremely-microscopic-silicon-volcanic-dust-disease' or, to rearrange things a bit more sensibly, 'lung disease (caused by) microscopic volcanic silicon dust'. (Incidentally, *microscopic* could itself be broken down into three elements: *micr* 'small', *scop* 'view', and *-ic*, which makes the word an adjective.) Notice that the meaning 'caused by' is not carried by any element in the word but must be inferred from the other meanings.

To approach such special words, we need to **parse** (i.e., analyze, break down, or take apart) the word into its proper components, and we need to know the meanings of the components. The same procedures for parsing and interpreting words can also serve to coin new words.

The rest of this book develops procedures and rules for putting this ability and knowledge into our hands. Long words need not be intimidating. In fact, the longer a word, the more likely it is that we can take it apart and figure out its meaning from the sum of its parts. You may or may not want to use your newfound skills to impress your family and friends, but you will definitely find that you have some powerful tools that will open up the worlds of technical and specialized vocabulary.

THE HISTORY HIDDEN IN WORDS

English words encode interesting and useful historical information. For example, compare the words

captain
chief
chef

All three derive historically from *cap*, a Latin word element meaning 'head', which is also found in the words *capital, decapitate, capitulate,* and others. The connection in meaning between them is clear if you think of them as 'the **head** of a vessel or military unit', 'the leader or **head** of a group', and 'the **head** of a kitchen', respectively. Furthermore, English borrowed all three words from French, which in turn borrowed or inherited them from Latin. Why then is the word element spelled and pronounced differently in the three words?

    The first word, *captain*, has a simple story: the word was borrowed from Latin with minimal change. French adapted it from Latin in the thirteenth century, and English borrowed it from French in the fourteenth. The sounds [k] and [p] have not changed in English since that time, and so the Latin element *cap* [kap] remains substantially intact in that word. (For the phonetic symbols inside the square brackets, see the section "International Phonetic Alphabet" under "Symbols and Abbreviations" in the Preface. Chapter 5, "Phonetics," covers the basics of English phonetics.)

    French did not borrow the next two words from Latin. As mentioned earlier, French developed from Latin, with the grammar and vocabulary being passed down from speaker to speaker with small, cumulative changes. Words passed down in this way are said to be **inherited**, not borrowed. English borrowed the word *chief* from French in the thirteenth century, even earlier than it borrowed *captain*. But because *chief* was an inherited word in French, it had undergone many centuries of sound changes by that time. Across the vocabulary, certain [k] sounds and [p] sounds became [tʃ] and [f] sounds, respectively, so that *cap* became *chief*. It was this form that English borrowed from French.

After English borrowed *chief*, French underwent further changes. Among these changes, [tʃ] sounds changed to become [ʃ] sounds, without changing the ‹ch› spelling, so that *chief* became *chef*. Subsequently English also borrowed the word in this form. Thanks to the linguistic evolution of French and the English propensity to borrow words from that language, a single Latin word element, *cap*, which was always pronounced [kap] in Roman times, now appears in English in three very different guises. These word triplets are so instructive, we will return to them later. Two others that follow the same pattern of [k] to [tʃ] to [ʃ] are *candle*, *chandler* ('candle maker'), *chandelier* (originally an elaborate candle holder), and *cant* ('singsong intonation, jargon'; also visible in *incantation*), *chant*, *chantey* (as in *sea chantey*). The history and relationships are diagrammed in table 1.1. Old French refers to that earlier stage of French, up to about 1300, when English borrowed a great many words. Modern French began in 1500. (The intermediate period was known as Middle French.)

For another historical sound correspondence, compare the originally Latin element *semi-* (as in *semicircle*) with the Greek element *hemi-* (as in *hemisphere*). Both *semi-* and *hemi-* mean 'half'. In this element and in many others, Latin [s] and Greek [h] go back to the same ancestral sound,

Table 1.1 CHANGES IN SOUND IN LATIN AND FRENCH AND THEIR RESULTS IN BORROWINGS.

Source	Sounds	English borrowings with these sounds		
Latin	[k]	*captain*	*candle*	*cant*
↓				
Old French	[tʃ]	*chief*	*chandler*	*chant*
↓				
Modern French	[ʃ]	*chef*	*chandelier*	*chantey*

one sign that Greek and Latin are **related** languages, that is, they descend from the same language. That language included the element *sēm-* 'half'. Over a long period of time, the two languages came to differ in certain respects, including the pronunciation of the first sound of this element. Later in the book, as we explore similar sound changes and their impact on English, we find that they give us a way to organize information about English words and offer clues to word relationships.

ADDITIONAL GOALS

While the book's immediate purpose is to teach new word elements and techniques for analyzing words, the overarching goal is to establish a path of vocabulary growth that will continue for a lifetime. The book should serve other purposes as well. Over the centuries, changes in pronunciation and meaning have been welcomed by some and resisted by others. Disputes arise when new usages come up that violate some people's sensibilities. For example, you may have run across objections to *hopefully* in a sentence like *Hopefully, it won't rain on our picnic.* The reason cited is usually that this adverb can properly modify only human actions and not the action of raining. The use of *hopefully* in this example so upset an English dictionary panel of experts in the 1970s that various members called it a barbarism and "popular jargon at its most illiterate level," complaining that it made them physically ill and that "Chalk squeaking on a blackboard is to be preferred to this usage." Even if you don't share these reactions, might you consider them valid or at least understand why someone else might? More generally, for any given new usage, including changes in pronunciation, meaning, or function, does it count as corruption or enrichment or something in between? And who gets to decide? It's hard to ignore the problem in a language like English, which adds new words and word meanings at a fast clip: lately, the Oxford English Dictionary (OED) has been adding well over two thousand new words, phrases, and definitions per year.

Complicating such questions, usage varies greatly from one region to another and even among different speakers in the same area. Answers demand a better awareness of attitudes and prejudices (others' and our own) concerning this variation. Confronting variations in later chapters also speaks to the issue of how to use sophisticated vocabulary properly for effective communication and understanding.

In the process of developing techniques for word analysis, we also introduce some of the principal areas of modern linguistics: phonetics and phonology (the study of speech sounds and how they function in language), morphology (the study of word structure), historical linguistics (the study of language change over time), lexical semantics (the study of word meaning), and sociolinguistics (the study of social factors in language variation and change). A final goal is spelling improvement. Word structure often correlates with standard spelling. For example, if you realize the words *pyromaniac* and *antipyretic* both contain the word element *pyr* 'fire', you will automatically know that there is a ‹y› (rather than an ‹i› as in *pirate*) between ‹p› and ‹r›. Similarly, if you know that *consensus* contains the element *sens* 'feel', you will remember that it has an ‹s› where many people mistakenly put a ‹c›. The secret to the correct spelling of *definitely*—too often seen with *ate* in place of *ite* before *-ly*—is recognizing that *definite* is the basis of the word *definition*, whose spelling is easier because its pronunciation makes clear that the vowel of the second-to-last syllable is *i*, not *a*. Similarly, the cue showing that the vowel of the middle syllable of *definite* is *i* is the vowel of the final syllable of the source word *define*. Knowing that *separate* has the same root as *pare* and *prepare* will keep you from misspelling it with an ‹e› in the second syllable, and knowing that *desperate* has the same root as *prosper* tells you that the correct vowel for the second syllable is ‹e›.

WORD ELEMENTS

The words in the *Examples* column in this section are there to illustrate the range of vocabulary words that a given element appears in. You need not memorize them, but they may help you memorize the element and its gloss. Among the examples appear familiar and unfamiliar words, and in them the word element of interest may be modified or unmodified from its basic form. Cases where word elements are modified are potentially the most interesting because they signal some of an element's typical variants, which will occupy us in later chapters.

Element	Gloss	Examples
anthrop	human	*anthropology, anthropomorphic, philanthropy*
bi	life	*biography, biology, bioluminescent, macrobiotic, microbial*
cac	bad	*cacophony, caconym, cacodemonic*
chrom	color	*chrome, monochrome, chromosome, chromatic*
chron	time	*chronic, diachronic, chronometer, anachronistic*
cosm	universe, adorn, order	*cosmic, cosmetic, macrocosm, cosmopolitan, cosmogony, cosmonaut, cosmecology*
gam	marry, unite	*monogamy, bigamy, exogamous, gamete, epigamic, gamogenesis*
iatr	heal	*pediatrician, iatrogenic, psychiatry, geriatric*
idi	personal	*idiosyncrasy, idiom, idiot, idiolect, idiomorphic, idiopathy, idiochromatic*
log	speak, study	*logic, logo, anthropology, analogy, eulogy, prologue, logorrhea*
macr	large	*macro, macron, macroeconomics, macrocephalic, macrocyte, macradenous*
micr	small	*microbe, microcosm, micron, microphotography, microscope, micranatomy*
mis	hate	*misanthrope, misogamy, misogyny, misology*
morph	form	*morpheme, morphology, amorphous, polymorphous, ectomorph, endomorph*
nom	law, system	*astronomy, autonomy, metronome, nomad, nomology*
path	feel, illness	*pathetic, pathology, pathos, empathy, sympathy*

Element	Gloss	Examples
petr	rock	*petrify, petroglyph, petroleum, petrous*
phil	liking	*philosophy, philanthropy, Anglophile, hemophilia, philately*
phon	sound	*phonics, phonetic, telephone, cacophony, euphony, symphonic, aphonia*
pol	community	*politics, police, cosmopolitan, metropolis*
pseud	false	*pseudonym, pseudopod, pseudoscience, pseudo-argument, pseudandry*
psych	mind	*psyche, psychic, psychiatry, psychopath, psychotic*
pyr	fire	*pyromaniac, pyrometer, pyrotechnics, pyrite, antipyretic*
the	god	*theology, theocracy, theogony, polytheism, atheist*
top	place	*topic, topical, topology, toponym, isotope*
xen	foreign	*xenophobia, xenon, xenogamy, xenoplastic, axenic, pyroxene*

All of the word elements in this list come from Greek. Notice that adjacent Greek roots in a word tend to be separated by an ‹o›, especially when the second root begins with a consonant. Another clue that some of these elements are Greek rather than Latin is the spelling: Latin elements rarely have the digraphs ‹ch›, ‹ph›, ‹th›; silent consonants or ‹x› at the beginning of a word; or the vowel sequence ‹eu›. Latin elements rarely have ‹y› except at the end of the word. The digraphs ‹ch› and ‹th› also occur in native English words, but ‹ch› reveals its Greek origin when it is pronounced [k].

It's important to watch out for **false friends**, letter sequences resembling an element that instead comes from a different source. For example, a **bi**cycle is not a **living** wheel; that word begins not with the root *bi* 'life' but the number element *bi* meaning 'two'. On occasion we explicitly point out homographic elements, but even when we do not, you need to keep your eye open for them because English has hundreds of them.

ELEMENT STUDY

1. *Cosm* generally means 'world' or 'universe'. It means 'adorn' only in the variant form *cosmet* appearing in *cosmetic, cosmetology,* and so on. What is the unifying concept behind the two meanings?
2. *Idi* is mostly found at the beginning of words and usually names something that does not follow the general system or was not subject to outside influences. Distinguish from *ide*, which means 'idea'. For each of these words, give the trait or feature that is characterized as unusual:
   a. *idiosyncrasy*
   b. *idiolect*
   c. *idiopathy*
   d. *idiom*
   e. *idiot*
3. The element *log* 'speak, study' and the wooden *log* are totally unrelated elements. Which of the two is the source of the word *log* referring to a written record, as when we log hours on a job? If you are uncertain, look up your answer.
4. Although *log* is glossed as 'speak' or 'study', it has a wider range of meanings. To get an idea of where these meanings show up in real words, answer these questions:
   a. What general meaning does *log* have at the beginnings of these words: *logic; logistical; logarithm*?
   b. What very general meaning does *log* have in these words: *catalog; Decalogue; dialogue; prologue; travelogue*? Ignore the variation in the spelling of *log*.
   c. What general meaning does *log* have before the endings *-y* and *-ist* in the words *anthropology, geology, psychologist,* and *biologist*? Does it have the same meaning in *analogy* and *apology*?

5. *Nom* sometimes means 'law' in the sense of rule or control. But very often it refers to scientific law. Which of the two meanings best fits the definition of each word below?
   a. *anomie*
   b. *astronomy*
   c. *autonomy*
   d. *Deuteronomy*
   e. *economics*
   f. *heteronomy*
   g. *taxonomy*
   h. *theonomous*
6. In each word below, replace the noun suffix *-y* with a new ending that makes it into an adjective.
   a. *astronomy*
   b. *autonomy*
   c. *economy*
7. The element *nom* is unrelated to the element *nomen~nomin* 'name' found in *nominal* and *nomenclature*. In which of the following words does *nom* mean 'law'? Verify your answers by looking them up.
   a. *autonomic*
   b. *binomial*
   c. *gastronomy*
   d. *nominate*
8. The element *path* in this chapter is an element from Greek with no connection to the native word meaning 'way'. Combined with the suffix *-y* at the end of a word, *pathy* sometimes names a type of feeling, sometimes a disease, and sometimes a system for treating disease. For each word in the following list, determine which of these three meanings comes closest to capturing the meaning of *path* in that word.
   a. *antipathy*
   b. *apathy*

c. *arthropathy*
   d. *cardiopathy*
   e. *empathy*
   f. *homeopathy*
   g. *hydropathy*
   h. *myopathy*
   i. *naturopathy*
   j. *neuropathy*
   k. *sympathy*
   l. *telepathy*
9. List five words beginning with the element *phil* and five words ending in *phile*. A good place to look for words satisfying a pattern like one of these is https://www.rhymezone.com/, where you can search for strings using a wildcard character, e.g., *phil** or **phile*. Some online dictionaries have a similar function. Describe the range of meanings of *phil* and its variant *phile* in these words. Do any meanings correlate with position at the beginning versus the end of a word?
10. What is the root in these words? Look up each word, and include a brief sentence about the relation between the root's literal meaning and its meaning in this word.
    a. apophony
    b. misoxene (Note: Identify both roots!)
11. Replace the question marks with the appropriate word elements and glosses you have memorized. For example, in *a* below you'd write "pseud" for "?$_1$" and "shape" for "?$_2$." Then spell out the full word, incorporating any extra letters you are not asked to gloss. For *a*, you would write out "*pseudomorph*."

a. **elements**	?$_1$	o	morph		
glosses	false		?$_2$		
b. **elements**	?$_1$	o	phag		e
glosses	large		eat		

c.	**elements**	the	o	gam	-ous
	glosses	?₁		?₂	A
d.	**elements**	?₁	o	metr	-y
	glosses	mind		measure	N
e.	**elements**	?₁	anthrop	e	
	glosses	hate	?₂		
f.	**elements**	?₁	o	?₂	-y
	glosses	bad		sound	N

EXERCISES

1. For each of the borrowed words in the following list, give a synonym that is a single native word. The native word will generally be less formal. You may be able to guess the answer yourself or find likely candidates in a thesaurus or at https://www.rhymezone.com/. Check an etymological source (e.g., https://www.etymonline.com/ or a good dictionary) to verify that your answer really is a native word. Borrowed words are identified as such. Native words are instead traced back to earlier English and Germanic sources.
   a. *inter*
   b. *depart*
   c. *velocity*
   d. *rapid*
   e. *decay*
   f. *illumination*
   g. *terminate*
   h. *converse*_V
   i. *canine*
   j. *injure*
   k. *perambulate*

2. Indicate which word is native and which is the borrowed word in each of the following pairs. Besides their etymologies, what kinds of clues to their origins do the form and structure of the words themselves provide?
    a. *wordy, verbose*
    b. *chew, masticate*
    c. *vend, sell*
    d. *malady, sickness*
    e. *answer, respond*
    f. *old, antique*
    g. *tell, inform*
    h. *watch, observe*
    i. *durable, tough*
    j. *eat, consume*
    k. *emancipate, free*
    l. *deadly, mortal*
    m. *sad, dejected*
3. In this chapter *fatherly* and *paternal* were seen to have similar meanings but different connotations. Consider *donate* and *give* in this light. When and why might one choose to use one over the other?
4. What, if anything, differentiates a *chronometer* from a *watch*?
5. Given what you've learned from the word elements for this chapter, what do you think the word *philophony* might mean? (You won't find this word in a dictionary.) Explain your answer.

Two
The History of English and Sources of English Vocabulary

The last chapter mentioned English's very large vocabulary and its flexibility in adapting new words, giving English a special place among the languages that originated in Europe. How did English get this way? Part of the answer lies in the history of the language, which expanded its native Germanic vocabulary to include massive numbers of foreign elements, especially from Latin, Greek, and French.

The phrase *English language* refers to something that is at the same time the American language, the Australian language, the Canadian language, the language of England, Scotland, and Wales, and so on. According to Ethnologue.com, English is the native tongue of more than 379 million people in many independent nations. It is also a major second language, primary, or alternative official language for an even larger number of people throughout the world. So, what is it that is "English" about this major world language? The answer is its history, because for almost a thousand years it was spoken almost entirely in England. During this period, the language evolved in ways that helped to make it a fitting tool for communication around the world. The globalization of English is quite recent. Among languages of European origin, English ranked only fifth in the number of speakers at the end of the nineteenth century, after French, German, Spanish, and Italian.

As we look at historical events, we see that they have had a variety of linguistic repercussions, and we may ask what English would have been like if its history had been even slightly different.

BACKGROUND TO THE HISTORY OF ENGLISH

Origins of Language

Human language goes back at least fifty thousand years. That is roughly when fully modern humans emerged from Africa and started developing recognizably modern human culture around the globe. The remarkable success of this new type of human—us—is thought to be due in large part to the development of a brand-new type of communication system: language as we know it. Unfortunately, we know no details about the original human language. Language, being very ephemeral, left no traces at all before the invention of writing about five thousand years ago. Furthermore, language constantly changes. If only a few words are lost and replaced with new ones in each human generation, virtually the entire original vocabulary would be lost over the course of fifty thousand years.

Another result of constant language change is that the original language (or languages) has by now diverged into over seven thousand distinct languages, according to the latest count by Ethnologue.com. As humans spread around the world, they formed independent communities that were no longer in intimate contact with each other. Relative isolation generally kept innovations in the language of one community from spreading to others. After only a few centuries, the speech forms of separate communities became so different as to leave them with essentially different languages. Because of the obscuring effects of time, all theories about remote language origins are highly speculative. However, linguists can make some reasonably solid conclusions about prehistoric languages, provided they don't try to trace things too far back in time—more than, say, ten thousand years. By comparing **attested** languages—those currently spoken or for which there exist historical records—linguists may find common traits that demonstrate that certain languages diverged from a common earlier form. To describe the connections between languages, they make liberal use of biological metaphors. If a language, say, Latin, diverges in time into, say, French and Spanish, linguists say that French and Spanish are **genetically related** (or simply **related**) to each other, that they **descend** from Latin, that Latin is an **ancestor** or **parent** of French and Spanish, and that French and Spanish are **descendants** of Latin. Furthermore, French and Spanish and all the languages that are related to them are said to form a **family**. All this biologically inspired terminology is straightforward enough, provided one does not try to read too much into it. Languages are not formed by the union of a mother and father language. They don't come into being suddenly, as humans do. And the fact that two languages are genetically related does not mean that their speakers are genetically related, since speakers can adopt the language of a group they're not genetically affiliated with.

Indo-European

The method of comparing languages to discover their prehistory (called the **comparative method**) has led linguists to discover that English is related to dozens of other languages. That family is called **Indo-European** because even in prehistoric times the family had already ranged from as far as India in the east to the Atlantic coast of Europe in the west. The ancestor of all the Indo-European languages is called Proto-Indo-European.

Proto-Indo-European was spoken before the invention of writing, so it is not directly attested, but a great deal of the language can be **reconstructed** by the comparative method. The language was highly inflected, meaning that most words could appear in many different forms depending on how they were used in the sentence. Where English has two forms for nouns—*horse, horses*—Proto-Indo-European had perhaps two dozen forms. Where English has on average four or five different forms for verbs—*love, loves, loving, loved*—Proto-Indo-European verbs could take hundreds of different forms.

Eventually the speakers of that language spread through much of Europe and western Asia, replacing the languages formerly spoken there. A speaker of an Indo-European language might like to think that Indo-European languages won out because they were superior to the earlier languages, but it is doubtful whether any language is objectively superior to another. Rather, languages gain territory because their speakers have military or socioeconomic superiority. An intriguing possibility is that Proto-Indo-European spread so widely because its speakers were among the first to use horse-drawn war chariots.

Linguists have divided the Indo-European languages into about a dozen groups, or **branches**, of languages, each of which must have shared a common ancestor that descended from Proto-Indo-European (see figure 2.1). For example, the **Italic** branch includes Latin and its descendants the **Romance** ('originating in Rome') languages (e.g., Italian, French, Spanish, Portuguese, and Romanian), as well as other extinct languages. Other groups important in the history of English include **Celtic** (e.g., Welsh, Irish, and Scots Gaelic) and **Hellenic** (Greek). These branches are very much like families: groups of related languages with a common ancestor. We even refer to their common ancestor languages with the *Proto-* prefix: *Proto-Italic, Proto-Celtic, Proto-Hellenic.* The only difference between a branch and a family is that a branch's protolanguage has an identified ancestor: the ancestor of Proto-Italic was Proto-Indo-European, but we don't know what the ancestor of Proto-Indo-European was.

Germanic

English belongs to the branch of Indo-European called the **Germanic** group. Proto-Germanic was probably spoken in northern Germany and southern Scandinavia. It was not as highly inflected with grammatical case endings and tense markers as Proto-Indo-European had been. Indeed, simplification of the inflectional system is a constant theme in the history of English.

The History of English and Sources of English Vocabulary 23

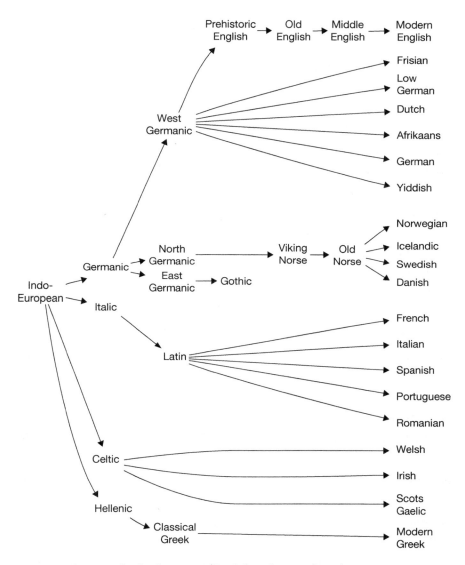

Figure 2.1 Stages in the development of English and some of its relatives.

We also know that a great many of the consonants changed in Proto-Germanic. For example, in Proto-Indo-European, the word for 'foot' began *ped* or *pod*, and these are still the forms in Latin and Greek. But English is typical of the Germanic languages in having quite different consonants in the word *foot*. To a casual observer these differences seem great. One of the earliest achievements of modern linguistics was Grimm's law, which revealed how systematic and transparent the correspondences between Germanic consonants and those of other Indo-European languages were. Grimm's law is presented in chapter 10.

Proto-Germanic developed into not only English, but also several other languages we are familiar with. Some Germanic tribes migrated eastward, into what is now Romania and Ukraine, and developed the language branch known as East Germanic. The most important language in this group was **Gothic**, the first Germanic language in which we have a significant amount of written text: a translation of part of the New Testament. All speakers of East Germanic languages eventually abandoned them in favor of other languages, and so we say that that branch is now **extinct**—another biological metaphor.

After the East Germanic branch split off, we begin to find in the core Germanic area a small body of short inscriptions written in **runes**, highly modified variants of the Latin letters. A typical old Germanic inscription is the following, from one of the golden horns of Gallehus: ᛖᚲᚺᛚᛖᚹᚨᚷᚨᛊᛏᛁᛉ᛬ᚺᛟᛚᛏᛁᛃᚨᛉ᛬ᚺᛟᚱᚾᚨ᛬ᛏᚨᚹᛁᛞᛟ: Rendered in ordinary Latin letters, this reads *ek hlewagastiz holtijaz horna tawido* 'I, Hlewagast of Holt, made [the] horn.'

The Germanic area was bordered by the Roman Empire, and the history of the two sociopolitical groups was strongly intertwined. Germanic borrowed from Latin several words for cultural items that were new to the Germanic tribes or that were distinctively different in the Roman and Germanic worlds. Among these earliest words borrowed from Latin and still present in English are the practical, familiar terms *wine, street, mile, pit, cheese, chalk, kitchen, dish, pepper, kettle, cheap, pound, tile,* and *mint* (both the plant and the place where money is coined).

After East Germanic branched off, the Germanic language that remained diverged into two new groups, **North Germanic** and **West Germanic**. The West Germanic group, which includes English, is discussed in the next section. The North Germanic branch comprises **Viking Norse** dialects, which developed into literary Old Norse and eventually into modern

Scandinavian languages, among them Icelandic, Norwegian, Swedish, and Danish.

Note that our history of English still has not taken us to England! Until the fifth century, England was inhabited by Celts, whose language developed into modern **Welsh**. Eventually England was incorporated into the Roman Empire as the province of Britannia—a name of Celtic origin. It is easy to mistakenly assume that early Latin influence on English occurred because England was part of the Roman Empire. But the chronology would be wrong; Roman presence in Britain during the Celtic period can only explain Latin influence on Welsh. Latin influence on (the ancestor of) English occurred because of social and economic contact between the Romans and Germanic peoples on the European mainland, peoples who, on the whole, were not part of the Roman Empire.

West Germanic

In the fifth century, Germanic expansion brought about the fall of the Roman Empire. Subsequently, without the Roman army to defend them, many lands passed under the control of Germanic tribes. The movements of the West Germanic tribes are particularly important to the story of English. By the end of the fifth century, West Germanic speakers had taken control of much of France and England. In France, many words of the conquering Frankish Germans were incorporated into the vocabulary. These words included the name of the land itself: called *Gallia* (*Gaul*) under the Romans, it now came to be called *Francia* (*France*) 'land of the Franks'. Still, Latin (or an increasingly modified descendant of Latin) remained the language of France. It is perhaps surprising that the conquerors adopted the language of the conquered people, but the high prestige of Latin as the language of a great empire and civilization may have contributed to its survival.

As for England, most of its invaders came in the fifth century from what is now northwestern Germany—including Lower Saxony, the region whose name reappears in *Anglo-Saxon*—although some invaders must have set out from other nearby areas around the North Sea as well. The languages spoken in this area are very closely related to English, especially Frisian, which is spoken along the North Sea coasts of the Netherlands and Germany. Other West Germanic languages include Dutch and its South African variety Afrikaans. Yiddish and standard German, which developed in southern Germany, are somewhat more distantly related to English, although the Low German dialects of northwestern Germany are still more similar to English than to standard German in several respects.

MAJOR STAGES IN THE HISTORY OF ENGLISH

Prehistoric English

In the fifth century, Germanic invaders from the east conquered and occupied the eastern part of the British island. The Celtic language originally spoken in that area was replaced by the West Germanic dialects spoken by the invaders, as the original inhabitants were killed or relocated, or adopted the language of the now dominant society. The western part of the island, as well as much of the far north, was not subjugated at this time. This is why the island to this day contains not only England but also the separate countries of Wales and Scotland, which still use native Celtic languages alongside English. The Celtic language of Scotland, Scots Gaelic, was introduced from Ireland, but that of Wales, called Welsh, is the descendant of the language spoken throughout southern Britain at the time of the Germanic invasions.

Although, as we have seen, the Germanic tribes occupying France adopted Latin, those occupying Britain retained their own language. Why the difference? After all, both regions had an ostensibly similar sociopolitical background—Celtic populations who had been incorporated into the Latin-speaking Roman Empire. Apparently, the difference is that Latin never really took hold among the native population in Britain, which lay on the periphery of the empire and was conquered by Rome quite a bit later than Gaul was. Furthermore, the Latin-speaking soldiers, administrators, and governors all retreated from Britain early in the fifth century. Consequently, the people conquered by the Germanic tribes were speakers of a Celtic language that was not associated with a wealthy and prestigious empire. The invaders did not adopt the native language or even borrow very many words from it.

Roughly speaking, the tribes that settled in Britain formed three groups: the Angles north of the Thames, the Saxons south of the Thames, and the Kents in the southeast. The Angles and the Saxons occupied by far the greatest part of the country, so that the Germanic civilization that emerged in Britain is often called Anglo-Saxon. The Angles lent their name to the language—English—and to the whole of the territory held by the invaders—England.

Because we have very few written records of this stage of English, it is called **Prehistoric English**. The Germanic speakers did bring with them their runic script. But we have only about a dozen legible inscriptions from this period (400–700), and they are all very short. Presumably, relatively few inscriptions were produced, and most of those were on materials like wood that have rotted away. By contrast, runic inscriptions on durable stone were produced prolifically by the North Germanic speakers who spread through Scandinavia.

It was during the Prehistoric English period that England was converted to Christianity. Latin, the official language of the church, provided not only ecclesiastical vocabulary (e.g., *abbot*, *mass*, *pope*, and *priest*) but also a surprising number of what are now everyday words (e.g., *candle*, *cap*, *fennel*, *school*, and *spend*). These were added to the stock of Latin words that earlier had passed into Germanic during the period of the Roman Empire.

Old English

Around the year 700 there began to appear substantial English texts, written in a version of the Latin alphabet that was introduced from Ireland. This is therefore the approximate date of the beginning of historical

English—that is, English for which we have reasonably detailed historical records. It is conventional to divide the history of a language into three equal parts, referred to as Old, Middle, and Modern. When this system was adopted around 1900, there were twelve centuries of history to work with. So the first four hundred years or so of historical English (700–1100) is referred to as **Old English**.

Old English is the direct ancestor of the English spoken today and serves as the source of some of the most basic elements of English vocabulary. While it may at first appear quite alien to the modern reader, closer examination shows its deep resemblance to modern English.

In Old English the sentence *He has a white tongue* would have been written "he hafaþ hƿite tungan" and pronounced [heː ˈhavaθ ˈhwiːtɛ ˈtʊŋɡan] (refer to "Symbols and Abbreviations" in the preface for the sound values of these symbols). We see that some things haven't changed much since Old English, while others are rather different. Alongside the obvious differences in pronunciation are differences in spelling—for example, Old English ⟨f⟩ for the [v] sound, and two survivals from the runic script: ⟨þ⟩ for the [θ] sound and ⟨ƿ⟩ for the [w] sound. Note also the Old English inflectional endings *-aþ*, *-e*, and *-an* on these words. These endings marked such things as the function of words in a sentence, so that, for example, the ending *-an* on the word *tungan* 'tongue' indicated that it was the direct object of the verb *hafaþ* 'has'. All of these disappeared on the way to present-day English, and of them only one is likely to seem familiar to a speaker of modern English: *-aþ*, an earlier form of the ending *-eth* in words like Shakespearean *holdeth* 'holds'. It marked the person and number of the subject of the verb, which in our sentence is the third person singular pronoun *he* 'he'. In current English, *-s* has replaced *-eth* in this function.

One of the most important periods in the development of Old English was the reign of Alfred the Great in the ninth century. Alfred was concerned about the poor state of Latin learning in his day. He undertook a massive campaign to revive learning by making English translations of Latin books. One result of this campaign was the flourishing of English-language literature, with the eventual emergence of a literary standard based on the West Saxon dialect of King Alfred and his successors, whose court was in Winchester. From the ninth to the eleventh centuries, English language and culture were among the most vibrant and active of the Western world. With every new cultural, material, technological, religious, scholarly, or artistic development, the language grew and changed, especially in vocabulary. The more sweeping the change, the more dramatic the influence on the language.

Throughout the ninth and tenth centuries and into the eleventh, Vikings invaded and settled large parts of England. English again responded by borrowing words, this time from the North Germanic tongue of the invaders, Viking Norse. This created an interesting mixture, because Old English was still very similar to this close Germanic relative. Like languages themselves, words can be related to each other, or **cognate** (literally, "together born"), meaning that their origin traces back to the same word in an ancestor language. A fair number of words borrowed from Viking Norse closely resembled cognates that already existed in Old English, but they often had somewhat different pronunciations and meanings. These pairs of native and borrowed cognates are called **doublets**. A few English–Norse doublets are illustrated in the following word pairs:

Native	**Norse loan**
shirt	*skirt*
no	*nay*
shrub	*scrub*
lend	*loan*
rear	*raise*

In addition, several hundred Norse words with no surviving native English cognates were also incorporated into Old English, among them *ill, till, flat, they, skin,* and *egg*.

Middle English

The Middle English period is defined as lasting the four centuries from 1100 to 1500. Arguably the most important single event to affect historical

English, the **Norman Conquest**, took place at the end of the Old English period. The monumental changes that this invasion produced in the shape of English society were accompanied by tantamount effects in the vocabulary of Middle English.

The Normans were originally Vikings—their name comes from *North man* (i.e., 'Norse'). In a sense, then, the Norman conquest can be seen as yet another Germanic invasion. But there was a difference this time. The Normans had earlier been ceded control of a large duchy along the northern coast of France—Normandy. As French subjects, they had adopted French culture. So the language they brought with them was not a Germanic language, but French. As we have seen, French is an Indo-European language, being a descendant of Latin. But that degree of relationship to English is not nearly as close as that of Viking Norse.

After their victory in 1066 at the Battle of Hastings under William the Conqueror, the Normans quickly assumed leadership and privilege in England. The Norman dialect of French thenceforth was the language of the upper class, while English was relegated to use by the peasants. As a result, the English language lost most of its literary and scholarly vocabulary. When English again came to be used widely for literary purposes a few centuries later, writers naturally turned to their knowledge of French to supplement the vocabulary. Especially during the 1200s, English assimilated a multitude of Old French words, especially those dealing with areas of life in which French language and culture were dominant. These included government (where we find French borrowings such as *court, duke, baron, county, crown, trial,* and *village*), war (*peace, enemy, arms, battle, moat*), and the finer things (*gown, robe, emerald, diamond, feast, savory, cream, sugar*).

The story of borrowings from French is complicated by the fact that some French words are themselves borrowed from Latin. The French word *animal* would not have preserved the shape of the Latin word *animal* so perfectly if it had been passed down in the normal lines of transmission from ancestor language to descendant language, subject to almost a thousand years of change. Instead, the French borrowed it from Latin, which language was still used for many secular and religious purposes during the European Middle Ages. Medieval speakers of Latin tried, with varying degrees of success, to keep words the way they were during the Roman Empire. For a historian it may well matter whether English speakers borrowed the word from French or directly from Latin, but for our purposes, the most important thing is that the English word *animal* looks and behaves like a Latin borrowing, so we call it Latin. In cases where we are not sure, or do not care, whether a word is really Latin or was modified by its descent through French or other Romance languages, we can always hedge and call it **Latinate** (i.e., borrowed from Latin, whether directly or indirectly).

Middle English differed from Old English not only in vocabulary but also in its grammatical structure. Most of the vowels in inflectional endings became [ə] (spelled ⟨e⟩), which change obliterated the distinction between many of the endings. The following lines from Geoffrey Chaucer, the greatest and most renowned of Middle English writers, illustrate how the language looked after these changes.

And Frenssh she spak ful faire and fetisly,
After the scole of Stratford atte Bowe,
For Frenssh of Parys was to hire unknowe.
Canterbury Tales, General Prologue, The Prioress

We can make this passage more understandable by substituting the modern forms of the Middle English words while keeping the Middle English word order:

And French she spoke full fair and featously,
After the school of Stratford-at-the-Bow,
For French of Paris was to her unknown.

(The word *featous* 'elegant' was borrowed from French and is now obsolete.) Only a few changes in word choice and order are required to translate this into Modern English prose:

And she spoke French very pleasantly and elegantly—
according to the Stratford-at-Bow school, for Parisian
French was unknown to her.

Chaucer is poking fun at a prioress who strives to be a sophisticate but whose French was obviously learned in an English convent. While this passage is relatively easy to follow, even in its original written form, hearing it spoken would be quite another matter, for it was pronounced approximately like this:

[and frɛnʃ ʃeː spaːk fʊl faɪr and ˈfɛːtɪslɪ
aftər θə skoːl ɔf ˈstratfɔrd ˈatːə bʊʊ
fɔr frɛnʃ ɔf ˈparɪs was toː hɪr ʊnˈknɔʊ]

During virtually the entire Middle English period, England and France were closely connected. But gradually the ruling classes of England began to think of themselves as English, especially after losing Normandy for the first time in 1204. They began to look more favorably on English and began to use that language more widely, even for literary purposes. But the connection with Old English traditions had been severed, and the members of the new literate class didn't even speak the dialect that the old literature had been written in. The language of King Alfred in Winchester had been a southern, Saxon-based dialect, while the new language of the London court was based mostly on Anglian dialects of the English Midlands. Native verse forms were abandoned, and even the script and spelling system took on a radically different shape. Much had been lost, but Middle English writers had at their disposal the tradition of spoken and literary French to help them create a vigorous and rich national language. With the Hundred Years' War spanning the fourteenth and fifteenth centuries, enthusiasm for things French waned considerably, but English retains many hundreds of French words, not to mention thousands of Latin and Greek words that entered the language indirectly through French.

Table 2.1 THE GREAT VOWEL SHIFT.

ME sound	ModE sound	ME example word	Same word in ModE
[iː]	[aɪ]	*fine* [fiːnə]	*fine* [faɪn]
[eː]	[i]	*me* [meː]	*me* [mi]
[ɛː]	[i]	*cleene* [klɛːnə]	*clean* [klin]
[aː]	[e]	*name* [naːmə]	*name* [nem]
[uː]	[aʊ]	*hous* [huːs]	*house* [haʊs]
[oː]	[u]	*moone* [moːnə]	*moon* [mun]
[ɔː]	[o]	*goote* [ɡɔːtə]	*goat* [ɡot]

Modern English

The current stage of the language, **Modern English**, is conventionally said to have begun in 1500. Thanks to the advent of movable type, books began to be produced in English on a massive scale, leading to greater standardization of the language and to its acceptance as a major language. During the English Renaissance, from the late fifteenth century to the beginning of the seventeenth century, great numbers of Latin and Greek words were added to English, along with continued borrowings from French.

One of the most extensive linguistic changes in the history of English is known as the **Great Vowel Shift**, which marks the transition from Middle English (ME) to Modern English (ModE). These major sound changes affected the pronunciation of **long vowels**. These changes are shown in table 2.1, which tells us, for example, that the older sound [iː] became [aɪ]. One example is that the word *fine*, formerly pronounced [fiːnə], is now pronounced [faɪn]. (The sound [ə] was lost from the ends of words at roughly the same time, but that deletion is not considered a part of the Great Vowel Shift.)

By Shakespeare's time (around 1600), the Great Vowel Shift was complete. Here is an example of the written language of that period:

The king hath on him such a countenance,
As he had lost some Prouince, and a Region
Lou'd, as he loues himselfe.
> *The Winter's Tale*, act 1, scene 2

Few if any of these words are hard to recognize, especially if we take into account that the letters ‹u› and ‹v› were often interchanged in this period. The words were pronounced then very much as they would be today in American English, and even words like *hath* that have dropped out of general use may still be familiar from poetry or the King James Version of the Bible. The presence of such Latinate loanwords as *countenance, province*, and *region* shows the continued importance of the French and Latin loanwords borrowed throughout the Middle English period.

External influences continued to augment English vocabulary. The Renaissance opened a new age for art and science in England and the rest of Europe. Along with many new words from French and Latin, Greek words now began to make their greatest impact. The scholarly disciplines owe much of their vocabulary to classical Latin and Greek. Among the first contributions to Modern English from Latin were *exterior, appendix, delirium, contradict, exterminate*, and *temperature*. At about the same time, Greek provided *tonic, catastrophe, anonymous, lexicon*, and *skeleton*.

As the European colonial empires expanded throughout the world, English borrowed words from many other languages. Among these words are names for animals and places (*moose, skunk, woodchuck, Michigan, Chicago, Manhattan*) from American Indian languages encountered by English settlers; food terms (*yam, gumbo, banana*) from African languages spoken where the foods originate; new species and technologies (*kangaroo, koala, boomerang*) from Australian languages; unusual weather phenomena and customs (*typhoon, kowtow*) from Chinese; and many others.

Still, English continues the tradition of the Renaissance in its heavy reliance on Latin and Greek. This is fortunate for our purposes here, since it means that the systematic study of scientific and other special vocabulary can concentrate on these two languages out of the many that English has drawn from in its history. Because the Latin of ancient Rome itself borrowed words from Greek, many Greek words entered English indirectly through Latin. As a result, the three most important sources of borrowed vocabulary—French, Latin, and Greek—have contributed to English along the paths illustrated in figure 2.2.

In the Renaissance period, English did not just borrow actual words from Latin and Greek. To handle new cultural and technological developments, entirely new vocabulary was created using parts of older borrowings, resulting in the large-scale formation of words that had never existed in Latin and Classical Greek when they were living languages. This process of innovation remains alive in English today and is one way that the classical word stock can be so valuable. Anyone can cannibalize the elements of borrowed words to invent words such as *phrenolatry* 'the act of worshipping the mind' or *somnivorous* 'sleep devouring' or *steatocephalic* 'having a fatty head'. This is because English, along with borrowing huge numbers of words, in effect also borrowed the rules relating forms to each other. For example, Greek usually put an *o* between word elements when it formed compound words like *philosophia*, from *phil* 'liking' and *sophia*

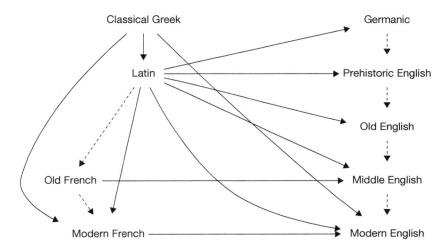

Figure 2.2 Major paths of borrowing from Greek and Latinate sources into English. Dashed lines indicate descent between different stages of the same language.

'wisdom' (borrowed by English as *philosophy*). Consequently, when we make up new compounds from Greek elements, we usually apply the same rule, as when we made up the word *phrenolatry* from *phren* 'mind' and *latri* or *latry* 'worship'. An example of the complexity of developments in borrowing and neologism is the path taken by an ancient word (and, later, word element) for 'wine', borrowed from an unknown source by both Ancient Greek and Latin during the first millennium BCE, from which it was in turn borrowed by Germanic and English at several points in its history. Dashed lines indicate descent within a language over time; darker lines indicate borrowing between languages; and the arrowhead pointer indicates derivation from the word above it, within the same language (figure 2.3).

With so many layers of borrowing into English, one could easily get the impression that English has turned into a non-Germanic language. Admittedly, English does rank high in its hospitality to loanwords. But it remains at its core typical of Germanic tongues. In general, the most

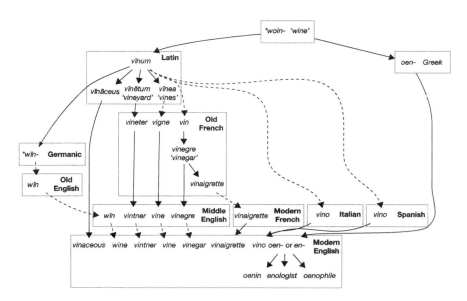

Figure 2.3 Developments involving word elements meaning 'wine' up to Modern English. Dashed lines indicate descent between different stages of the same language. White arrowheads indicate derivation.

basic, most frequently used, and simplest words of Modern English are inherited from its Germanic ancestor languages. Words such as *sun, moon, lamb, life, death, mother, health,* and *god*; prefixes such as *un-* and *be-*; suffixes such as *-ness, -ly, -some, -ship,* and *-hood*; and thousands more words and elements are all native to English. And, unlike many other languages, English retains an utter fascination with forming compound words. Recent additions to the *OED* include *bird colonel, chicken glove, flag-off, hen-day,* and *onboarding.* Compounding is something English inherited from Germanic, though Modern German famously outstrips English in the length of the compounds it will tolerate. No English compound is likely to match German *Rindfleischetikettierungsüberwachungsaufgabenübertragungsgesetz,* a legal term for 'the law for the delegation of monitoring beef labeling'.

We have largely focused our attention here on the sources of vocabulary, but there are other mechanisms of linguistic change as well. For example, words can acquire new meanings. The word *bead* used to mean 'prayer', and the word *edify* used to mean 'construct a building'. We examine many similar developments in the chapter on semantic change. Borrowing can also bring into the language new sounds and new relationships between sounds. The [t] at the end of words like *democrat* and *pirate* becomes an [s] in *democracy* and *piracy* because of a change that took place in postclassical Latin. Changes in meaning and sound are discussed more fully in chapters 6 and 9 through 11.

SUMMARY

Historical events and political and cultural factors have left their linguistic traces on the development of English. The original Indo-European and Germanic vocabulary is still found in abundance, but the language has also undergone a series of changes in grammatical structure and pronunciation. Its original Germanic word stock has been enhanced by copious borrowings from many languages, most notably Latin, Greek, French, and Norse. The major stages of word borrowing into English are listed below.

- **Germanic** (before ca. 450): Borrowings from Latin, mostly words for types of everyday objects new to the Germanic peoples.
- **Prehistoric English** (ca. 450–700): More borrowings of names of everyday objects from Latin. Beginning of an influx of ecclesiastical terms accompanying Christianization.
- **Old English** (700–1100): More literary borrowings from Latin. Large influx of everyday words from Viking Norse.
- **Middle English** (1100–1500): Steady flow of borrowings from literary Latin are joined by heavy borrowing from French, especially terms from law, government, the military, and higher culture.
- **Modern English** (1500–present): Heavy influx of scientific vocabulary, including many neologisms based on elements from Latin and Greek. Borrowings from many other languages with which English has had contact in Europe, Asia, Australia, Africa, and the Americas.

WORD ELEMENTS

Learn the following elements and their meanings.

Element	Gloss	Examples
anim	soul	*animate, animosity, animadversion, unanimous*
corp	body	*corps, corpse, corpus, corpuscle, corpulent, incorporate*
culp	fault	*culpable, culprit, exculpate, mea culpa*
duc	to lead	*educate, induce, introduce, duct, conduct, product, ductile, duke*
fug	flee	*fugitive, fugue, centrifuge, refuge, fugacious*
grat	goodwill	*grateful, gratis, gratuity, congratulate, ingrate, ingratiate, grace, gracious*
greg	social group	*gregarious, congregation, egregious, segregate*
hom	human	*homicide, hominid, Homo sapiens*

Element	Gloss	Examples
leg	law, deputize	*legal, legacy, allege, relegate, privilege, legislature*
libr	balance, weigh	*equilibrium, Libra, libration*
liter	letter	*literal, literary, literati, alliteration, obliterate, transliterate*
nov	new	*novelty, nova, novice, novitiate, innovate, renovate*
omn	all	*omnipotent, omniscient, omnivorous, omneity*
par	give birth to, produce	*parent, prepare, separate, parturition, apparatus, oviparous, postpartum*
pet	seek, go to	*petition, appetite, centripetal, impetus, perpetual, compete, repeat, petulant*
pot	able, powerful	*potent, potential, impotent, omnipotent, possible*
prob	good, test	*probe, probable, probity, approbation, reprobate*
sci	know	*science, conscious, omniscience, prescient, plebiscite, adscititious, sciolism*
sec	cut	*sect, sector, secant, bisect, insect, transect*
somn	sleep	*insomnia, somnambulism, somnolent, soporific*
ven	come	*venue, provenance, intervene, contravene, eventual, prevent, venture*
ver	true	*verify, aver, verdict, veritable, veracity, verisimilitude*

All of these elements are taken from Latin. For a few of them this is obvious, because classical Greek elements never contain the letters ‹f› or ‹v›.

ELEMENT STUDY

1. What is the root in these words? Look up each word, and include a brief sentence about the relation between the root's literal meaning and its meaning in this word.
   a. *aggregate*
   b. *literacy*
   c. *conscience*

d. *vermifuge* (Note: two roots; the first is *verm(i)* 'worm')
e. *omniparent* (Note: two roots)
2. Identify the root or roots, which could be from either chapter 1 or chapter 2.
   a. *misarchy*
   b. *dialog*
   c. *catalogue*
   d. *cacophonic*
   e. *biomorph*
3. The element *anim* has developed the following meanings: (1) 'life'; (2) 'soul, mind'; (3) 'hostility'; (4) 'courage'. Which words below exemplify which of these meanings?
   a. *animalcule*
   b. *animate*
   c. *animation*
   d. *animism*
   e. *animus*
   f. *animadversion*
   g. *animosity*
   h. *magnanimous*
   i. *pusillanimous*
4. *Leg* meaning 'law, deputize' is easily confused with another element of the same spelling meaning 'read' or 'gather'. In which of the words below does *leg* (or an altered form of it) mean 'law' or 'deputize'?
   a. *legislate*
   b. *college*
   c. *legate*
   d. *delegate*
   e. *legend*
   f. *league*
   g. *colleague*

5. a. *Par* often occurs in *parous* at the ends of words describing reproduction. Find three such words.
   b. There is a closely related element *par* meaning 'prepare' in *apparatus, disparate, pare, prepare,* and *separate*. What do the two meanings 'reproduce' and 'prepare' have in common?
6. The element *sci* 'know' is historically related to *sec* 'cut'. Elements containing *sci* that still mean 'cut' are *scind* and *sciss* 'split'. What is the connection between the basic meaning 'cut' and the extended meaning 'know'?
7. False friends: One of the challenges of word analysis is determining the correct word element when two or more candidates are similar or identical. These are called *false friends*.
   a. The element **par** in *parent* has a meaning more akin to 'produce' in *prepare, separate,* and *apparatus*. English also has many words in **par** that derive from other sources. Among these is *apparent*, which, like its source word *appear* and like *transparent*, derives from a different root entirely that goes back to the Latin verb for 'show'. As the example *appear* shows, this root appears sometimes as *par* but elsewhere as *pear*. Yet another spelling of this root appears in the related verb *peer*. Words like *parity* have yet a third version of the root *par*, deriving from the Latin word for 'equal', which is also the source of the word *pair*. Look up each word below and identify the etymological root: **par** 'give birth to, produce'; **pear** ~ **par** 'show'; or **par** 'equal'.
      i. *subpar*
      ii. *preparation*
      iii. *apparition*
      iv. *parity*
      v. *compare*
   b. As noted in this chapter, *libr* 'weigh, balance' is easily confused with *libr* 'book' (as in *library*) and *liber* 'free' (as in

liberty). (*Libr* 'weigh, balance' is the source of the abbreviation *lb.* for 'pound'.) For each of the words below, identify the etymological root.

   i. *library*
   ii. *liberal*
   iii. *deliberate*
   iv. *liberty*
   v. *equilibrate*
   vi. *libretto*
   vii. *libertine*

8. After studying this chapter's word elements, test your knowledge by replacing the question marks with the appropriate word elements or glosses you have memorized. Then spell out the full word. With the aid of a dictionary, give a brief definition that partly or fully reflects the meaning of the individual elements. If you cannot find the word in your dictionary, you may find portions of it that allow you to imagine what the full word might mean.

elements	*extra-*	*corpor*	*-eal*
glosses	'outside'	?	A
elements	?	*-ent*	*-ate*
glosses	'powerful'	A	N
elements	*centri-*	?	*-al*
glosses	'center'	'seek'	A

EXERCISES

1. Which part or parts of the verb in the sentence *She perspires in the heat* marks the person and number of the subject?
2. Look up the following words in your dictionary. On the basis of the etymologies given there, state for each one

a. whether it is a native Germanic word (i.e., one present in Old English with no evidence of borrowing from any other language) and
   b. if it is not native, indicate: (1) what language the word originally came from and (2) when it was borrowed: Old English or earlier, Middle English, or Modern English.

To answer these questions, you may have to read the introductory material in your dictionary to learn how to interpret the **etymologies** in individual word entries. Be sure you understand how the dictionary distinguishes between when a word is borrowed from another language and when a word is related to or akin to a word in another language.

   a. *time*
   b. *face*
   c. *want*
   d. *canoe*
   e. *finger*
   f. *theology*
   g. *chant*
   h. *critic*
   i. *wise*
   j. *stigma*
   k. *vest*
   l. *corn*
   m. *barn*
   n. *great*
   o. *joke*
   p. *taste*
   q. *bazaar*
   r. *please*
   s. *sweet*
   t. *grain*
   u. *crown*
   v. *tomato*

w. *poem*

x. *canine*

3. These are Modern English words and the Middle English words they descend from. Using phonetic symbols, give the pronunciation of each word. You may assume that any sound not discussed in this chapter was pronounced roughly the same in Middle English as in Modern English. Be sure to consult "Symbols and Abbreviations" in the preface for the correct IPA symbols. As an example, for the first pair below you would transcribe ModE [tek], ME [taːkə].

   a. ModE *take*, ME *take*

   b. ModE *reed*, ME *reed*

   c. ModE *shoe*, ME *shoo*

   d. ModE *hone*, ME *hoone*

   e. ModE *shine*, ME *shine*

   f. ModE *town*, ME *toun*

   g. ModE *cake*, ME *cake*

Three

Morphology

The Structure of Complex Words

THE BASICS OF MORPHOLOGY

This book is largely about learning to analyze **complex** words into their **morphological elements**.

Word	Elements
blackbird	*black, bird*
refresh	*re-, fresh*
bookish	*book, -ish*
warmth	*warm, -th*
past	*pass, -t*
elephantine	*elephant, -ine*

The hyphen after *re-* in the second column here indicates that *re-* is a prefix, while the one before the elements *-ish*, *-th*, *-t*, and *-ine* indicates that they are suffixes. Many of the word parts here happen to be single syllables, but it would be a mistake to confuse word elements with syllables, as can be gathered from the elements *-th* and *-t*, which are not syllables at all. Furthermore, *elephant*, the root component in *elephantine*, has three syllables. What we are dealing with here clearly goes beyond syllables or sounds.

Recognizing morphological elements helps us remember new words and can provide some explanation for their meaning. Even if we have never run across the term *pancarditis* before, recognizing at least some of the parts will give a hint at its meaning. The ending *-itis* may be familiar from names of other forms of inflammation, such as *tendinitis* or *tonsilitis*. We may also recognize the element *card,* meaning 'heart', from *cardiogram* or *cardiologist*. (Later in the book, we will find that *heart* and the root *card* are actually the same word.) So *pancarditis* probably involves inflammation of the heart. What meaning is added by *pan*? This is the same prefix found in *pan-American* and *pantheist* with the meaning 'all, everywhere'. Thus a reasonable guess—which would prove to be right—is that *pancarditis* is inflammation of all of the tissues of the heart. Compositionality—a word's meaning deriving from the meaning of its parts—extends to even the most common words. A *blackbird* is a *bird* species typified by *black* coloration. *Warmth* is the state of being *warm*. As will become evident, this information is hardly ever perfect: not all black birds are blackbirds, and not all blackbirds are black. Still, the parts of a complex word reveal far more about meaning than we could learn from trying to take apart a **simplex** word like *eat, people,* or *elephant*. The complex word *bookishness* has the immediate components *bookish* and *-ness,* and *bookish* itself has the components *book* and *-ish*. A form that cannot be broken down further, like *book, -ish,* and *-ness,* is called a **morpheme**. Each of the elements listed for study in our word element sections is a morpheme. Dividing a word into constituents—our ultimate objective in hundreds of cases to come—is called **parsing**. We separate constituents from one another with a space and put a hyphen after prefixes and before suffixes, as here:

Word	Elements
bookishness	*book -ish -ness*
unreadable	*un- read -able*
translucent	*trans- luc -ent*
hyperthermesthesia	*hyper- therm esthes -ia*

Morphology

PRACTICE

If these morpheme breaks make sense to you, try your hand at analyzing the following four words. As above, separate elements with a space and add a hyphen after prefixes and before suffixes. See how you do on your own, and then feel free to check your answers in a dictionary.

befriended
infuriate
subatomic
uvulopalatopharyngoplasty

Here's a bit of discussion on some questions that may have arisen during that practice exercise. For *infuriate*, removing the prefix *in-* and suffix *-ate* leave us with *furi*. This is the same morpheme as *fury* with a tiny spelling difference. If you analyzed the root of *subatomic* as *atom*, that's reasonable enough, but *atom* itself can be broken down even further to *a-* 'not' and *tom* 'cut', reflecting the earlier notion that the atom was an indivisible entity. For the last example, you may have wondered what to do with the *-o-* of *uvulo-*, *palato-*, and *pharyngo-*. Later we suggest parsing these combining forms as a root plus a meaningless element *-o-* that is commonly inserted between roots of Greek origin.

The two previous chapters showed that over time words can undergo a complex set of changes—changes that can make it hard to pick out their roots and affixes. To make things easier, the next few chapters focus on a few dozen common changes that serve to obscure the identity of roots and affixes. An example is the weakening of the vowel of the root *fac* 'do, make' of *fact* and *facile* in words like *defect* and *infect*. We see a similar pattern in word pairs like *gradual/ingredient*, *sacred/desecrate*, *status/obstetric*, and many others. In the next chapter, we formulate a vowel weakening rule general enough to apply to whole classes of morphemes.

Changes in form and meaning over the centuries can cause a single etymological root to split into distinct ones. For example, recall from chapter 1 that *captain*, *chief*, and *chef* all go back to a Latin root *cap* 'head.'

Does that mean that all three are the same morpheme? Despite their common origin, subsequent changes over the centuries have obscured their etymological status as three forms of an identical root. True, we can still detect the historical meaning relation among the three words, but the connection has become remote because the remaining similarities among consonants and vowels of the threesome are not regular enough to lead us to identify the root element of *captain, chief,* and *chef* as one and the same morpheme in current English. How do we determine this? The simple answer is that the words have migrated so far apart in form and meaning that any rule trying to connect them would fail to apply to other cases with any generality. Our goal is instead to identify recurring regularities that help to account for form and meaning in the largest possible variety of English words. For this reason, we analyze *captain, chief,* and *chef* as having distinct roots despite their etymological connection. Same for *skirt* and *shirt* and similar doublets from chapter 2. The important lesson to keep in mind is that parsing words in this text stops short of performing an etymological analysis.

Word etymologies are fascinating, though, and tracing words back to their origins raises many types of questions, including hypotheses about prehistoric cultures. For example, some scholars consider the element *agr* 'field', a root in the word *agriculture*, to derive from the Proto-Indo-European root *ag-* 'drive (cattle)'. This might imply a connection between herding and farming. But following up on this type of question would take us too far from the more immediate goal of understanding and remembering unfamiliar vocabulary. Thus, our policy is to treat *agr* and *ag* as distinct roots, just as we've done with *captain, chief,* and *chef* and with *skirt* and *shirt*. Still, it's hard not to be impressed by how much linguistic history can be retraced over a period of about six thousand years, and later in the book, we trace the history of select word elements back to their origin, often as far back as Proto-Indo-European.

For now, we aim for more accessible word analyses that—unlike etymologies—don't require extensive comparative and philological information. Our main thrust over the next few chapters will be developing procedures for breaking down words into components. Ideally, the principles will apply equally well to familiar words like *bookishness* as to unfamiliar ones like *hyperthermesthesia*. Dictionary etymologies will help us along, even though they are not the end product we're seeking. Still, completing this text and doing the exercises may in the end take readers a step closer to recognizing word etymologies. In fact, one reason we recommend consulting the *American Heritage Dictionary of the English Language* is precisely because it traces many morphemes back to their ultimate etymological source.

To many linguists, a key issue in word analysis is whether native speakers of English intuitively recognize subcomponents, or whether they can use subcomponents to create new words that other native speakers will understand. These are worthy criteria, but the focus on parsing words in this book calls for some new terminology. While most of us can break apart *unreadable* into *un-read-able* and make new words with each of those three parts, we might not be aware that *fan* originally derived from *fanatic* or that *mildew* is based on the word *dew*. Yet connections like these are one of main things we learn from word analysis. To emphasize our interest in unearthing new connections among words that may not be obvious to speakers, we introduce a neutral term—**element**—to sidestep debates among linguists about what is or is not a **morpheme**. As you progress through the course, word elements will become easier to isolate as you spot them in more and more words. For instance, each constituent of *hyperthermesthesia* is found in many other words:

hyper- is the same prefix as in *hyperactive* and *hyperbole*.
therm is the root of *thermal* and *thermometer*.
esthes is the root of *anesthesia* and, in slightly different form, *aesthetics*.
-ia is a suffix for medical conditions.

Our aim is to help you perform a similar analysis on as many different kinds of words as possible. We noted briefly above that dictionary etymologies provide too much information on word etymologies. For example, we will learn to analyze the word *student* as a simple root plus suffix: *stud-ent*. By contrast, the *American Heritage Dictionary*'s etymology for *student* is highly detailed and includes citations of whole words from Latin and Old French that don't separate the root from the suffixes:

> [Middle English, alteration (influenced by Latin *studēre*, to study) of *studient, studiant*, from Old French *estudiant*, one who studies, from present participle of *estudier*, to study, from Medieval Latin *studiāre*, from Latin *studium*, study; see **STUDY**.]

Based on this account, we might analyze the historical Latin root as *studi*, whose final vowel was preserved in French. This *i* is not preserved in English *student*, and this argues for *stud* as the basic representation of the root. The *i* does turn up in *studious*, though, and accordingly in the next chapter we treat *studi* as a variant form of the root *stud*. As for the word *study*, we analyze it as *stud-y*, where *-y* is the noun-forming suffix of *synonymy* and *family*.

The farther we move along in this book, the more evident the advantages of knowing a little Latin and Greek will become, because the inventors of our learned vocabulary were consciously working with Latin and Greek vocabulary components. Some of the later chapters of this book provide some basic word elements from these languages along with their modern reflexes in English words.

FUNCTIONS OF MORPHOLOGICAL ELEMENTS

Roots and Affixes

In addition to finding word elements in complex structures, we can categorize elements by their function. A **root** is a basic word element whose function is primarily to provide meaning. Every word has a root, at the very least. For example, *book* is a root. Complex words can be formed by adding prefixes or suffixes to roots. Since prefixes and suffixes perform similar functions, the label **affix** is used to designate both. We'll also encounter a few cases where affixal material is inserted between word elements. An example is the *-o-* in *photograph*, inserted between the roots *phot* 'light' and *graph* 'write, draw'. In *bookish*, the suffix *-ish* vaguely tells us that the word describes a tendency, but the bulk of information about the meaning comes from the root *book*. Because the root tells us more about the meaning of a word than anything else, the first thing we ask about a complex word is often, what is its root or roots?

In our structurally simplest vocabulary, roots are themselves independent words. But in many English words, including the vast majority of unfamiliar ones, roots are not words in themselves. For example, in *transgress* subtracting the prefix *trans-* leaves us with *gress*, which is not a word. However *gress* is a morpheme, the same root found in *progress* and *regress*. Roots that can serve as words by themselves are called **free**; roots lacking this property are called **bound**. Because bound roots are harder to isolate than free roots, we devote much effort to learning how to identify them. That is the purpose of the list of common word elements at the end of chapters, which we urge you to memorize and to practice finding in English words.

Affixes

Besides roots, the **prefixes** *con-*, *ex-*, and *pre-* and **suffixes** *-ness*, *-ent*, *-able*, and *-ia* are examples of the other major class of word element, which attaches to roots to perform a variety of semantic and grammatical functions. As mentioned earlier, prefixes and suffixes belong to a more general grouping called **affixes**. This category also includes infixes, interfixes, and superfixes, all to be introduced later in the text. The very term *affix* (= *ad-fix*) 'something attached' indicates that it is an appendage to a more basic part of the word. The more basic component can be a simple root, such as *book*, or it may be a complex form that already has an affix. In *exoplanets*, the affix *-s* attaches to the base *exoplanet*, which already has the affix *exo-*.

Structure

Word structure looks linear because it's written and read from left to right, yet it must instead be hierarchical if it is to account for the range of different interpretations we assign to words. We interpret *unreadable* to mean 'impossible to read'. In other words, *un-* is prefixed to *readable*, which was formed by suffixing *-able* to *read*. But now suppose that English also had a verb *unread* for the act of wiping a previously read passage from memory. In that case, we could also suffix *-able* to the hypothetical *unread* to mean 'able to be unread'. This theoretical possibility is actually instantiated by *undoable*, which can mean either 'not doable' or 'able to be undone'. The trees in figure 3.1 capture the ambiguity by representing whether the main structure break occurs between *undo* and *-able* or between *un-* and *doable*.

Hierarchical structure is key to resolving this ambiguity, but even more importantly, it potentially serves to differentiate human language from animal communication, where no evidence of hierarchical structure has been found.

To save space and avoid extra artwork, we can display hierarchical structures linearly with labeled bracketing to indicate the parts of speech and boundaries of constituents, as here, with *V* for *verb* and *A* for *adjective*:

[un- [[do]$_V$ [-able]$_A$]$_A$ vs. [[un- do$_V$]$_V$ -able$_A$]$_A$

This notation provides an excellent way to specify the internal structure of a word like *atomic*, where the prefix and suffix attach to different entities. As the representation [[a-tom]$_N$ -ic$_A$]$_A$ shows, *-ic* goes onto the word *atom*, while the prefix *a-* goes onto the root *tom*.

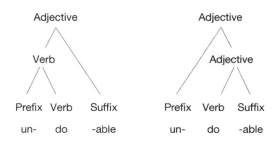

Figure 3.1 Representing the ambiguity of *undoable*.

Affix Meanings

Affixes vary widely in the amount of intrinsic meaning they convey. In many words the suffix *-ish* indicates a tendency or inclination; *-ee* often indicates someone who is the object of an action, as *employee* or *trustee*; sometimes it indicates an indirect object, as in *donee*, or even a subject, as in *standee* and *escapee*. Consistency of meaning is even more important in negating affixes, such as *-less*, *un-*, or *non-*, since they reverse the meaning of the base word. With most affixes, though, meaning is fuzzy and varies from word to word. This is true of the *-ous* in words like *famous* and *pompous*, where the only consistent "meaning" we can apply is that it forms adjectives. If we try to pin the meaning down further, we soon find exceptions. In *tetrapterous* 'having four wings' (like insects), the roots are *tetra* 'four' (compare *tetralogy* 'a literary work in four parts') and *pter* 'wing' (as in *helicopter*, literally 'helix-wing'). If we try to conclude from this example that *-ous* means 'having', a look at other *-ous* words shows that this won't work. The word *disastrous* does not mean 'having disaster' and *miraculous* does not mean 'having a miracle'. These examples push us back to a vaguer meaning such as 'characterized by'. But such a notion, common in dictionary definitions, doesn't capture the different meanings themselves. Instead, it's at best a kind of least common denominator, an attempt to capture what all of the different meanings of *-ous* share. Thus, all that actually unites the different occurrences of *-ous* is that they all form adjectives. On the other hand, quite a few suffixes that characteristically mark part of speech also have relatively constant meanings. An example is *-er*, a noun-forming suffix expressing agency as in *borrower* and *lender*. Another is *-able*, which creates adjectives, usually with passive force, as in *expendable* and *relatable*.

Finally, a few affixes have no meaning or function at all. Later in this chapter we briefly mention words built on adjacent Greek or Latin roots with a meaningless **interfix** separating the two roots. In *philosophy* and *omnipotent*, the interfix *-o-* appears between the roots *phil* and *soph*, and interfix *-i-* appears between roots *omn* and *pot*. While interfixes have no meaning, they do have roles in word derivation, and we tend to fill them in when forming new words structured analogically along the lines of existing words like *philosophy* and *omnipotent*. That is why in recently coined words we find *-o-*, as in *smellorama*, or sometimes *-a-*, as in *foodaholic*.

ROOT MEANINGS

It is not just derivational elements that can have fuzzy meanings. Even roots are seldom as well behaved as the simple glosses in the word element lists might lead one to expect. The glosses provide mere hints of a basic meaning that English vocabulary, in all its richness, may manipulate in imaginative ways. An example is *curr*, glossed above as 'run'. The fact that this root doesn't literally mean 'run' in the word *concurrent* may not be too disturbing, because it is easy enough to connect the actual meaning of *concurrent* with the image 'running together'. But other instances of this root present new images, related in other ways to the literal meaning 'run'. In *recurrent*, whose prefix means 'again', there is normally no running in the literal sense, yet the notion of running makes for a more picturesque image of the bland event 'happen'.

Very often the use of morphological elements relies on our ability to see ways in which one thing stands for another. In *astronomy*, the root *astr* means 'star'. This strikes us as entirely appropriate, even though astronomy is the study of all heavenly bodies, not just stars. The 'point' designated by the lexical component *punct* (a variant of the root *pung*) in *punctuation* refers not just to a period but to a variety of marks, even blank spaces. In *punctual* the connection with a literal point is different. And in both cases the semantic connection becomes even more tenuous when one realizes that the ultimate root of the component *punct* means 'poke'. In the rest of this chapter and in chapter 7 we explore the ways in which word elements depart from their literal meanings.

AFFIX MEANINGS AGAIN

Affixes often present special meaning problems. When they come at the end of a word, they generally have a grammatical function, determining what part of speech a word belongs to, and in all positions they often add to meaning as well. For example, *-ity* creates nouns and often adds the meaning 'quality or state of being' to the base it is attached to. Thus, *sincerity* means 'the quality of being sincere', and *ability* means 'being able'. Some *-ity* nouns designate objects characterized by a certain quality: examples are *monstrosity* 'something monstrous' and *oddity* 'something odd'.

The suffixes *-like, -ish, -esque,* and *-y* all form adjectives, such as *childlike, yellowish, picturesque,* and *risky*. These four suffixes are in fact similar semantically; they describe an attribute through its resemblance to some object. But there are also meaning differences among them. *Childlike* can be used in flattering ways (as in *We found his childlike manner disarming*), but *childish* tends to have negative connotations (*Your childish behavior has to stop*). *Spongelike* and *spongy* derive from the same noun, but with different shades of meaning. Something *spongelike* is similar to a sponge, while something *spongy* may simply be springy but not really like a sponge. Thus, it is probably good for a cake to be spongy but bad for it to be spongelike.

As we see, some suffixes have greater ranges of meaning than others. The meaning of *-like* is quite uniform from example to example, while *-y* varies in meaning from 'like' (as in *yellowy*) to 'containing an appreciable amount of' (as in *meaty*). Several suffixes, in fact, have a number of distinct meanings or functions. For example, besides the adjective-forming suffix *-y*, there is a noun-forming suffix *-y*, which appears in *monogamy, democracy,* and *comedy,* and also a suffix *-y* that forms diminutives, as in *kitty, Billy,* and so on. These three separate occurrences of *-y* obviously have very different meanings. Such cases are best regarded as accidental resemblances in form between different suffixes.

OTHER VARIATIONS IN THE MEANINGS OF WORD ELEMENTS

One good reason for so much variation in meaning is that language must constantly stretch to fit new situations in a changing world. A word element starts out with a particular meaning, but once it is used in different words, the meaning may lose its original simplicity, and as those words continue to be used in different situations, the word element may accumulate additional meanings. The root *ship* once meant specifically 'oceangoing vessel', but in the compound *spaceship* it loses that 'oceangoing' qualification and simply means 'vessel'. Thus, although word elements remain meaningful over time, their actual meaning will become less constant from word to word.

Easing the problem, variation in meaning often follows patterns. For example, *pyr* sometimes means 'fire' (as in *pyrotechnics* 'fireworks') and sometimes 'fever' (as in *antipyretic* 'a medication that reduces fever'). The meanings are not the same, but they are related; in this case, the relationship has come about from the use of *pyr* 'fire' as a metaphor for the "burning" of a fever's heat. Patterns in meaning change are the subject of chapter 7.

WORDS AS SYMBOLS

The word *apteryx* denotes the kiwi, a flightless bird of New Zealand with only rudimentary wings. We can parse this word into its components: the negating prefix *a-*, which means 'without' or 'not', as in *atheist* 'without (belief in) God'; the root *pter* 'wing'; and the suffix *-yx* (a rather rare noun-forming suffix, as in *calyx*). If we assumed that the meaning of a word is completely determined by the meanings of its parts, *apteryx* would mean something like 'wingless thing'. But kiwis aren't literally wingless, and even if they were, there is much more to a kiwi than the state of its wings. Such incompleteness in representation of meaning is the rule, not the exception. This is natural enough, since words are mere symbols, not complete linguistic representations of the physical or conceptual world.

Another example is *bibliophile* (from *bibli* 'book' and *phil* 'liking'), a very general term for someone who likes books. Would it, by the same token, be reasonable to infer that a *pedophile* (*ped* 'child') is anyone who likes children? Hardly. In *pedophile*, the liking is of a very specific kind, one involving sexual attraction, a sense that does not apply to *bibliophile*.

Morphology

Therefore, even where we succeed in breaking a word down into parts, the task of figuring out its meaning may not be over. We may get significant clues to the complete meaning, but the rest is left up to general knowledge, or common sense, or the idiosyncrasies of the word as a whole. A word's surrounding context can also provide clues.

WHY ANALYZE WORDS?

Parsing words provides clues to the meaning and function of unfamiliar words while deepening our knowledge of familiar ones by revealing the images on which our vocabulary is built. For example, *reject* literally means 'throw back', and *salient* means 'jumping'. Furthermore, recognizing the element *sal* in *salient* helps us spot it in words like *sally* and *salacious*. Recognizing that a multitude of words are built on images like these may enhance the language's expressive power for us. Analyzing words can even provide reliable spelling clues. If we realize that *renovate* contains the element *nov* 'new', we know that the middle vowel in that word is spelled with an ‹o› rather than an ‹a› or some other letter. Finally, skill in word analysis also strengthens the ability to recall words that are not yet thoroughly familiar. Even though many characteristics of the kiwi are not expressed by any particular part of the word *apteryx*, it is easier to recall its relationship to the notable "wingless thing" because of its very common key elements: *pter*, which appears in many words having to do with wings or flying, and *a-* 'not, without'.

HOW WE MAKE WORDS

New Components from Old

People coin words in many ways, often spontaneously and idiosyncratically, but it is useful to think of words as being built up in the following, ideal way.

Word formation begins with a root. Suppose we wish to coin a word to describe a place with a lot of wind. We might start with the root *wind*, then affix the adjective-forming suffix *-y*, forming *wind-y*, with a hyphen marking the dividing line between the morphemes. Our newly minted *wind-y* is a candidate for further derivation, for example suffixation of *-ness* to create yet another word, *wind-i-ness*. (The change from *y* to *i* is just a spelling rule of English.) To make this two-stage derivation explicit, we can enclose each component within square brackets. Thus, [wind] plus [-y] makes [[wind][-y]], and [[wind][-y]] plus [-ness] makes [[[wind][-i]] [-ness]]. The bracketing gets cumbersome fast, and so we tend to use it only to make a point about the internal structure of a word.

Compounding

A **compound word** is built by putting together two or more lexical elements. Most English compounds are formed by putting together existing words. Many combine a noun with a noun to form another noun, but compounds can be built from different parts of speech and can form any part of speech:

doorstep$_N$	*door$_N$ + step$_N$*
footstep$_N$	*foot$_N$ + step$_N$*
window-shop$_V$	*window$_N$ + shop$_V$*
comparison shop$_V$	*comparison$_N$ + shop$_V$*
stir-fry$_V$	*stir$_V$ + fry$_V$*
killjoy$_N$	*kill$_V$ + joy$_N$*

These examples of compounds functioning as nouns and verbs illustrate the wide variety of internal relations that can be expressed among their elements. *Doorstep* and *footstep* look similar in structure, yet the relation between their first element and *step* is different. The *step* of *doorstep* is an object leading up to a door, while in the second, *step* names an action by a foot. In *window-shop*, the first word expresses the location of the action of

Morphology

the second, while in *comparison shop*, the first element states the method used for the action of the second element. We see different sets of relations in *killjoy*, where the second element is the thing affected by the killing, as compared to *kill zone*, where the second element is the location of the action of the first.

While the examples just presented use nouns and verbs to create noun and verb compounds, there are many other possibilities. Here are a few examples:

jet-black$_A$	*jet*$_N$ + *black*$_A$
outsource$_V$	*out*$_{ADV}$ + *source*$_V$
easygoing$_A$	*easy*$_{ADV}$ + *go*$_V$ + *-ing*$_A$
able-bodied$_A$	*able*$_A$ + *body*$_N$ + *-ed*$_A$
in between$_{PREP}$	*in*$_{ADV}$ + *between*$_{PREP}$

Compounds need not even be restricted to two words, as seen in *pick-me-up* and *jack-in-the-box*. Due to their versatility, compounds are marvels of expression. Consider the wealth of grammatical and cultural information conveyed by very simple compounds like *soccer mom*, *lounge lizard*, *strip mall*, and *Facebook*. To see the point more clearly, try expressing the content of each of these four compounds by using the two words of the compound and adding all of the words not expressed but implied by their meaning. This reinforces our earlier point that the elements of a word give hints as to its meaning but rarely reveal a word's full semantic content.

Compounds can also be built from constituents other than full words. The most common examples in English are built on one or more borrowed Greek- or Latin-derived elements, like *micr-o-scope* and *ped-i-cure*. In chapter 2 we noted that English has been adopting Greek and Latin elements ever since the Renaissance to form new words, and often these words are compounds. Ancient Greek formed compounds freely, normally inserting interfix *-o-* between elements, forming words that come down to us as *phil-o-soph-y*, *the-o-log-y*, and the like. Latin did similarly with the interfix *-i-*. Examples are *aqu-i-fer*, a compound of root elements *aqu* 'water' and *fer* 'carry', and *agr-i-cult-ure*, a root *agr* compounded with the word *culture* (which is further analyzed as *cult-ure*).

Another compound-forming element is *tele-*, as in *tele-scope* and *tele-path-y*, cases without an interfix because the vowel interfix is inserted only between consonants. Interestingly, in a case that should have gone the same way, the original spelling *artefact*, based on Latin *arte* ('by art'), has mostly given way to the spelling *artifact*, though both are still in common use.

PRACTICE

Create five new compounds by combining these Greek-derived elements from chapter 1 along with an interfix. What would your new compounds mean, based on the glosses of the constituent elements?

cosm
log
morph
path
psych

You may have noticed variation in the way compounds are punctuated. Sometimes they are written as one word:

workbook
blackboard
mailman

But others are ordinarily written as two words:

exercise book
bulletin board
mail carrier

And in still others the compounded elements are (or can be) separated by a hyphen:

lean-to
work-around
sister-in-law
jack-in-the-box

The rules for punctuating compounds are arbitrary enough to lead to lots of variation in practice and lots of change over time. Microsoft Corporation first incorporated itself as *Micro-Soft* but quickly shifted to the smoother-flowing *Microsoft*. When the term *website* first appeared, it was written as two words, and occasionally hyphenated. For a time we'd see all three, *web site*, *web-site*, and *website*, sometimes in the same document (and often with a capital *W* on *web*). But nowadays the two-word version, separated by either a space or a hyphen, is well along the way to being a relic of the past (and *web* is now normally all lowercase). The progression from separating compound elements with a space to writing them together is natural enough. When a new concept first comes up, we may find it easier to grasp by viewing it as a compound of two separate elements. Then, as the two elements get linked conceptually, we may opt for a hyphen to express the link. As the compound gains familiarity, it develops into an entity unto itself, which we show by eliminating the space or hyphen. The evolution can be gradual—as happened with *goodbye*, which for centuries was written as two words, followed by hyphenated version *good-bye*, which had its heyday in 1920 before ceding ground to the unpunctuated spelling *goodbye*, which has been the most frequent since 1960. The earlier variants still survive, sometimes defended by passionate adherents. This, as we'll see in chapter 8, is typical of the route to language change.

Conversion

English is well known for converting one part of speech into another with no visible or audible change in the word. This is called **conversion**.

table$_N$	The committee laid the bill on the table.
→ table$_V$	The committee tabled the bill.
TiVo$_N$	I recorded this program with a TiVo brand device.
→ TiVo$_V$	I TiVoed this program.
control$_V$	The new treatment controls things excellently.
→ control$_N$	The new treatment provides excellent control.
overnight$_A$	Better request overnight delivery on this package.
→ overnight$_V$	Better overnight this package.
other$_A$	This group's needs have been labeled and treated as other for too long.
→ other$_V$	This group has been othered for too long.
out$_{ADV}$	The president was forced out of the closet.
→ out$_V$	The president was outed.

Conversion usually creates a noun or a verb out of some other part of speech. Over the centuries it has created many nouns from verbs, including *feel*, *release*, and *reveal*, and even more verbs from nouns, including *sense*, *figure*, and *curse*. It is still highly productive today, though we may be able to sense the newness of the examples from the fact that they sound more artificial than the established ones. An example that appeared just a few decades ago is the verb *trial*, a conversion from the noun, as in "Scientists are *trialing* a new procedure to obtain patient samples."

Converting a verb to a noun can sometimes lead to a shift in stress. Compare the stress patterns of the verb and noun forms of the following words.

addict$_V$	*Clarence is addicted to reality TV.*
addict$_N$	*Clarence is a reality addict.*
progress$_V$	*Aviation progressed rapidly in the 1910s.*
progress$_N$	*Aviation made rapid progress in the 1910s.*
separate$_V$	*I wish the store would separate the ensemble and sell the blouse and skirt as individual pieces.*
separate$_N$	*I wish the store would sell the blouse and skirt as separates.*

When there is a stress difference, nouns are stressed on the first syllable, while verbs get a stress (primary or secondary) on a subsequent syllable. Because stress can signal conversion in a way not unlike the way that prefixes and suffixes can signal a difference in part of speech, it can be thought of as an affix—specifically, as a **superfix**, because it neither precedes nor follows the word but floats above the entire word.

Clipping

So far, we have been discussing classical patterns of word formation. Affixation, compounding, and conversion account for virtually all word formation in Latin and Greek, and the great bulk of the English vocabulary as well. But present-day English vocabulary has a number of ways of forming new words and word elements. One is **clipping**, which cuts down a word to a bare minimum that still allows it to be recognizable. Clippings from the last part of the twentieth century like

dis	*disrespect*
hyper	*hyperactive*
info	*information*
hood	*neighborhood*
morph	*metamorphose*
neocon	*neoconservative*
Y	*YMCA*

joined a host of earlier clippings that now seem very ordinary:

ad lib	*ad libitum*
auto	*automobile*
blitz	*blitzkrieg*
bus	*omnibus*
flu	*influenza*
graph	*graphic formula*
intercom	*intercommunication system*
lab	*laboratory*
phone	*telephone*
tux	*tuxedo*
typo	*typographical error*
van	*caravan*

The element *cran*, which until a few decades ago existed in only one English word, *cranberry*, was clipped from that word and used to form new compounds by the makers of Cran-Apple and Cran-Grape juice. The clipping of *YMCA* to *Y* is doubly interesting because here clipping feeds on the result of another shortening process, taking just the initials from *Young Men's Christian Association*. While one might regard the use of initials as a form of clipping, we see later that it goes by a special term, *initialism*.

Clippings can vary in their uses and in where they are recognized. For example, at the time of writing, Urban Dictionary glosses *graf* as both 'paragraph' and 'graffiti'. Recent clippings can sound informal and even colloquial, but the process has a long history in English. Clipped words that have been in the language for centuries are likely to lose their connections with their source words. An example is *fan*, originally from *fanatic* but now without a pejorative meaning. Even more surprising is *soccer*, coined late in the nineteenth century by clipping *soc* from *association football*, the official name for the game, and then adding the suffix *-er*, as used colloquially in words like *rugger* 'rugby' and *fiver* 'five-pound note'.

Significantly, the clipped form does not respect morphological structure. If it did, we'd object to clipping *in-form-ation* right in the middle of the second element to get *info* or clipping *web-log* in the middle of the first element to get *blog*. We'd also be at a loss to clip *caravan* at all, since the entire word is just a single root. Of course, now that *van* has become a well-accepted word in its own right, it can serve as a root in new words such as *vanpool*. It's worth keeping in mind that this makes it tempting to mistakenly analyze *caravan* as if it were ˣ*cara-van*.

Practice

Clipping is a highly active process in current English, but at the time of writing, clipped forms of the following words had not yet become widespread. Using your knowledge of English and drawing on the examples in the preceding section, what would you yourself choose as the clipped form for these words? Are you by chance aware of your strategy in arriving at these answers?

recognize
scholarship
manuscript
etymologist
giraffe

Blending

Blending creates a new word by fusing together parts of two or more words. Once in a while a blend juggles some of the consonants and vowels around, as with *chortle* from *chuckle* and *snort*, but more standard is *smog*, a blend of *smoke* and *fog* that leaves the order of its parts intact, helping us to identify their source, as we can see from the following:

motel	*motor, hotel*
homophobia	*homosexual, phobia*
squiggle	*squirm, wiggle*
spam	*spiced, ham*
netiquette	*Internet, etiquette*
pixel	*pictures, element*

Blends of two source words often retain sounds or letters common to both original words, as with the *et* of *netiquette*, making the source words easier to find. Blends can also be subtle, and some readers may be surprised to see pixel and squiggle on the list. The same goes for the blending process behind *billion* (which originally meant 'a million millions') from *bi-* and *million* and *trillion* (originally meaning 'a million million millions') from *tri-* and million. *Million* itself is not a blend but a borrowing from French *million*, which French borrowed from Italian. As we'll see in chapter 6, French *milli* is the source of our prefix *milli-* in words like *millimeter* and *milliwatt*.

In recent decades, blend activity has been on the rise, adding words like *chocoholic* from *chocolate* and *alcoholic*, and *emoticon*, a blend formed from a clipped form of *emotion* and the word *icon*. A fairly recent addition is *fignature*, a signature drawn with a finger on an electronic pad.

Blends often have an aura of frivolity, but they serve the vital purpose of allowing us to succinctly refer to concepts that would otherwise be a mouthful. The members of the International Criminal Police Organization are not joking around when they refer to themselves as *Interpol*. Blends are crucial in fields like chemistry and molecular biology, where words like *aldehyde* and *aflatoxin* are much more convenient than the alternatives (*alcohol dehydrogenatum* and *Aspergillus flavus toxin*).

The last few examples show that blending, like clipping, does not respect the internal structure of the source words. *Afla* is neither a root nor an affix. It gets its first *a* from *Aspergillus*, and *fla* is a convenient, one-syllable clip from *flavus*. It may be disappointing to learn from a book about internal word structure that internal word structure is not a factor in blends. Yet our language is all the better for it, because blending gives rise to new word parts that in turn lead speakers to create entirely new words. The prefix *wiki-*, originally a clipped version of *WikiWikiWeb*, was adopted for the names of other free sources of information on the web, including Wikipedia, wikiHow, and WikiLeaks, and it is also used by itself as a full-fledged word, *wiki*, for a website that anyone can edit or add content to. At the same time, *-pedia,* clipped from *encyclopedia,* became a suffix in names of online information sources, including concoctions like *Techopedia, Investopedia,* and *Webcam-pedia*. A similar trend has operated over the five decades since the scandals of the Watergate era, which gave rise to the suffix *-gate*, contributing words like *nannygate* and *Monicagate* for newer scandals. Along similar lines, the suffix *-ponics* has been used for new practices based technically or metaphorically on hydroponics, including aeroponics, geoponics, and organoponics.

Recent decades have brought an explosion in English of blended compounds formed by clipping words in pairs, such as *sci-fi, romcom, FedEx,* and *Bed-Stuy,* from *science fiction, romantic comedy, Federal Express,* and *Bedford-Stuyvesant*. (Note the differences in punctuation paralleling the ones noted earlier in word-word compounds.) As with *info* and *van*, clipping here does not go out of its way to respect morphological structure. The *fi* of *sci-fi* is not a morphological component of *fiction*, and the fact that *sci* is an actual word root is coincidental, because it happens to be a syllable in the base word *science.*

Another wildly popular type of blending in current English involves substituting a clipped form for a syllable or two in an existing word. *Chocoholic,* based on *alcoholic,* wryly connects a fondness for chocolate to dependence on alcohol. A *mockumentary* is a kind of documentary whose intent is to imitate or satirize a real one. *Docudramas* and *docucomedies* are dramas and comedies structured as documentaries. Modern technology has given rise to a number of new terms structured along similar lines. Examples are *webinar* from *web seminar* and *phablet* from *phone tablet,* along with *emoticon* and *netiquette* cited earlier.

Structurally similar words are sometimes inspired by pure frivolity. The inventor of a robot that makes pizza dough named his device a *doughbot*, while the conductors of some organized pizza tours call themselves *doughcents*. For a time, the popular media fused the names of the two members of celebrity couples as a way to symbolically unite them: *Brangelina* for *Brad* and *Angelina* and *Kimye* for *Kim* and *Kanye*. That particular trend had cooled by the time of writing, as did the marriages of those two couples.

Initialisms and Acronyms

Another way of reducing potentially long names to something manageable is to represent a phrase by its initial letters. Words so formed are called **initialisms**.

USA	*United States of America*
GAO	*Government Accounting Office*
YMCA	*Young Men's Christian Association*
IBM	*International Business Machines*
WWW	*World Wide Web*
OK	*Oll korrect*

Often people do not think of initialisms as words, because they seem so much like abbreviations. The difference is that abbreviations, like *Dr.* and *ME*, are intended to be pronounced in full when read aloud (*doctor, Middle English*), whereas an initialism has a pronunciation of its own, the sequence of the names of its component letters. Indeed, the initialism often becomes more frequent than the full phrase or replaces it entirely. We see this happening today with the spate of initialisms coming from the rise of the Internet and social media, including *LOL, BFF,* and *SMH*.

Some initialisms are read off by the actual sounds of their letters rather than by the letters' individual names. This type of initialism is called an **acronym**, a compound name formed from elements *acr* 'height, tip' and *onym* 'name'. Here are a few examples:

radar	*radio detecting and ranging*
scuba	*self-contained underwater breathing apparatus*
Qantas	*Queensland and Northern Territory Aerial Services*
WYSIWYG	what you see is what you get

As these examples suggest, acronyms are even more likely than initialisms to completely supplant the original phrase they were derived from. While the examples in the preceding list are all built on the initial letters of the constituent words, acronyms can also be constructed from longer sequences than initial letters—syllables, for example, or arbitrary sequences of letters at the beginning of a word. As mentioned earlier, these tiny sound chunks are another example of clipping, as in FedEx, which clips the initial syllables of *federal* and *express* and joins them into an acronym. An acronym can become so compelling and popular that it leads to the creation of others along similar lines. The Manhattan district known since the middle of the twentieth century as *Soho* (clipped from 'South of Houston') has since given rise to others, such as *Tribeca* ('Triangle below Canal'), and *Nolita* ('North of Little Italy'). In each case, the components are all clipped from the beginning of the words they stand for. But acronyms can also take on a more complex form, as in the recent coinage USINDOPACOM, composed of a two-syllable initialism, *US*, prefixed to an acronym formed from the first three syllables of *Indo-Pacific* and the first syllable of *Command*. The pairing of an initialism with an acronym makes this a hybrid.

Perhaps the ultimate development in acronymy is when the acronym makes sense as a word that describes some aspect of its meaning.

zip (code)	*Zone Improvement Program*
NOW	*National Organization for Women*
ACT	*American Conservatory Theater*
MADD	*Mothers Against Drunk Driving*

However, the full phrases are often invented afterward as a justification for the acronym and sometimes as a joke. The search engine Bing has been facetiously analyzed as an acronym for "because it's not Google". We return briefly to these so-called reverse acronyms in the later section on back-formation.

Onomatopoeia and Sound Symbolism

The normal situation in language is for sound and meaning to be totally divorced from one another. In *cat*, nothing inherent in the individual sounds or sound combinations suggests the meaning 'cat'. But occasionally the sounds do suggest meanings.

In **onomatopoeia**, a word attempts to mimic the sound it describes, or occasionally the object that makes that sound.

pow
creak
blip
flap
clash
bleat
cuckoo
bobwhite
cough
babble

Many onomatopoeic words go back to Middle English, Old English, or beyond. Their antiquity may help explain why some onomatopoeia doesn't sound very natural. The word *cough* may sound more like a cough if you pronounce the ‹gh› not with the modern [f] sound but in the Middle English fashion, as a raspy *k*-like sound as in the first consonant of *Hanukkah* or the final consonant of *Bach*. A sheep's bleat may sound more like *bleat* if you pronounce the vowel in its Old English form, rhyming with the modern pronunciation of *bat*.

Some onomatopoeia has been borrowed from other languages. For example, *barbar*, the root of *barbarian*, came to us from Ancient Greek, where it referred to all people who did not speak Greek. The

Greeks thought foreign speech sounded like *bar-bar*, a meaningless stammering, or perhaps they thought that was what foreigners sounded like when they spoke Greek. (Nowadays, extras in movies are said to mutter "rhubarb" repeatedly when generating indecipherable background conversation.) A similar process was probably behind the word *Berber*, which comes from an Arabic term for peoples of North Africa who didn't speak Arabic. Onomatopoetic words have also found their way into our technical vocabulary. The medical term for a stomach rumble, *borborygmus*, is an onomatopoetic term that ultimately goes back to Ancient Greek.

Slightly different from onomatopoeia is **sound symbolism**. Here, the connection between the sound of the word and its meaning is less direct. Some probable examples are

putrid

foul

mother

teeny

humongous

The etymological root of *putrid*, *pu*, dates back to a Proto-Indo-European exclamation of disgust. The root is sound symbolic because it mimics the natural (nonlinguistic) sound humans might make on smelling rotten food; if it were onomatopoetic it would name the sound itself, or the person making the sound. *Foul* has the same origin but has been significantly altered by Grimm's law and the Great Vowel Shift. The element *cac* from chapter 1 may also be a symbolic cry of disgust; compare *caca* 'excrement' in baby talk. A huge number of the word's languages have an [m] in their word for *mother*, because this is the sound a baby most easily makes when making sucking movements.

Some sound-symbolic words don't mimic sounds at all. In *teeny*, the consonants and especially the [i] vowels suggest smallness synesthetically; that is, the thin, sharp sound of the [i] indicates smallness in other, nonacoustic domains. In *humongous*, the opposite is true.

Sound symbolism is especially beguiling because when one knows English so well that it becomes second nature, one starts to feel that most words sound like what they mean—even though in fact their sounds are completely arbitrary, as in *cat*. Often some crosslinguistic investigation can tell us whether a sound-meaning correspondence is really sound symbolism. For example, experiments beginning with Wolfgang Köhler's *Gestalt Psychology* (New York: Liveright, 1927) have shown that people presented with two totally made-up words—like *takete* and *maluma*—overwhelmingly choose the first as the name of an angular object and the second as the name of a curvy one—whether the people are speakers of English, Spanish, Tamil, or Swahili, among other languages. Thus, awareness of the possible effects of sound symbolism might offer subtle clues to the meanings of some words.

Analogy

The structure of existing words often inspires the creation of new ones. If we are looking for a word to describe an aversion to reading tweets on Twitter, we might well use existing words for aversions, such as *agoraphobia*, *acrophobia*, and *xenophobia*, as models for a new word *tweetophobia*, whose structural resemblance to the originals even includes a vowel interfix between the roots *tweet* and *phob*. This is just what happened with the verb *prepone* 'move to an earlier time', which showed up early in the twentieth century and was modeled on the verb *postpone*. It was used frequently enough to be listed in the *OED*, but it's rarely heard nowadays. An adjectival form of *shambles* appeared a few decades ago—*shambolic*—which may have been formed on analogy to *symbolic*, from *symbol*. We have even heard of dogs being said to *caninify* certain qualities. If a person can personify bravery then a dog, apparently, should be able to caninify it. The word *caninify* obviously owes its origin to analogy, but in structure it looks no different from *personify*, a noun plus the affix *-ify*.

Analogical reasoning applied to word structure may result in **back-formation**, where a simpler word is derived from a more complex word. The words *edition* and *editor* existed in English long before the simple word *edit*. Clearly somebody noted that *-or* and *-ion* often are used to derive nouns from Latinate verbs ending in *-t*, and so inferred that an *editor* is one who **edits editions**. That is completely logical, but historically speaking what has happened was not affixation: it was the undoing of a supposed affixation. Similarly, *televise* was formed from *television* and *metamorphose* was formed from *metamorphosis*. You may occasionally run across the word *incent*, a back-formation from *incentive* that means 'incentivize' but is two syllables leaner. The availability of a potential back-formation by no means guarantees its acceptance, however. Hans Marchand (*The Categories and Types of Present-Day English Word-Formation*, 2nd ed. [Munich: Beck, 1969]) lists a number of attempts that never caught on. Examples of missed opportunities include:

to auth
to ush
to buttle

The examples of analogy we have given so far would be hard to identify without special historical information. Just looking at the word *arachnophobia* will not tell you that it was coined, in part, by analogy with *agoraphobia* and not the other way around. However, some back-formed words leave us clues:

*This tape will **self-destruct** in five seconds.*
*Nobody would **carjack** my beat-up Hyundai.*

At first glance, *self-destruct* and *carjack* seem like ordinary compounds, with a little blending added in the latter case (*car, hijack*). But there's something a little strange with these words. Since when have English verbs expressed their objects by compounding? We don't ˣdinner-eat after we ˣself-wash-up. We would expect that Mr. Phelps's tape should *destroy itself*, and that people should not **hijack** my old car. But we do have lots of English nouns that compound with objects, in particular, *self-destruction* and *carjacking*. People have back-formed verbs from the nouns by simple analogy:

reaction N is from *react* V + *-ion* N

::

self-destruction N is from *self-destruct* V + *-ion* N

without noticing that the compound verb would not normally have existed in the first place.

The verb-adjective pair *react/reactive* is the likely analogical source of *proact*, a back-formation from *proactive* that at the time this book was written was established enough to appear in only a few dictionaries, among them Wiktionary and the OED.

Another type of back-formation is the reverse acronym, known also by the whimsical blend word *backronym*. One often hears that *phat* comes from *pretty, hot, and tempting*, or that *posh* comes from *port out, starboard home*, purportedly an observation about how posh travelers book sea voyages between England and India. Some think that the word *news* is an acronym formed from the points of the compass, which misses the much more obvious explanation that *news* is information about *newly* occurring events. Without historical information it can be hard to judge which came first, the phrase or the acronym. Often, we can spot a backronym from the fact that it just sounds much better than the full phrase. The *Lisa*, an early Apple computer, was said to be an acronym for *Local Integrated Software Architecture*, whatever that might mean, until it was revealed that it really was named after Steve Jobs's daughter. Also, acronyms more than a few letters long rarely arise by sheer coincidence. One strongly doubts, for example, that the authors of the USA PATRIOT Act were surprised to discover that that acronym just happened to emerge from the official title *Uniting and Strengthening America by Providing Appropriate Tools Required to Intercept and Obstruct Terrorism* (U.S. Congress, H.R. 3162, October 24, 2001). Acronyms can be fun, but beware acronymic etymologies picked up on the street.

Morphology

Analogy can lead to **reanalysis**, a revision of the morphological composition of a word. The word *sovereign* picked up its ‹g› because someone imagined that the final syllable of that word was from *reign* (the suffix is actually *-an* as in *Mississippian*). Similarly, *marijuana* picked up the ‹j› in English because it was misinterpreted as coming from the names *María* and *Juana*; the original Spanish word was *marihuana* or *mariguana*. So many people have taken *covert* as containing *overt* that its pronunciation has been affected: traditionally [ˈkəvr̩t], being a derivative of *cover*, but now mostly [ˈkovr̩t] or [koˈvr̩t], to rhyme with *overt*. Enough people have somehow found the word *bosom* in *buxom* that one would now be foolish to use *buxom* in its original sense of 'obedient'.

Widely accepted restructurings of established words due to reanalysis are called **folk etymologies**. The word *pea* was *pease* in Middle English, where it was originally a singular noun. But the final [z] sound came to be taken as a plural ending, and so the ending was eventually subtracted to give a new singular form, *pea*. Some words are sitting ducks, their surface features practically begging for a folk etymology. It's nearly impossible to imagine an *uproar* without connecting it with our English word *roar* even though etymologically English *uproar* derives from an unrelated Dutch word for a tumult or confusion. *Babel*, traditionally pronounced to rhyme with *label*, is the English rendering of the Hebrew name for *Babylon*. *Babble*, which rhymes with *rabble*, is a native English word that means to talk incoherently. On top of the similarity in spelling and sound, there is also a semantic connection. In the Bible, people in Babel undertook to build a very tall tower, and God distorted their speech, giving everybody a new language so they couldn't understand each other. Those two words are so similar that they began to influence each other, to the extent that in the United States today they are almost universally pronounced the same, as if there were a Tower of Babble.

For the term *chaise lounge*, English speakers modified the French expression *chaise longue* by substituting the English word *lounge* for the French adjective *longue*. Because the French adjective means 'long' and has no connection with lounging, this is quite a switch. Why English speakers didn't also change the first word, *chaise*, is anyone's guess. Finally, the only connection between Jerusalem artichokes and the city of Jerusalem is the similarity in sound of the name of this city with the Italian term *girasole*, which means 'sunflower'; the Jerusalem artichoke is in fact a kind of North American sunflower.

Most surprising of all perhaps is how little sense many folk etymologies make. What could a sockeye possibly be? How could anyone think a cockroach (from *cucaracha*) has anything to do with cocks (male chickens) or roaches (a type of fish)? Apparently, the main motivation in many cases is simply to transform long strings of unfamiliar syllables into familiar English word elements that sound vaguely similar; the fact that the parts have little or nothing to do with the meaning of the whole is often neglected. Nevertheless, folk etymologies should not leave us shamefaced, for even the term *shamefaced* is a folk etymology, coming from Middle English *shamefast*, 'bound by shame'.

While reanalyses could easily be branded as errors arising from insufficient information, it's also possible to see them in a more positive light. Much as modern technology seeks to make some of its new devices backward compatible, so that updated technology still works in your old system, reanalysis attempts to help a strange new word fit in by making its parts more compatible with existing word structures.

What we need to add at this point is that all these examples fail to show that most reanalysis is undetectable and thus without any effect. Someone you know might be harboring suspicions that *antagonism* is somehow connect with *ants* and *agony*, but this would only come out in the open if they happened to mention it.

Morphology or Etymology?

As we've seen, morphology studies the components of words; etymology studies the history of words. When the definitions are stated so starkly, the distinction between morphology and etymology seems very clear. But in practice, a morphological analysis of a word is often very hard to tell apart from an etymological analysis. Consider the following pairs of statements:

morphology: *Blackbird* is a compound of *black* and *bird*.
etymology: *Blackbird* was formed by compounding *black* with *bird*.

morphology: *USA* is an initialism of *United States of America*.
etymology: *USA* was formed from the initials of the main words in *United States of America*.

In these sentences, the difference between morphology and etymology is trivial, and it disappears entirely when the statements are brief enough. More often than not, you'll find that the sorts of concise etymologies that appear in most dictionaries serve very well as a morphological analysis. The confluence of etymology and morphology is particularly strong in a book like this one, where the history of a word is taken as an important piece of evidence for its morphology.

But often there is a sharp distinction between morphology and etymology. Here are some examples of etymological statements that would be out of place in a morphological analysis:

The word *pantheon* was borrowed from Latin and first appeared in English during the Old English period.
Oak comes from the Old English word *āc*. It is related to the German word *Eich*.

This kind of information is also included in many dictionaries, and students need to be careful not to automatically copy out such information when asked to do purely morphological research. These facts say nothing about what the functional elements of the words might be. By the same token, morphological statements such as the following would be considered laughably inadequate by etymologists:

Pantheon has the structure *pan- the -on*, where the root is *the* 'god'.
Oak is a morpheme.

In some cases morphology conflicts with etymology. Historically, *cockroach* derives from *cucaracha*, yet today it is a compound of *cock* and *roach*. *Scissors* originated from the Latin root *cid* 'cut', putting it in the same company as *decide* and *incisor*; but in its modern spelling it groups more naturally with *scissile* and *scission*, so arguably it now shares with those words the root *sciss*, which means 'split' or 'cut'.

This book deals with both morphology and etymology, which, though easily confused, are distinct. Perhaps the biggest source of confusion comes from the fact that in analyzing a word's structure, we often talk about whether elements are native, Latin, or Greek. Understandably enough, this looks a lot like etymology. But the purpose of appealing to a source language like Latin or Greek when analyzing a word is not primarily to uncover its history, as it would be if our main concern were etymology. Instead, recognizing the original source language of a root provides keys to its behavior when different affixes are attached—the subjects of chapters 4 and 6. Besides, finding Latin and Greek elements in words does not actually trace words back to the ancient Roman and Greek era. Most such words are, in fact, modern creations, a point made earlier in this chapter and in chapter 2. The word *anemometer*, for example, was coined in the eighteenth century. Knowing that *anem* 'wind' and *met* 'measure' are Greek roots helps us understand why the interfix *-o-* is used in this compound.

SUMMARY

Unlike etymology, which studies the history of words, morphology is the study of the functional composition of words. Components may be complex, consisting of other components, or simplex, in which case they are called morphs. Lexical components, including every content word, contain at least one root, which provides the core meaning. Affixes may accompany the root. They add to the meaning or provide grammatical information such as the part of speech. Affixes are either inflectional, creating different forms for a vocabulary word—such as singulars versus plurals or present versus past tense—or derivational, forming different vocabulary words from a base word, such as *childish* from *child*. Affixes can also be classified by where they attach to their bases: prefixes attach before, suffixes after, interfixes between, and superfixes cause change of stress in English.

The meanings of a word element may vary from word to word. Its contribution to the meaning of a specific word can often be identified from general knowledge, context, or an understanding of the systematic ways in which meanings vary.

The most frequent types of word-formation process are affixation and compounding. Compounds combine two words, sometimes with an interfix between them. Another process, analogous to affixation except that it does not add a visible affix, is conversion, which shifts a word from one part of speech to another with no other changes apart from an occasional adjustment of stress pattern. Processes that are more active now than earlier in the history of the language include clipping, which is often accompanied by blending; initialisms and acronyms; and onomatopoeia and sound symbolism. In practice, word formation often considers the analogy of existing words as well. Analogy can also lead to back-formation of simpler words from more complex ones and can be easily detected only if the product is irregular. Finally, analogy can cause people to assign false structures to words, sometimes bringing about folk etymology, where a word changes its spelling or pronunciation to agree better with the reanalyzed structure.

RELATED READING

Our source for the notion that hierarchical structure in human language may differentiate it from forms of animal communication is Adam R. Fishbein, William J. Idsardi, Gregory F. Ball, and Robert J. Dooling, "Sound Sequences in Birdsong: How Much Do Birds Really Care?," *Philosophical Transactions of the Royal Society B* 375, no. 1789 (2020): 20190044. At the time of writing, the article could be found at https://royalsocietypublishing.org/doi/pdf/10.1098/rstb.2019.0044.

WORD ELEMENTS

Learn the following derivational affixes and their glosses. The glosses A, N, and V indicate that the element makes words having a specific part of speech: adjective, noun, and verb, respectively.

Suffix	Gloss	Source	Examples
-ance	N	L	*penance, brilliance*
-ant	A, N	L	*tenant, Protestant, valiant*
-ary	A, N	L	*library, mortuary, temporary, tertiary*
-ate	N, A, V	L	*delegate, irate, navigate, novitiate, precipitate, prelate, roseate*
-ence	N	L	*science, intransigence, patience*
-ent	A, N	L	*ambient, parent, proponent, incumbent*
-ic	A, N	L, G	*arithmetic, chronic, dramatic, neurotic, psychic, topic*
-ion	N	L	*action, nation, attrition*
-ity	N	L	*stupidity, alacrity, monstrosity, paucity, variety, loyalty*
-ive	A, N	L	*native, laxative*
-ize	V	G	*Americanize, extemporize, vocalize, systematize*
-oid	resembling (A, N)	G	*android, pterygoid, spheroid, adenoids*
-ory	A, N	L	*sensory, auditory, oratory*
-ous	A	L	*porous, poisonous, abstemious, pendulous, tremulous*
-sis	N	G	*analysis, praxis, thesis, tmesis*
-y	N	L, G	*astronomy, privacy, sympathy*

Prefix	Gloss	Source	Examples
ab-	from, away	L	*abdicate, ablative, abolish, absolute, abstain, abstruse*
ad-	to, toward	L	*adapt, adit, abbreviate, adduce, affect, annul, arrive, attract*
an-	not, without	G	*anarchy, anhydrous, anaerobic*

Morphology

Prefix	Gloss	Source	Examples
ana-	up, again, back	G	*analyze, anabolic, anachronism, anaclastic, analeptic, analog*
ante-	before	L	*antebellum, antecedent, antedate, anterior*
apo-	away from, off	G	*apology, apogee, apoplectic, apostasy, apastron, aphelion*
cata-	down, backward	G	*cataclysm, catacomb, catalepsy, catalog, catapult, catalyst*
con-	with	L	*convene, concomitant, concord*
contra-	against, facing	L	*contraceptive, contradict, contrapositive*
de-	reverse, from	L	*decode, demand, denote, deport, descend, destruction*
dia-	through	G	*diameter, dialog, dialysis, diathesis, diocese, diorama*
ec-	out	G	*appendectomy, ecstatic, tonsillectomy, exegesis, exodus*
ecto-	outside	G	*ectoplasm, ectoderm, ectomorph, ectoparasite*
en-	in	G	*energy, encephalitis*
endo-	inside	G	*endogamy, endomorph, endoscopy, endarteritis*
epi-	on, over	G	*epitaph, epigram, epitome, epencephalic, ephemeral*
eu-	good	G	*eulogy, euphemism, euphony, euphoria, euthanasia, eugenic*
ex-	out	L	*exact, excavate, except, exfoliate, extend, educe, egregious*
extra-	outside	L	*extraordinary, extramarital, extraneous, extraterrestrial*
hetero-	other	G	*heterogeneous, heterodont, heterodox, heteronomy, heterosexual*
homo-	same	G	*homogenize, homologous, homosexual, homatomic*
hypo-	under, below	G	*hypodermic, hypothermia, hypothesis, hypogeal, hypalgia*
in-	in, into	L	*incite, inception, incinerate, invade, inoculate*

Prefix	Gloss	Source	Examples
in-	not	L	*inert, inauthentic, incompatible, inequity, illegal, impossible, irreverent, ignorant*
infra-	below	L	*infrared, infrastructure, infralapsarian*
inter-	between	L	*interfere, intercalate, interior, interject, internal*
intra-	within	L	*intramural, intrauterine, intravenous*
iso-	equal	G	*isometrics, isosceles, isopathy, isobar, isandrous*
meso-	middle	G	*Mesolithic, mesobiotic, mesomorph, Mesopotamian, mesosphere*
meta-	beyond	G	*metadata, metamorphosis, metaphor, metaphysics, method, metonymy*
ob-	toward, against	L	*object, obdurate, obit, obloquy, obstacle, omit*
para-	beside, nearly	G	*parallel, paramedic, paranormal, paragraph, parenthesis, parody*
per-	through, thorough	L	*perturb, pernicious, perspicacity, pervade*
peri-	around, near	G	*perimeter, perihelion, periscope*
post-	after, behind	L	*posterior, posterity, postpartum, postpose, postprandial, postwar*
pre-	before	L	*prehistoric, preadolescent, prewashed*
pro-	forward, for	L, G	*proceed, prowar, provide, procure, produce*
re-	again, back	L	*reappoint, redo, review, redundant*
se-	apart	L	*separate, select, seduce, segregate, sedition*
sub-	under	L	*subhuman, subclass, subreption, success, suffuse, suborn*
super-	above	L	*superpower, supercilious, superficial, supersede, supreme*
syn-	with	G	*synergy, synchronize, syllogism, sympathy, symphony, systolic, system*
trans-	across, through	L	*transaction, trans-Atlantic, transfigure, translucent, transparent, traverse*

ELEMENT STUDY

1. The suffix -*ate* on nouns has several meanings or functions:
    a. 'one who has been (VERB) ed', e.g., *delegate* 'one who has been delegated'
    b. 'one who (VERB)s', e.g., *deviate* 'one who deviates'
    c. 'thing that has been (VERB)ed', e.g., *aggregate* 'thing that has been aggregated'
    d. 'place for (VERB)', e.g., *novitiate* 'place for novices'
    e. 'chemical derivative of (NOUN)', e.g., *opiate* 'chemical derivative of opium'

    Mark each of the following nouns in -*ate* with one of the letters (a) through (e) to indicate which of the functions just introduced best captures its meaning; if the meaning is better expressed in another way, give that meaning.
    a. *advocate*
    b. *caliphate*
    c. *certificate*
    d. *chromate*
    e. *concentrate*
    f. *electorate*
    g. *isolate*
    h. *moderate*
    i. *sulfate*
    j. *surrogate*

2. Many adjectives in -*ic* have a noun counterpart. Which of the following words function both as adjectives and nouns? Where does stress normally go on words ending in this suffix? Is the rule for stress more regular for adjectives or for nouns?
    a. *comic*
    b. *historic*
    c. *eccentric*
    d. *concentric*
    e. *arithmetic*

f. *basic*
   g. *sardonic*
   h. *automatic*
3. The suffix *-ize* is one of our most common and most productive endings. To get a feel for its productivity, list ten adjectives or nouns that this suffix can be attached to and list another ten that it cannot be attached to. For any answer that doesn't take a suffix in *-ize*, check to see whether the word can already function as a verb. For example, *table* can't take the suffix *-ize* because *table* can function as a verb without *-ize*, as in *table a motion*. Look for cases that don't already function as verbs without *-ize*.
4. Replace the prefixes in the following words with a different prefix from the element set from this chapter. In each case, show how prefixes affect meaning by contrasting the meaning of the original word with the meaning of the word you turned it into.
   a. *catabolic*
   b. *contravene*
   c. *diagnostic*
   d. *ectoderm*
   e. *hypomanic*
   f. *infrasonic*
   g. *metapsychology*
   h. *periscope*
   i. *persist*
   j. *secede*

EXERCISES

1. Identifying and distinguishing roots, morphemes, and morphs. Here is how the glossary defines these terms:

   root The smallest meaningful part of a word.
   affix A morphological component that does not contain a root but is only attached to

Morphology

a base form that has one or more lexical components. For example, prefixes, infixes. and suffixes are affixes.

morph The smallest unit of meaning or function in word construction. In other words, every root or affix is ipso facto a morph. For example, in *pretend* the prefix *pre-* as well as the root *tend* are morphs.

Look up each word below in a dictionary, divide it into its morphological components, and answer these questions for each component: Is it a root? Is it an affix? Is it a morph?
   a. *parapsychologist* (Consider *psycho* to be a single constituent.)
   b. *apathy*
   c. *hypersomnia*
   d. *hypersomnic*

2. The glossary defines **stem** as a lexical base to which an inflectional affix may be attached. For example, *book-* and *booklet-* are both stems to which the inflectional affix *-s* may be attached. In other words, we need to be able to identify inflectional affixes in order to identify stems. Inflectional affixes express grammatical functions like number, degree, tense, person, and case, and stems are simply what is left after all inflectional affixes have been removed from the word. Apply these definitions to identify stems in the words below.
   a. *swimmers*
   b. *philosophizing*
   c. *inflectional*

3. The glossary defines a **bound morph** as a morph that cannot appear as an independent word. For each bound root below, add a prefix to make this bound form into a word. (You may well need to adjust the spelling from the bare form of the root.) If you cannot find a prefix that accomplishes this task alone, feel free to add a suffix or suffixes along with a prefix.
   a. *duc* 'to lead'
   b. *fug* 'flee'
   c. *nov* 'new'
   d. *ven* 'come'
   e. *log* 'speak, study'

4. These three words look roughly similar in linear composition yet differ in internal structure. Using tree diagrams or bracketing, compare the word structure:
   a. *compensatory*
   b. *unambiguous*
   c. *disproportionate*
5. Here are some examples showing that some roots function as both bound and unbound: *re-lease* versus *release*, *resent* versus *re-sent*. Does this happen only with *re-* or do other prefixes behave similarly? The account of word structure in this chapter does not give a way to explain this difference. How might we expand the account to cover cases like these?
6. There are many types of internal relations between the elements of a compound. Combine any two random common nouns into a compound and imagine what the resulting compound would mean. If you're not happy with the compound, see if it helps to reverse the elements, or simply choose a different pair of input words. Now express the relation between the elements in words. For example, if you create *word kind*, you might capture the relation with 'the kind **of** word a word is'. For *pocket place*, the relation would be given as 'a place **for** a pocket'. Repeat this exercise for a total of five compound words, aiming for word combinations revealing different internal relations.
7. Starting with the word *arm* 'weapon', list a dozen other English words related to it by regular word-formation processes, for example, *arms* and *disarm* but not *harm*. Be aware that *arm* 'upper limb' is an unrelated word and so you should not include words related to it, such as *armpit*. It is all right to include words like *armament*, in which the word formation actually took place in another language (Latin).
8. Using each of the following suffixes, give four examples of words to illustrate what part of speech they form. In general, what is the part of speech of the base that each suffix is added to? Is there a general pattern to the meaning of the suffix besides the part of

speech which it forms? (For example, -*like* in *childlike, lifelike, dreamlike*, and *doglike* forms adjectives from nouns. These adjectives all mean 'similar to or resembling [the noun] in some respect'.)

   a. -*ish*
   b. -*ity*
   c. -*ize*

9. Each entry in the following list actually represents two or more distinct suffixes that happen to have the same spelling and, in some cases, the same pronunciation. For each one, determine the different suffixes it represents by naming the different type of word (e.g., noun, verb, adjective) that each is used to form. Give examples and explain the differences in meaning the suffixes give a word. For example, for -*y* we would say that there is one suffix -*y* that attaches to a noun and forms an adjective meaning 'having or associated with [the meaning of the noun]', as in the word *dirt-y*; and that there is another suffix -*y* that attaches to a proper noun to make another proper noun with a diminutive or affectionate sense in the names, as in *Bill-y* and *Joe-y*.

   a. -*er*
   b. -*ly*
   c. -*ate*
   d. -*al*

10. Using a dictionary or appendix 1 of this book, parse and gloss the word *antidisestablishmentarianism*: divide the word into parts and write the meaning or other function of each part underneath it. You can treat *establish* as a single element. How many prefixes does the word have? How many suffixes? Using the discussion of the word *apteryx* in this chapter as a model, indicate what portion of the meaning of the word given by the dictionary definition comes directly from the glosses of the individual morphs. What portion of the word's definition

is not contained in the morphs themselves but inferred from general knowledge or the actual use of the word? (Note that *disestablishment* is the withdrawal of especial state patronage and control from a church.)

11. Identify prefixes, roots, and suffixes in the following words. Looking them up is not cheating.

dia-	*chron*	*-ic*
'through'	'time'	A

    a. *anaerobic*
    b. *catastrophe*
    c. *equilibrate*
    d. *contrapositive*
    e. *helicopter*

12. What words were used to form the following recent blends?
    a. *flexitarian*
    b. *taploid*
    c. *flawsome*
    d. *Brexit*
    e. *greige*
    f. *hip-hopera*
    g. *planetesimal*

13. The following adjectives ending in *-y* show how highly productive this suffix is in English. They also illustrate that productiveness is no guarantee of uniformity. Examine this list for patterns of any kind. Some properties worth considering include predominant parts of speech the suffix is attached to, segments of the vocabulary that the suffix draws from (e.g., is it formal or informal? Technical or nontechnical?), variations in meaning in the suffix itself or in the elements it attaches to, predominance of metaphorical or nonmetaphorical uses, and any restrictions on the kinds of words that can be formed by adding *-y*. If a pattern admits a few exceptions, give the exceptions along with the pattern.

Morphology

These examples all begin with ‹a›, ‹b›, or ‹c›. Feel free to add any words that help you make a point, regardless of what letter they start with.

achy

airy

angry

balmy

batty

beefy

billowy

bloody

boozy

bosomy

bossy

bouncy

brainy

brawny

breathy

brushy

bumpy

busty

buttery

carroty

catty

chesty

chocolaty

choky

choosy

crabby

creaky

creamy

creepy

Four

Allomorphy

In the last chapter, we saw that morphemes do not always hold their meaning constant from word to word. Now we learn to deal with another characteristic that can make them even more elusive: morphemes may change their form from word to word.

Consider plural endings. Several similar morphs can make a noun plural:

peach-es	[ˈpitʃ-əz]
plum-s	[pləm-z]
grape-s	[grep-s]

All have the same function and similar pronunciation, so despite their differences they can be thought of as variant forms of the same thing. This "same thing" is what we are calling a **morpheme**. Using the term **morph** for each of the variant forms, we can regard a morpheme as a set of one or more morphs. The suffix *-eme* indicates that the *morpheme* contains no smaller linguistic units of its kind. In addition, *-eme* means that the item is somewhat abstract, in that a morpheme itself does not strictly have a pronunciation. Rather, each of a morpheme's member morphs will have its own pronunciation.

The morpheme is such a useful concept that most discussions of morphology talk about morphemes much more than about morphs. Even when a morph has no alternative forms—*walk*, for example, stays the same no matter what word it is part of—we still usually refer to the *walk* morpheme rather than the *walk* morph. This is because meaning and function tend to be more central to communication than tiny differences in sound. The following chart illustrates the relationship between morphemes and morphs.

Function	Morpheme	Morphs
plural	-əz ~ -z ~ -s	-əz -z -s
'do, make'	fac ~ fec ~ fic	fac fec fic

It's easy to understand the importance of morphs. A learner of English who learns only one pronunciation for each morpheme and forms the plural of *peach* by adding only *s* for ˣ*peachs* might be understood but would attract stares. Allomorphy figures just as strongly when it comes to learning the Latin and Greek elements presented in this book. When Latin and Greek morphemes are borrowed into English, their allomorphy usually comes along with them. These rules are rarely intuitively obvious, but learning them can pay dividends. Knowing allomorphy rules can

- vastly reduce memory load,
- prevent incorrect analyses of unfamiliar words, and
- help to coin new words that others will understand.

Consider what would happen if someone didn't know the rules of English plural allomorphy. They would have to learn the plural of each noun separately. When hearing a word like *dense*, they might think it is a plural of *den*, while we who know the rules realize the plural of *den* must be *dens*, ending in a [z] sound. A goal of this chapter is to help you avoid such problems with Latin and Greek elements, even though there are no Latin and Ancient Greek native speakers left to stare you down. Knowing the different variants of a morpheme will help immensely in finding morpheme divisions within words and building confidence in word analysis.

ALLOMORPHS

Morphs that are variant forms of the same morpheme are called **allomorphs**. The morphs [əz], [z], and [s] are allomorphs of the plural morpheme.

Recall from chapter 3 that there is no universal agreement as to how finely a word can be chopped up into morphs. The same flexibility applies to deciding whether two morphs are allomorphs of the same morpheme. To a historically inclined linguist, it would be obvious that *inter**nec**ine*, *per**nic**ious*, *in**noc**ent*, and *n**ox**ious* all share the same Latin root; that is, their root morphs are all allomorphs of the same morpheme, *nec* 'harm'. To a psychologically inclined linguist, it would be equally obvious that the vast majority of English speakers don't understand the connections between these morphs, and so they wouldn't be considered as belonging to the same morpheme. Since this book is about word analysis, the first approach suits our goals better because it leads us to see structure wherever it can be found.

Morphs that are allomorphs of the same morpheme all have the following properties:

1. Allomorphs of the same morpheme all have the same function.
2. The choice of allomorph depends on other morph(s) in the word.
3. Allomorphs share a common history and similar pronunciation.

The first principle may come as a surprise, because earlier we found that morphs can have rather different meanings in different words; *cosm* is an example. But there is always a thread connecting the meanings of morphs in different words, and when there is no thread, they are different morphemes, no matter how close the morphs are in spelling or sound. Thus the *path* of *socio**path*** has nothing to do with the *path* of *foot**path***;

they are different morphemes. Clearly, this principle applies as well to morphs that differ in pronunciation. As we saw at the start of this section, *nec* as in *internecine* and *noc* as in *innocent* are allomorphs of the same morpheme. Still, no one would dream of considering *pet* 'seek' and *pot* 'able' as being allomorphs of the same morpheme, because they have completely different meanings.

The second principle, that choice of allomorphs depends on other morphs in the word, serves to restrict what can be regarded as allomorphs. To take the simplest possible case, whole words, such as *vend* and *sell*, are not allomorphs of each other even if they seem to mean the same thing. This is necessarily so, because nothing in the word itself could be cited as conditioning the substitution of one for the other. By contrast, we identify *in-* and *im-* as allomorphs of the same morpheme because we can identify as a conditioning factor the first sound in the next morpheme (e.g., *inviolable* before [v] but *impossible* before [p]). We explore phonological conditioning in chapter 6.

The third principle warns us that allomorphs, due to their shared history, should ordinarily be similar phonetically. For example, we have learned that *chron* is a morph meaning 'time', and so is *tempor*. That similarity in function is not enough to make them allomorphs of the same morpheme, however. *Chron* was borrowed from Greek and *tempor* was borrowed from Latin, and they have no deeper common history, as their completely different pronunciation suggests.

It helps to be as systematic and exhaustive as possible in spotting allomorphy. For example, if we didn't know that the prefix *re-* had the allomorph *red-* before some roots beginning with a vowel, we would likely strike out in attempts to parse words like *redolent*. We might be tempted to analyze it as *re-dol-ent*, but this turns out to be wrong; there is no root *dol* in this word. The correct parse is *red-ol-ent*, where the root *ol* means 'smell', as it does in *olfactory*. The word *redolent* means 'fragrant'; by metaphorical extension, it means 'reminiscent'. A similar case is *sedition*, which it would be tempting to analyze with the root *sed* 'sit', as in *sedentary*. But this would be wrong. Sedition in fact has nothing to do with sitting, and the morph *sed* is instead an allomorph of the prefix morpheme *se-* 'apart'.

The correct analysis of *sedition* is *sed-i-tion*, where *i* is the root morpheme meaning 'go'—the same root found in *ex-i-t*.

Because morphemes can take several different forms, we need special measures for referring to them. The three adopted in this book cite the morpheme

- by listing some or all of its allomorphs, separated by the symbol ~ (e.g., "the morpheme *mit~miss*"),
- by using parentheses to mark letters or sounds that are found in some allomorphs but not others (e.g., "the morpheme *re(d)-*"), and
- by choosing one allomorph to stand for all (e.g., "the morpheme *nec*").

PHONOLOGY-BASED ALLOMORPHY

Allomorphy has two main sources. First, a morpheme with only one form may come to have two or more different forms as the language changes. This may be thought of as a **morph split**. In the second, what was originally a sequence of morphs comes to be reinterpreted as a single morph. This can be thought of as **morphemic merger**.

Morph splits are almost always due to phonological factors. In many cases, a huge list of allomorphic variations in many different morphemes can be explained by a single phonological principle, which can seriously simplify the task of learning allomorphs. Here we present a general overview of allomorphy that arises from phonological causes before returning to the topic in chapter 6.

Phonological Repairs

Certain combinations of morphs would create pronunciations that are **ill-formed**—that is, they would violate the general rules and constraints of the language. If we tried to apply the most common allomorph of the prefix *con-* to all words containing this morpheme, we would end up with forms like ˣ*conplete* and ˣ*conbine*. The prefix allomorphy makes sense if viewed simply as a result of rules for repairing illegal pronunciations.

Yesterday's Phonology Is Today's Allomorphy

Allomorphy makes the most phonological sense when one looks at an earlier stage of the language. Here are some striking examples:

foot	*feet*
goose	*geese*
tooth	*teeth*
man	*men*
mouse	*mice*

In this list, the different vowels in the plural arose in Prehistoric English. At that time, the plurals had an [i] ending. English also had a phonological rule (known by the German word **umlaut**) whereby vowels preceding an [i] became closer to the [i] in pronunciation. At a later date, the ending was lost. From the perspective of Modern English, the current allomorphy is doubly senseless. First, there is no overt ending to explain the alternation in the stem. Second, even if there were, English has lost the umlaut rule. This is why we feel no pressure at all to turn *Ann* into ˣ*Enny* when we add the suffix *-y* [i].

Thus one big source of English allomorphy is the phonology of English. When English loses the phonological rule, or when sounds in the word change so that the rule no longer applies, the alternation often remains in place, and from then on it is a rule of the morphology.

Borrowed Phonology

The phonological factors behind allomorphy are also hidden from us when the phonology is that of a foreign language. English has borrowed so many words from Greek and, especially, Latin that English has incorporated many of the rules of those languages. Those rules, though, which may have been totally regular phonological principles in the languages we borrowed from, come into English as allomorphic rules, applying only to restricted classes of borrowed morphemes.

We see this with the Latin prefix *in-* meaning 'not'. This prefix has the allomorphs *in-* [ɪn] as in *ineligible*, *im-* [ɪm] as in *imprecise*, *il-* [ɪ] as in *illegal*, and *ir-* [ɪ] as in *irregular*. This allomorphy applies to hundreds of words, and while it was a fully general phonological rule in Latin, it is not as general in English, as shown by the native prefix *un-*. This prefix has the same meaning and almost the same form as *in-* and yet does not undergo the same changes: compare *unprovable*, *unloved*, and *unreal*, which would change to *umprovable, *ulloved, and *urreal if *un-* behaved like *in-* . Because this pattern of changing the final *n* in the prefix applies only to Latin prefixes, speakers of English tend not to perceive it as a phonological pattern but as just another allomorphic rule to memorize.

Other English allomorphy stems directly from Latin and Greek patterns that lacked clear phonological motivation in those languages. Our terms *apnea*, *atheist*, *asymmetry*, *anesthetic*, and *anhydrous* all begin with a prefix meaning 'not', which was borrowed from Greek. English follows the original Greek by realizing this prefix as *an-* before vowels and [h], and *a-* before other consonants. No other Greek prefix behaves quite like *an-*, which owes its behavior to ancient phonological changes in Prehistoric Greek.

A very widespread pattern in Latin is **Latin Vowel Weakening**:

factor	*defect, infect*	*deficient*
capture	*receptive*	*recipient*
apt	*inept, adept*	
spectator	*respect*	*conspicuous, despicable*
sacrifice	*desecrate*	
status	*obstetric*	*constitute*
tenuous	*content*	*continent*

Basically, any vowel is allowed in the root when it is the first syllable of a word, but the vowel may be weakened to an *e* (before two consonants) or *i* (before one consonant) when prefixation makes the root move to a later syllable. In many languages vowel weakening is caused by the loss or absence of stress: compare the first vowels in the English pronunciations of *species* and *specific*. Latin Vowel Weakening is a holdover of the precursor to Classical Latin, Old Latin, where word stress was always on the first syllable. This explains why vowels were weakened only in noninitial syllables: they weren't stressed.

To summarize, many instances of allomorphy have their origin in phonology, whether within English itself (often in an earlier stage of it) or in Latin or Greek. Over time, the phonological conditioning becomes invisible due to other changes. The difference in sounds persist as allomorphy: the conditioning factor shifts from adjacent sounds to adjacent morphs.

SUPPLETION

Normally the various word forms of a **lexeme**—the word without any inflections—are based on the same root. However, occasionally this rule is violated:

go, went
be, is, was
good, better

Any child could tell you that the past tense of *go* "should" be ˣ*goed*, but in fact it is formed by adding *t* to *wen*, which means we have an odd-looking allomorphy *go~wen*. The appreciable difference in sound and spelling in this lexeme is due to the fact that *went* was historically a totally different word. Originally, *went* was the past tense of *wend* (compare *spend* and *spent*), a word that the poets among us still occasionally use to mean 'proceed' or 'go' even in the present tense (*Leopold Bloom wends his way through the urban landscape*). The process of incorporating a totally different word in part of another word's inflectional system is called **suppletion**.

A few English allomorphies can be traced directly to Latin suppletion. The words *essence* and *future* come from different (suppletive) forms of the verb *be*. The curious fact that the adjective *Jovian* is so different from *Jupiter* is also due to a suppletion in Latin.

MORPHEME MERGER

Allomorphy by Fusion

We have witnessed yesterday's phonology becoming today's morphology. Often enough, today's morphology restructures yesterday's morphology as well, distancing a word's structure from its etymology. Two adjacent morphemes in English can come to be perceived as a single one, especially in cases where one of them loses its connection with meaning. A simple example is the second *or* at the end of *or* in *corporal* and *corporate*. At one time this *or* was a separate morpheme, a relic of an older pattern in Latin, but in English this *or* has no meaning and *corpor* is simply an allomorph of *corp*.

Possibly the most common morpheme extension in English is *t* in these Latin-based examples, all built on the vocabulary elements at the end of this chapter: *fact, defect, mental, respect, state, tact,* and *extent*. As you work your way through the remaining vocabulary elements in the text, be on the lookout for allomorphs formed from Latinate roots by adding a *t*. You'll find abundant such cases in the Examples column in the Word Elements lists at the end of this chapter, for example, *captive, except, secret, discrete*. In these and similar examples, *t* creates a new allomorph of the element in question. To emphasize that this *t* is not an inherent part of the element, our normal practice is to introduce the new allomorph with a space before the *t*. But as soon as the allomorph has been introduced in this way, we move to a representation with no space before *t* to emphasize that *t* is part of the allomorph and not a separate morpheme.

Such morpheme extensions used to be meaningful, signaling changes in tense, part of speech, and other distinctions. Today the meanings are mostly gone entirely or have wandered from their original state. For example, *duc* and extended form *duct* have very different meanings in *induce* and *induct*, in *deduce* and *deduct*, and in *conducive* and *conductive*. Another case, from Element study 1 in chapter 1, is *cosm*, with a different range of meanings from the extended form *cosmet*.

Here are a few more examples from the word element list at the end of this chapter. The Greek root *nec* 'die' has the allomorphs *nec* and *necr*. The *r* in *necr* was originally a suffix, and this *r* appears in most of the English words whose origin goes back to the Greek morpheme, as in *necrology* 'a list of people who have died' and *necrophilia* 'attraction to corpses'. English has also borrowed a cognate root from Latin, where it meant 'harm'. One allomorph of that Latin root is *noc*, which appears in *innocent* (which literally means 'not causing harm'). When extended by [s], which was originally a suffix, we get *nox*, as in *noxious*.

The root *ten* 'stretch, thin', which appears in words like *tenuous* and *extenuating*, is extended by *d* in *extend*. The allomorph *tend* in turn is the source of yet another allomorph, *tens*, which appears in the words *tensile* and *intense*. The change of ‹d› to ‹s› comes about as a result of another rule of allomorphy that is introduced in a later chapter.

Sometimes the required allomorph sounds better to us than one that is not called for. For example, *bathyscope* arguably is more mellifluous than ˣ*bathscope*. But our language has dozens of words that are about as awkward sounding as ˣ*bathscope*, such as *landscape*. The choice of the allomorph *bathy* over *bath* in *bathyscope* is simply a relic from earlier times.

In the above examples, allomorphs are seen to add either a vowel (like *bathy* from *bath*) or a consonant (like *necr* from *nec* and *tend* from *ten*) or a vowel-consonant sequence (like the *or* of *corporal*). Because there are so many possible variations and so little carryover from one pattern to the next, we do not here explicitly memorize lists of extensions or rules for applying them. When parsing a word, you will consequently be tempted to ascribe any difficult letter or letter sequence to a neighboring morpheme. That could be true in some cases, but first you should try to rule out the alternative that the problematic sequence is a morpheme all by itself. To

Allomorphy

save you lots of guesswork, we include the most frequent allomorphs in the word element lists at the end of each chapter.

Nasal Infixation

In nasal infixation, an ⟨n⟩ or ⟨m⟩ is placed immediately after the vowel in the root:

in-cub-ate	*in-cumb-ent*	'lie'
con-tag-ion	*tang-ent*	'touch'
frag-ile	*frang-ible*	'break'
vic-tor	*con-vince*	'conquer'

In Proto-Indo-European, this consonant was a derivational affix, much like prefixes or suffixes. Because of its placement inside the root, it is called an **infix**. It was one kind of marker of the present tense in Latin and Greek, but there is no trace of this function left in English.

Ablaut

In Proto-Indo-European, most roots contained the vowel *e* in their basic form. Some of the morphological processes of that language involved changing the vowel to *o*. Other changes consisted of deleting the vowel or making it longer. These changes are all known as **ablaut** (not to be confused with *umlaut*).

In native English words, this alternation between *e*, *o*, and nothing (usually called **zero**) is disguised by millennia of sound changes. But it can still be detected in verbs whose vowels change to make the past tense and past participle, such as *sing, sang,* and *sung*. The clearest examples of ablaut can be found in elements borrowed from Greek, which hasn't changed its vowels as much as Latin and the Germanic languages have. Some examples of the different ablaut forms (or **grades**) in Greek elements:

Root meaning	e-Grade	o-Grade	Zero Grade
'birth'	*genetic*	*cosmogony*	
'cut'	*temnospondyl*	*atom*	*tmesis*
'throw'	*belemnite*	*symbol*	*problem*
'work'	*energy*	*organ*	

From Latin:

'hang, weigh'	*dependent*	*ponderous*	
'birth'	*indigenous*		*pregnant*
'think'	*memento*	*admonish*	
'accept'	*decent*	*docent*	

Empty cells in these tables simply mean that there are no clear examples that were borrowed into English. Several examples of ablaut have been left out because sound change has made them difficult to recognize.

Linguists aren't completely sure what the function of ablaut was in Proto-Indo-European, and as far as Greek and Latin word elements in English are concerned, we can consider ablaut to be another source of allomorphy with no inherent meaning of its own.

PRACTICE

For each of the following word pairs, identify the type of root allomorphy as Latin Vowel Weakening, suppletion, nasal infixation, ablaut, or a combination of two of these:

effective, efficient
embolism, emblem
mentor, monitor
am, are
fragment, infringement

DOUBLETS OR ALLOMORPHS?

English borrowed a lot of its Latin vocabulary through Old French, introducing yet another source of allomorphy. As we saw in chapter 1 with *captain* and *chef*, often the same morpheme was borrowed into English from both languages. Sometimes the form that has come into English combines elements from both Latin and Old French. Such cases commonly use Latin morphs throughout except for the very end, which takes an Old French form. For example, the word *faculty* comes from the Latin base *fac-ul-* 'easily done', plus a respelled form of the Old French suffix *-té*, which forms nouns. This suffix is the French descendant of Latin *-tat*, which appears in the related word *fac-ul-tat-ive*. The use of French allomorphs at the end of words is the source of many alternations in English.

French	Latin	Examples
-le	*-ul-*	angle, angular; circle, circular
-le	*-il-*	able, ability
-ous	*-os-*	generous, generosity
-ence	*-ent-i-*	preference, preferential
-ance	*-ant-i-*	substance, substantial
-fy	*-fic-*	glorify, glorification

This pattern of French/Latin allomorphy is most noticeable in suffixes, because they occur in hundreds of words, but minor patterns appear in some roots. For example, the Latin root *ten* 'hold', as in *abstention, content, detention, pertinent* (by Latin Vowel Weakening), and *retentive*, takes on the Old French allomorph *tain* at the end of the word: *abstain, contain, detain, pertain,* and *retain*.

The pairs discussed so far are clearly allomorphs by any definition. But should we say that any French morph should be considered an allomorph of the Latin morph it descends from? As chapter 11 shows, many French morphs have changed considerably from Latin. For instance, the Latin morph *fid* 'trust', as in *confident* and *fidelity*, is the ultimate source of the French loanword *faith*, and it appears also as *fi* in *defiant* and as *fe* in *fealty*. Are they all the same morpheme? At least the common *f* unites all these morphs, but consider now the Latin morph *cav* 'hollow', found in *cave* and *cavity*, which is also the root, via French, of the word *jail*. Is this allomorphy?

For our purposes, it's best to regard these Latin versus French variants as doublets, not allomorphs. Recall from chapter 2 that the doublets *shirt* and *skirt* entered the language through different routes and, despite their similarity in form and meaning, there is no evidence for a connection between them apart from the etymological one. From the standpoint of the present language, they don't participate in any systematic alternations: instead, they behave as independently of one another as *blouse* and *jacket*. Hence there would be no point in analyzing them as allomorphs of the same morpheme. *Cav* and *jail* are analogous. The morphs derive from the same parent morpheme, but their different paths of borrowing led them to have distinct forms and usages. Such cases are analyzed as doublets as long as they don't alternate with each other systematically.

The word element lists in this book don't contain many French forms, so we won't see many difficult cases like *cave* versus *jail*. The doublets we do find will be from Latin and Greek, their similarity due to the shared Proto-Indo-European ancestry of Latin and Greek and their differences due to divergent changes in each language. By separately adopting both morphemes, English acquired new doublets.

Doublets are found for three of the number terms in chapter 6: *hemi-~semi-* 'half', *hexa~sex* 'six', and *hepta~septem* 'seven'. The morphs in ‹h› are from Greek, and those in ‹s› are from Latin. The root for 'to creep' is another example: *herp* in Greek and *serp* in Latin.

A different set of variants distinguishes Latin *nomen* from Greek *onom*, two morphemes meaning 'name'. The Latin root *nomen* has the allomorph *nomin* (as in *nominal*, *nominate*). This is an example of Latin Vowel Weakening, mentioned earlier in the section on borrowed phonology. The Greek root *onom* has the allomorphs *onomat* (as in *onomatology* "the study of the origins of names") and *onym* (as in *synonym* and *antonym*).

Another doublet pair is *dent* and *odont* 'tooth'. Latinate *dent* is the root in the more familiar *dentist*, and Greek *odont* appears in the more scholarly *odontologist* 'one who studies teeth'. The pattern of using Latin roots for more common things and Greek roots for more specialized purposes is one that occurs very often in this book. Latin *fa* 'speak' appears in *fable* and *famous*; the Greek doublet *pha* appears in the medical conditions *aphasia* and *dysphasia*.

Some variant forms of morphs are so idiosyncratic, they simply have to be learned individually. Cases from our word element lists are *de~div* 'god', *aut~taut* 'same', and *lith~lit* 'stone'. Still, most alternations in the form of English morphemes are quite regular, since they are, or used to be, governed by phonetic principles. This gives us a good reason to master some basic concepts of phonetics in the next chapter.

SUMMARY

Allomorphs are morphs that fulfill the same function in building words but alternate systematically with each other based on the other morph or morphs in the same word. The abstract functional entity that comprises the set of allomorphs is called the morpheme. Some patterns of allomorphy apply regularly to a wide range of morphemes. Others may apply idiosyncratically to only a few or even just one morpheme, in which case shared allomorphy can help identify morphemes. Allomorphs may be caused by phonological changes that split one morph into many; among the dozens of such patterns are cases illustrated in this chapter: English umlaut, Latin and Greek prefix alternations, and Latin Vowel Weakening. At other times allomorphs come about through suppletion, incorporating parts of one word into another word's inflectional patterns. Finally, an allomorph can result from a morph's being extended by what used to be a morpheme, such as old Proto-Indo-European suffixes, ablaut vowels, and nasal infixes. Morphemes borrowed from distinct but related languages can function as allomorphs, as when French allomorphs at the end of a lexeme vary with Latin allomorphs nonfinally. More often, though, they act as different morphemes and may be considered doublets.

WORD ELEMENTS

Learn the following elements, their meanings, and variant forms.

Element	Gloss	Source	Examples
al~ol	nurture, grow	L	*alimentary, alma mater, alumnus, abolish, adolescent, adult*
am~im	love	L	*amorous, amative, amicable, inimical*
ann~enn	year	L	*annals, per annum, perennial, millennium*
apt~ept	fit	L	*adapt, aptitude, coapt, adept, inept*
bol~bl	throw	G	*diabolical, hyberbole, metabolism, symbol, parabola, parable, emblem, problem*
cap~cep~cip~cup	take	L	*capacious, captive, except, incipient, principle, occupy, recuperate*
cid~cis	cut, kill	L	*homicide, incision, excise, concise, caesura*
cri	judge, separate	G	*critic, criterion, crisis, hypocrisy, endocrine*
cri~cre~cer	separate	L	*certain, discern, secern, secret, discrete, secrete*
cub~cumb	lie down	L	*cubicle, concubine, incubate, incumbent, recumbent*
de~div	god	L	*deity, deification, divine, divinity, diva*
equ~iqu	even	L	*equal, equate, equity, equidistant, equanimity, adequate, iniquity*
erg~org~urg	work	G	*energy, ergative, organ, orgy, georgic, demiurge, liturgy, metallurgy*

Allomorphy

Element	Gloss	Source	Examples
fac~fec~fic	do, make	L	*fact, factor, factory, facsimile, factotum, defect, perfect, prefect, artificial, deficit, suffice*
frag~frang~fring	break	L	*fragile, fragment, fracture, frangible, refringent, infringe*
fund~fus	pour, melt	L	*refund, fuse, fusion, fusile, diffuse, effusive, infuse*
gen~gn~na	birth	L	*general, genus, genius, genial, genital, gentile, genuine, indigenous, progeny, benign, pregnant, innate, native, nation, natal, agnate*
gen~gon	birth	G	*gene, genesis, genocide, heterogeneous, gonad*
i~it	go	L	*ion, initial, exit, transit*
men~mon	think	L	*mental, dementia, memento, mention, admonish, monster*
mne	remember	G	*amnesia, mnemonic*
mov~mo	move	L	*motor, motion, emotion, motility, motive, promote, mobile*
nec~necr	die	G	*nectar, nectarine, necrology, necrosis*
nec~noc~nic~nox	harm	L	*internecine, pernicious, innocent, innocuous, noxious*
pend~pond	hang, weigh	L	*depend, appendix, expend, pendulum, vilipend, ponder, preponderate*
sacr~sanc~secr	holy	L	*sacred, sacrifice, sanctify, consecrate, desecrate*
semen~semin	seed	L	*semen, inseminate, seminal, disseminate, seminary*

Element	Gloss	Source	Examples
spec~spic	look	L	*spectacle, spectrum, specious, speculate, inspect, retrospect, despicable*
sta~ste	stand	G	*static, thermostat, ecstasy, stasis, system*
sta~ste~sti~st	stand	L	*status, stationary, statute, stable, stamen, obstetrician, constitution, institute, prostitute, insist, interstice*
tag~teg~tig~tang~ting	touch	L	*contagion, contact, tax, integer, tangent, tangible, contingent*
tempor	time	L	*temporary, temporize, contemporary, extemporaneous*
ten~tin	hold	L	*tenable, tenure, tenacious, retention, continuous, retinue*
tom~tm	cut	G	*anatomy, atom, microtome, entomology, epitome, tmesis*
vic~vinc	conquer	L	*victor, evict, conviction, convince, evince, invincible*
vor	eat	L	*carnivore, omnivore, voracious*
zo	animal	G	*zoology, protozoon, zoomorphic, azotometer*

ELEMENT STUDY

1. *Walk* is an example of a word element and morpheme that does not vary in form, as shown by *walked, walking, walker*. Give a few more examples of such English morphemes.
2. What is the root in the following words? Where the element has several allomorphs, choose the one that most closely matches the

Allomorphy

morph in the word in question. Look up each word, and include a brief sentence about the relation between the root's literal meaning and its meaning in this word.

Part 1: Chapter 4 elements:
a. *iniquity*
b. *critic*
c. *precise*
d. *allergy* (Note: of the two roots, the first is all 'other'—chapter 10)
e. *receptive*
f. *pendant*
g. *epitome*

Part 2: Cumulative elements. Identify all prefixes and roots.
a. *necrobiosis*
b. *psychogenic*
c. *isopyre*

3. The root *am* 'love' is easily confused with other sequences *am*. Which of the following words contain the root *am* 'love' or one of its allomorphs?
a. *amaze*
b. *ameliorate*
c. *amend*
d. *amenity*
e. *amiable*
f. *amity*
g. *amoral*
h. *amour*
i. *amphitheater*
j. *amulet*
k. *amuse*
l. *enamor*
m. *enemy*
n. *imitate*
o. *paramour*

4. Which one of these words does not contain a form of the root *ann*?
   a. *annual*
   b. *annul*
   c. *biennial*
   d. *perennial*
   e. *superannuate*
5. False friends: *cap* 'take' vs. *cap* 'head':
   Two very common roots are easily confused because both have the allomorphs *cap* and *cep*: one meaning 'take' and the other meaning 'head'. Practice distinguishing the two by giving the meaning of the root in each of these examples:
   a. *capital*
   b. *reception*
   c. *deceptive*
   d. *decapitate*
   e. *capture*
   f. *captain*
   g. *capacity*
   h. *capitulate*
   i. *incipient*
   j. *precipitate*
6. False friends: *gen~gon* vs. *gon* 'angle':
   English has relatively few words with the allomorph *gon*. The most common are probably *gonad*, *gonorrhea*, and *epigone*. More frequent in English is a different root entirely, *gon* 'angle', as in *pentagon* and *diagonal*. Complicating the picture is that *gon* 'angle' has an allomorph *genu*, as in *genuflect*, and the allomorph *gen* of *gen ~ gon* itself occasionally appears as *genu* in several words.
   Sort out the differences by looking up these words and deciding which element they represent, *gen ~ gon* or *gon*.
   a. *genuine*
   b. *ingenuity*

c. *genius*
d. *genus*
e. *orthogonal*
f. *goniometer*
g. *pathogony*

7. Doublets *gen~gn~na* 'birth' and *gen~gon* 'birth';
Both elements derive from the same ancient root, each having undergone some different changes on their way into Latin and Greek. We list them separately in this chapter because they have different allomorphy. The allomorph *na* often has a /t/ at the end, as in *native, nation*.

Once you're able to distinguish Latinate affixes from Greek ones, it's easy to tell the source of a given allomorph of these two elements. Identify whether the root in each of the words in the next list is Latinate or Greek. We use the term *Latinate* to allow for the fact that many words of Latin origin came into English via a language that got the word from Latin, as happened especially often with French.

See how far you can get in this exercise without a dictionary, and then look up your answers.

a. *cognate*
b. *impregnate*
c. *benign*
d. *congenital*
e. *genesis*
f. *indigenous*
g. *generous*

8. What variations, if any, do you detect in the meaning of the root *al* in *alumnus, alimony, coalesce,* and *altricial*? In *proletariat* and *prolific* the vowel of *al* runs together with the prefix *pro-*, making the root very hard to detect. How would you relate the meaning of the root in these last two words to the basic meaning of *al*?

9. After studying the word element list for this chapter, test your knowledge of the elements presented so far by parsing the following words. Gloss the elements and give variants for the roots. You may assume that any components not in the element's entry are extensions of a neighboring morpheme. With the aid of a dictionary, give a brief definition for the whole word that partly or fully reflects the meaning of the individual elements. Follow this format in your answer:

hetero-	*gene*	*-ous*
'other, different'	'birth, type, origin'	A

'having dissimilar parts'
(where *gene* is an extended form of *gen*).
   a. *conspicuous*
   b. *deification*
   c. *equanimous*
   d. *energy*
   e. *incipient*
   f. *seminal*

EXERCISES

1. Define *allomorphy*. Illustrate your answer with three examples. What is the relevance of allomorphy to the goals of this course?
2. Give the root and any variant forms as listed in the word element list for this chapter or in appendix 1, and give the gloss of the root. Give a brief dictionary definition of each full word as well.
   a. *contiguous*
   b. *pertinacious*
   c. *cognate*

Allomorphy

3. Match each word in column A with one in column B that has the same root. Identify the process or processes relating the roots: vowel weakening, nasal insertion, or ablaut.

A	B
a. *genome*	g. *sacrilege*
b. *tangential*	h. *tenant*
c. *abstinence*	i. *theogony*
d. *edifice*	j. *contagious*
e. *nocuous*	k. *facile*
f. *desecrate*	l. *internecine*

4. Match each word in column A with one in column B that has the same root.

A	B
a. *organic*	g. *victory*
b. *oxygen*	h. *despicable*
c. *convince*	i. *benign*
d. *special*	j. *hyperbolic*
e. *parable*	k. *fragmentary*
f. *infringe*	l. *energetic*

Five

Phonetics

Our focus so far has been the morphemic content of words, but along the way we have found it useful to consider the sounds that make up a word element and that may vary from one allomorph to another. We've seen cases where the meaning of a word element differs from word to word, and now we need to look more closely at their pronunciation. Learning some English phonetics puts us in a better position to discuss and understand allomorphy, since most changes in pronunciation of word elements happen—or once happened—for phonetic reasons. Phonetic principles also bring out striking similarities between Latin, French, and English words despite several hundreds of years of sound changes. An example is Latin *cap*, the source of allomorphs *cep* and *cip*, as well as the root *ceive* in *deceive*, *conceive*, and *receive*, which came to us through French. Basic phonetics brings out striking similarities among the Germanic languages and Latin and Greek, even after several millennia of sound changes. For example, in chapter 10 we trace the English word *fire* back to the same source as the Greek root *pyr*, showing along the way that the difference in pronunciation between [f] and [p] is a highly regular one.

Many pronunciation changes are a form of **assimilation**, which makes one sound more *similar to* another sound, usually the immediately following one. The Latin negative prefix *in-* [ɪn] assimilates to *im-* [ɪm] before [p] (*impossible*) and [b] (*imbalance*). We will find that [p] and [b] share a phonetic property that leads [n] to change to [m] when it immediately precedes them. Before sounds like [t] and [d], the [n] of prefix *in-* does not change, and so we get the forms *intolerant* and *indecisive*, not ˣ*imtolerant* or ˣ*imdecisive*. In some cases assimilation is total, making the two sounds identical, as in *immodest* [ɪmˈmadəst], although we normally further reduce a sequence of identical sounds to a single sound in English: [ɪˈmadəst]. Understanding the principles behind assimilation is particularly helpful because they often apply quite generally, modifying several different word elements in many different words. To take just one example, compare the behavior of Latin-derived *in-* with that of the Greek prefix *syn-* 'with' before the same consonants in the words *sympathy*, *symbol*, *symmetric*, *syntax*, and *syndrome*.

Sometimes phonetic approximation goes beyond assimilation. For example, *presume* and *redeem* acquire an extra letter ⟨p⟩ when ⟨t⟩ is added, as in *presumptive* and *redemptive*. That is a clear rule of spelling, but in pronunciation some of us also insert an actual [p] sound when moving from an [m] to a [t]. As we will see, [p] can easily appear as a transitional sound because it shares some phonetic traits with [m] and other traits with [t].

Starting from our earliest experiences with the writing system, we discover gaps between spelling and pronunciation, thanks to "silent letters", vowel letters that do or don't "say their name", and the list of vowels ending with "sometimes *y*". Along the way, English spelling becomes ingrained in our consciousness, shaping and even distorting our perceptions of the sounds that letters represent. It may come as a surprise that the words *cats* and *dogs* generally do not end in exactly the same sound: the sound at the end of *cats* is essentially the one at the end of *hiss*, while the sound at the end of *dogs* is what we hear at the end of *buzz*. One reason we might not notice the difference between the two sounds [s] and [z] is that both are spelled the same way, ⟨s⟩, in the plural suffix. Just to clarify the point here, we do not mean to be attacking the spelling system of English for being phonetically inaccurate. There is so much variation in how different people speak that our much maligned spelling system would be even harder to deal with if it faithfully recorded all such distinctions. But when we focus on phonetics, we must be careful not to be misled by spelling, which is often a poor indicator of pronunciation.

Unlike the discrete letters on a keypad, the sounds of a language can be broken down into a small set of properties expressing phonetic relationships among sounds. For example, even though we noted above that [s] and [z] are not identical, they are indeed very similar, differing only in whether the vocal cords are vibrating or not.

The properties shared by sounds explain many assimilatory changes in language. As noted earlier, the [n] of *in-* becomes [m] before the initial [p] of words like *possible*, the initial [b] of *balance*, and the initial [m] of *modest*, but not before other sounds. This makes some sense, because [p], [b], and [m] all block the flow of air through the mouth but differ in where it is blocked (gum or lips). Note that the assimilatory change eliminates a distinctive property of [n], its normal **place of articulation**.

Breaking each sound down into a set of properties makes learning new sounds easier and less intimidating. Knowing how to produce a fricative sound like [s] and how to produce a velar sound like [k] puts us in a position to produce less familiar sounds, like the velar and uvular fricatives in German *Bach*, Hebrew *Ḥanukkah*, and Scottish *loch*.

BASICS OF SOUND PRODUCTION

Figure 5.1 shows the parts of the vocal tract that play a role in the description of consonants presented here.

The Airstream

Any speech sound involves an **airstream** whose flow is modified by the speech organs. All English sounds move air from the lungs through the larynx and **vocal tract** and out the mouth or nose. As the air passes along, its flow can be arrested, slowed down, or diverted by the movement of various speech organs or **articulators**. The nature of these effects and the location of the articulators that produce them are what differentiates speech sounds.

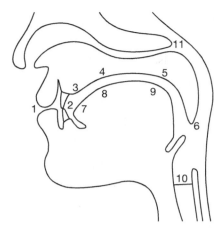

Figure 5.1 The articulatory apparatus: consonants. An idealized cross-section of the vocal tract (adjectival forms in parentheses): 1: lips (labial); 2: teeth (dental); 3: alveolar ridge (alveolar); 4: hard palate (palatal); 5: soft palate (velar); 6: uvula (uvular); 7: tip of tongue (apical); 8: blade of tongue (laminal); 9: back of tongue (dorsal); 10: vocal cords, in the larynx (glottal); 11: nasal passages (nasal).

Manner of Articulation

We begin with **oral** sounds, whose articulation involves the flow of air through the mouth.

One type of oral sound stops the airflow through the mouth temporarily by bringing two articulators together. These articulators may be the two lips, as with [p] and [b]. Another possibility is for part of the tongue to press against the teeth or roof of the mouth. Either of these articulations can stop the airflow abruptly, and so they are called oral **stops**. The oral stops used in Standard English are [p], [b], [t], [d], [k], and [g].

Slowly read the first sentence of the preceding paragraph aloud, and see if you can determine which sounds create temporary but total blockage of airflow. (The answer is at the end of this section.)

Most English sounds do not call for complete stoppage of air. Some consonants are produced by bringing the articulators close together but leaving enough of an opening so that air can pass through continuously. The narrowness of the opening causes the air to escape under some pressure, which results in a rushing or raspy effect that gives **fricatives** (with the root *fric* 'rub', as in *friction*) their name. The *fricatives* of English are [f], [v], [θ], [ð], [s], [z], [ʃ], [ʒ], and [h]. The word *fricatives* itself has three different fricative sounds in it.

The sounds known as **affricates** include a transition from a stop closure to a more open fricative sound without otherwise changing the position of the articulators. The fricative sound at the beginning of *shore* contrasts with the corresponding affricate at the beginning of *chore*. The affricate is represented as [tʃ], showing that it consists of a stop plus a fricative. The only other affricate in English is [dʒ], the initial and the final consonant of *judge*. Many English speakers make the same sound at the end of *garage*, while others follow the original French more closely, by producing a fricative, [ʒ]. Which sounds more natural to you?

Because the types of consonants discussed so far—stops, fricatives, and affricates—involve substantial **obstruction** of the airflow, they are called **obstruents**. For other consonants, the degree of oral constriction is less. The English consonants produced with the widest oral opening are the **approximants** [l], [r], [w], and [j].

If you pronounce [l] as in *love* attentively, you will notice that you make the sound with the tongue pressed against your teeth or alveolar ridge. This raises an interesting question: if there is firm contact between the articulators, how can [l] be an approximant rather than a stop? That is to say, how can the air flow past this area? To answer this question, pronounce an [l]. The answer will be more apparent if you inhale while pronouncing it. You should feel cool air as it flows past the sides of your tongue.

Sounds like [m] also permit relatively unrestricted flow of air. Is [m], then, an approximant? No. In fact, when you pronounce the sound [m], you can feel a distinct closure in the mouth. The lips are completely closed, just as for the oral stops [p] and [b]. The air that is totally blocked from exiting the mouth, however, can pass freely through the nose through a passage opened by lowering the velum. Because of this characteristic airflow through the nose, [m] is called a **nasal** stop. The other English nasal stops are [n] and [ŋ].

(The oral stops in the first sentence of the second paragraph of this section are: [t], [p], [d], [d], [t], [t], [p], etc.)

Place of Articulation

We have mentioned places of articulation in passing. In this section we consider in a little more detail the places of articulation used in English.

The oral airflow is manipulated by varying the distance or type of contact between **upper** and **lower** articulators. These are easiest to explore with stops, because the articulators come into firm contact with each other, making them easy to feel or to see in a mirror. For the stops [p], [b], and [m], the upper and lower articulators are the upper and lower lips, and so they are called **labial** consonants. For the other stops, the lower articulator is the tongue, and the upper articulator is the top part of the mouth (regions 2 through 5 in figure 5.1). For [t], [d], and [n], the tip or blade of the tongue presses against the alveolar ridge (the raised area just behind the upper teeth), and so these are called **alveolar** consonants. For [k], [g], and [ŋ], the back of the tongue presses against the soft palate, or velum, and so these are called **velar** consonants.

Because affricates begin with a stop, it is also easy to feel where they are articulated. Even though the affricates [tʃ] and [dʒ] are represented phonetically with the symbols [t] and [d], which are typically alveolar (cf. also the spellings in *etch* and *edge*), the position of the stop component is adjusted to match up with the fricative part of the affricate. You may be able to feel the difference by comparing the initial sounds of *tore* and *chore*. If you pronounce these two words as we do, you should feel that in *tore* it is the tip of your tongue that makes contact with the upper articulator, and it is pointed more upward than in *chore*. For *chore* a greater portion of the tongue makes contact, and contact extends to what is known as the **postalveolar** region—somewhat behind the alveolar ridge.

Fricatives are almost as easy to explore, because while the articulators do not press firmly against each other, you can usually feel the air rushing past the point of articulation. The fricatives [ʃ] and [ʒ] are postalveolar, just like the corresponding affricates [tʃ] and [dʒ]. If you move the tongue slightly forward, to the alveolar region, you will produce the alveolar fricatives [s] and [z], corresponding in place to the stops [t] and [d].

Imagine what it would take to make a labial sound that qualifies as a fricative. Try bringing your lips close enough together to produce noise when air passes through, without blocking the air entirely. You have produced a bilabial fricative, absent in English but present in many languages. The closest English comes to having this sound is the **labiodental** fricatives [f] and [v], which are made by bringing the lower lip into partial contact with the upper teeth. Try this and see if it produces something that sounds like a respectable English [f] or [v]. If not, try it again in front of a mirror.

Another place of articulation for fricatives involves touching the tip of the tongue to the front teeth. This produces what are called **dental** fricatives, written [θ] and [ð]. These occur in *thin* and *then*, respectively. More subtle is the **glottal** place of articulation, where the friction is made by air rushing through the glottis; this is used for [h].

The place of articulation for approximants can be a little bit harder to pin down, because the upper articulator is approached only very approximately. The approximant [l] is classified as alveolar. [r] tends to have a postalveolar articulation, though this greatly oversimplifies the facts about [r], the most variable consonant across English dialects.

For [j], the front and back regions of the mouth are relatively open, and a narrowing takes place in the middle of the mouth. This is done by raising the body of the tongue toward the hard palate. If you pronounce a sequence like *a yacht* [ə ˈjat] you will feel your tongue and your jaw moving upward after the first vowel and then downward on its way to the second. Sounds made in this part of the mouth are called **palatal**. In English, [j] is the only palatal consonant.

If you pronounce the [w] of *wet*, you will first notice that the lips are rounded. But there is more to its articulation than this labial gesture. Say the word *wet* very slowly—try to draw the [w] out very long—and feel what is happening. The lips are moving from a relatively rounded posture to a relatively spread one. But note also the movement of your tongue. At the beginning of the word, for the consonant [w], you should feel that the back of the tongue is raised toward the soft palate; as you move to the vowel [ɛ], this changes so that the back of the tongue is no longer raised at all. This shows that [w] is not only a labial sound but also a velar sound. Because of its twofold articulation, this sound is known as a **labiovelar**.

Practice

Give the IPA symbol for the first sound of the following words:

this
think
yet
wet
drip
jeep
cheep
sheep

Phonation

One key property of consonants remains to be described: **phonation**. The airstream must pass through the **larynx** (Adam's apple) on its way from the lungs to the oral articulators. The opening in the larynx through which the air passes is known as the **glottis** and is surrounded by flexible tissue known as the **vocal cords**. If the vocal cords are open, the air passes freely through the glottis, as it does when you are breathing and not talking. But it is also possible to position the vocal cords so that an airstream passing through them causes the vocal cords to vibrate. This is done by bringing the vocal cords together yet leaving them slack enough that the pressure of air below them briefly forces them apart. They then close and, again, are forced open by the airstream, a hundred or even several hundred times per second. It is this vibration that is known as voice or **voicing**. When you make a voiced sound, such as [v], it is possible to feel the vibration with your fingers. Place your fingers on your throat, at the sides of the bulge formed by the larynx, and pronounce a long and drawn-out [v]; now compare the voiceless sound [f]. Or if you use your index fingers to cover the openings of your ears as you produce a good [v], you will feel your whole head vibrate; again compare [f]. Using these cues, decide which of the consonants in this sentence are voiced and which are voiceless.

Here is a phonetic transcription of the previous sentence, pronounced in a very careful style: [ˈjuziŋ ðiz kjuz dɪˈsaid wɪtʃ əv ðə ˈkansənənts ɪn ðɪs ˈsɛntəns ar vɔɪst ænd wɪtʃ ar ˈvɔɪsləs]. (Note: Some people do not voice the beginning of the word *which*.)

You might notice that in normal speech, voiced sounds like [v] and [z] are not always voiced from beginning to end; voicing may start or stop part of the way into the sound. Languages vary quite a lot in how thoroughly they voice consonants; speakers of Romance languages like French and Spanish tend to voice consonants like [v] and [z] from beginning to end. In English, we need to be more attentive: we consider a consonant to be voiced if voicing is found anywhere within the sound, so voiced consonants may actually contain a bit of voicelessness.

Closely associated with phonation is **aspiration**. Oral stops such as [p], [t], and [k] may be so vigorously voiceless—that is, the glottis can be open so wide—that the voicelessness continues well into the next sound. This happens, for example, at the beginning of a word in English. In words like *pie*, *toe*, and *key*, you may even be able to feel a puff of air if you hold your finger up to your mouth, or see it if you hold a candle flame up to your lips. We say that the consonants are aspirated. We could indicate this in the International Phonetic Alphabet by adding a small [h] after the consonant, because that aspiration is a puff of air much like an [h]: [pʰ], and so on. One usually does not bother to do this for English, because no two words are ever distinguished in English solely by differences in aspiration. Some other languages, though, such as classical Greek, do use aspiration to distinguish words.

If you push the air out of your lungs fast enough, you may get your vocal cords to vibrate even if they are not very tense. The effect is **breathy** voice. You may get this naturally in English if you talk while exercising or are trying to sound sexy, but of course no two words are distinguished by whether your voicing is breathy. In some languages such as Hindi and Urdu, however, breathy voice is produced by aspirating voiced stops. A symbol like [b^h] signifies a [b] whose phonation is breathy and for which some period of breathiness follows the consonant. An example is [b^{h}ərət], the Hindi name for India. We will see later that these sounds were very important in the history of English.

In English, voicing may be the only property that distinguishes one obstruent from another, as with *safe* and *save*. The voiced obstruents of English are [b], [d], [g], [v], [ð], [z], [ʒ], and [dʒ]; the corresponding voiceless ones are [p], [t], [k], [f], [θ], [s], [ʃ], and [tʃ]. The obstruent [h] is normally voiceless, but—especially with vowels on either side, as in *ahead*—you may detect a bit of breathy voice. With consonants other than obstruents, the situation is different. They are normally voiced, although they can lose some of their voicing after aspirated obstruents.

By citing phonation, place, and manner of articulation, one can uniquely identify all the consonants of English.

Table 5.1 summarizes these observations about consonant properties.

Practice

Transcribe the final two consonant sounds of the following words, paying special attention to phonation. In these particular cases, the consonant

Table 5.1 PLACES AND MANNERS OF ARTICULATION OF ENGLISH CONSONANTS.

	Labial	Labiodental	Dental	Alveolar	Post-alveolar	Palatal	Velar	Glottal
Oral stop	p, b			t, d			k, g	
Fricative		f, v	θ, ð	s, z	ʃ, ʒ			h
Affricate					tʃ, dʒ			
Nasal	m			n			ŋ	
Approximant				l	r	j	w	

NOTE: Obstruents are cited in pairs, except for voiceless [h]; the sound before the comma is voiceless, and the following one is voiced. The remaining consonants are all voiced.

pairs will agree in voicing, though any consonant voicing may trail off toward the word's end.

ships
bibs
range
disc
leaves

Vowels

Figure 5.1 showing the vocal apparatus for consonants helps to describe vowels as well.

Unlike consonants, vowels are made with a relatively open vocal tract. English vowels are ordinarily voiced, as you can see by applying the voicing tests you learned for consonants to the vowels in words such as *I* and *we*. In some circumstances, however, particularly when an unstressed vowel is surrounded by voiceless obstruents, the vowel becomes voiceless. Pay attention to the first vowel of *potato* and see whether you pronounce it as a voiced or voiceless sound. Does the speed with which you say it have any effect?

Vowel sounds vary much more from dialect to dialect than consonant sounds do. Whether we are comparing different regional English dialects with one another or comparing generalized pronunciation tendencies across the Englishes of the United States, United Kingdom, and Australia, chances are good that we'll find more differences among the vowels than among the consonants. One big reason is that vowel articulation is inherently more open to variation than for consonants, which tend to have more discrete points of articulation. This makes it difficult to characterize English vowels in a way that does justice to their diversity. Still, the features that distinguish the vowel sounds are straightforward and easy enough to illustrate with real English examples. The problem is that your own vowel pronunciations may vary from what we describe in the examples. In that case, don't take our descriptions as prescribing how the different vowels *ought* to be pronounced—no one is in a position to do this. If your pronunciations differ significantly from the ones presented here, this account should at least provide the basic parameters for understanding how you produce your versions. The most important differentiating factor in vowels is the location of the body of the tongue. For the sound [i] of *heat*, the body of the tongue is raised toward the palate; for the sound [æ] of *hat*, the body of the tongue is lowered. The jaw is normally raised or lowered with the tongue. Starting with your tongue in the high position for [i], gradually lower it until you reach the position for the sound [æ]. What comes out may sound strange, but you should encounter some other English vowels in the course of going from the highest tongue position to the lowest.

The vowels [i] and [æ] are called **front** vowels, because they are made with the body of the tongue in a relatively forward part of the mouth. They are produced in approximately the same region of the mouth as palatal consonants, and in fact [i] is virtually the same sound as the palatal approximant [j]. Notice how the tongue moves little if at all when moving from the consonant to the vowel in the word *ye* [ji]. In table 5.2, the column labeled "Front" lists the front vowels in order from highest to lowest.

Other vowels are articulated with the back of the tongue; this is the case for the vowels [u] of *who* and [o] of *coat*. **Back** vowels tend to be pronounced with lip **rounding**. For most people nowadays, this rounding of

Table 5.2 Vowels of American English.

Height	Tenseness	Front	Central	Back
High	Tense	i (*heed*)		u (*loot*)
	Lax	ɪ (*hid*)		ʊ (*look*)
Mid	Tense	e (*wade*)		o (*coat*)
	Lax	ɛ (*wed*)	ə (*fun, sofa*)	ɔ (*horse*)
Low	Lax	æ (*cat*)		
	Tense	a (*spa*)		ɒ (*caught*)

the lips is rather slight and might only be noticed if you pronounce [i] and [u] in succession: your lips will probably be less spread for the latter sound.

The low back vowels tend to vary most across dialects and so are generally the most confusing. English dialects differ in how many distinctive low back vowels they have. Most speakers in England, for example, have three different vowels in the words *spa*, *spot*, and *caught*. Nowadays most Americans have the same vowel in *spa* and *spot*—most typically an unrounded vowel [a]. Consequently, most Americans have no more than two vowels where the English have three. But many North Americans have also changed the vowel [ɒ] as in *caught* so that it is pronounced the same as *cot*. For these speakers, all the words we have mentioned in this paragraph have the same vowel, approximately [a]. Are they alike in your own pronunciation?

American English has one more simple vowel that we haven't discussed yet because it is neither front nor back. The vowel [ə] is considered a **central** vowel. Its height depends a lot on the speaker and the context in the word, but in general it is of mid height. This vowel has the special honor of having its own name, **schwa**. Linguists have traditionally used this symbol only for unstressed vowels, but in contemporary American speech the stressed vowel in words like *fun* does not differ appreciably from the unstressed schwa at the end of *sofa*, so the symbol [ə] can thriftily be used for both.

Note how in table 5.2 some vowels share the same height and backness. The vowels [e] and [ɛ], for example, are both mid front vowels. To distinguish such sounds, linguists refer to an additional property of vowels, their **tenseness**. The vowels [i], [u], [e], [o], and [a] are **tense**, while the other vowels are considered lax. An easy way to remember the distinction is that in English, only tense vowels can be stressed at the very end of a word. For instance, there is a word [ˈde] (*day*), yet not only is there no such word as ˣ[ˈdɛ], but the very idea of such a word would seem strange to most speakers.

Many English speech sounds involve movement from one vowel position to another. For the sound [aɪ] of words like *I* and *might*, our articulators start out low, around the position for [a], and move toward the high front position of [ɪ]; for [aʊ] in words like *how* and *now*, we begin near the same position and move toward the high back position of [ʊ]. Vowels that involve significant movements like these are called **diphthongs**. In addition to [aɪ] and [aʊ], there is a diphthong [ɔɪ] in words like *boy* and *soil*.

We noted earlier that vowels are subject to a great deal of variation in English. The amount of diphthongization is probably the most variable aspect of vowels. Pronounce the tense vowels to see the extent to which they are diphthongs for you. Can you feel or see your tongue or jaw move during the vowel sound? To avoid the interfering effects of consonants, pronounce them in words whose consonants are not made with the tongue, such as [h] or [m]. In Standard English the amount of diphthongization on the high and low vowels is slight. Considerably more diphthongization occurs on the vowels of *ape* and *hope*, which start with a mid vowel and move toward a high vowel. In fact, these are often transcribed [eɪ] and [oʊ], respectively, but in this book, we keep to the simpler representations [e] and [o].

Practice

Transcribe the vowel of these words.

ship
sheep
coop
cup
bought
bot
bout
pan
pane
pine

SUMMARY

Consonants can differ in manner and place of articulation and in voicing. The basic characteristics of vowels are the height and backness of the tongue, rounding of the lips, and length or tenseness. Knowing about common features of different sounds explains the basis for a number of types of allomorphy, because sounds that are phonetically similar often behave in similar ways.

WORD ELEMENTS

Learn the following elements, their meanings, and alternate forms.

Element	Gloss	Source	Examples
ag~ac~ig	act, do, drive	L	*agent, agenda, agitate, exigent, intransigent, litigate, navigate, action, exact*
alt	high	L	*altitude, altiloquence, exalt, altithermal*
ambul	walk	L	*ambulance, perambulator, somnambulist, amble*
andr	male, man	G	*android, androgyny, polyandry, apandrous*
arch	first, govern	G	*anarchy, archaeology, archbishop, archetype, archive, monarch, oligarchy*
av	bird	L	*aviator, avian, avicolous, avine, auspice*
cad~cas~cid	fall	L	*cadence, casual, occasion, coincide, incident, Occident, recidivism*
ced~cess	go, let go	L	*cede, antecedent, intercede, secede, proceed, excess*
clud~clus	to close	L	*conclude, occlude, seclude, recluse*
doc	teach	L	*docent, docile, doctor, doctrine, document*
doc~dog	opinion	G	*doxology, orthodox, dogma*

Element	Gloss	Source	Examples
ero	physical love	G	*erotic, erogenous, Eros*
esth~aesth	feel	G	*anesthetic, kinesthetic, synesthesia, aesthetics*
grad~gred~gress	step, go	L	*grade, gradient, retrograde, gradual, ingredient, egress, regression*
heli	sun	G	*heliocentric, helium, aphelion, perihelion*
leg~lig	gather, read	L	*legend, legible, elegant, lectern, diligent, eligible*
lic	permit	L	*license, licentious, licit, illicit, scilicet*
ne	new, recent	G	*neofascist, neologism, neonate, neophyte, neoteny*
phot~phos	light	G	*photon, photosynthesis, aphotic, phosphor*
prac~prag	act, do	G	*practice, practicable, apraxis, pragmatic*
reg~rig	rule, straight	L	*regal, regent, regime, regimen, regular, dirigible, incorrigible, rex*
sent~sens	feel	L	*sentient, sententious, sentinel, consensus, insensate, sensory, sensual*
tele	far	G	*telepathy, telekinesis, telemetry, telephone, telesthesia*
ten~tend~tens	stretch, thin	L	*tenuous, tend, tendon, extend, extenuate, tense, tensile*
trud~trus	thrust	L	*intrude, extrude, protrude, abstruse, intrusive*

ELEMENT STUDY

1. What is the root in these words? For a root with several allomorphs, give the one that most closely matches the morph in the word in question. Look up each word, and include a brief

Phonetics 131

sentence about the relation between the root's literal meaning and its meaning in this word.
- a. *document*
- b. *exclusive*
- c. *illuminate*
- d. *practical*
- e. *maintenance* (Note: comment on *both roots* of this word.)

2. False friends: The root *leg* 'law, deputize' (as in *legal*) from chapter 2 comes from the same ancient etymological source as *log* 'speak, study' (as in *logic*) from chapter 1. So does *leg~lig* 'gather, read' (as in *legible*). Consequently these roots look alike, but we distinguish them by their different meanings. For each of the words below, identify the root as *leg* 'law, deputize', *lex~leg~log* 'speak, study', or *leg~lig* 'gather, read'.
   - a. *allege*
   - b. *allegory*
   - c. *collegial*
   - d. *elegant*
   - e. *elegy*
   - f. *legitimate*
   - g. *legato*

3. False friends: *ten~tin* 'hold, maintain' versus *ten~tend~tens* 'stretch, thin'. Both come from the same original root but via different historical paths, leading their meanings (originally 'stretch') to develop independently. These elements share the allomorph *ten*. What is the root in each of the following words?
   - a. *tender*
   - b. *tenure*
   - c. *tenant*
   - d. *tenable*
   - e. *tendency*
   - f. *tenement*
   - g. *tenet*

h. *intent*
i. *intensive*
j. *tennis*
k. *pretend*
l. *sustenance*
m. *tensor*
n. *tenuous*

4. False friends: As noted in an exercise at the end of chapter 5, the roots *cad~cas~cid* 'fall' and *cid~cis* 'cut, kill' both have allomorphs spelled *cid*. In the following set, which words have the root for 'fall', and which have the root for 'cut, kill'?
    a. *incisor*
    b. *accident*
    c. *precise*
    d. *decide*
    e. *genocide*
    f. *occasion*
    g. *cascade*
    h. *incident*
    i. *recidivism*
    j. *casual*

5. The meanings of the root *ced* go beyond the simple glosses 'go, let go'. Consider variations in the meaning of *ced* (including the alternate spelling *ceed*) in the following words. Using the basic meanings 'go' and 'let go' as a starting point, what differences in meaning do you detect? For example, are there differences in the kind of motion described, or in whether motion in the literal sense is involved?
    a. *accede*
    b. *cede*
    c. *concede*
    d. *exceed*
    e. *intercede*
    f. *precede*

g. *proceed*
h. *recede*
i. *secede*
j. *succeed*
6. The same gloss, 'man', is frequently given for the elements *anthrop* and *andr*. Compare the words *anthropocentric* and *androcentric*. How do their meanings differ, and what difference between the roots *anthrop* and *andr* does this illustrate?
7. After reviewing the word element lists for the preceding chapters, test your knowledge by parsing the following words. Under each element write a one-word gloss indicating meaning or function (e.g., part of speech) and categorize it as a root or tell what kind of affix it is: prefix, suffix, interfix, or superfix. With the aid of a dictionary, construct a brief definition for the entire word while staying as close as possible to the literal meaning of the individual morphs. Important aspects of the meaning that are not expressed by the word parts themselves can be included in parentheses.
    a. *amorphous*
    b. *omniscient*
    c. *conducive*
    d. *perinatal*
    e. *incidence*
    f. *extenuate*
    g. *acceptance*
    h. *adequate*

EXERCISES

1. Transcribe the following words using phonetic symbols. For example, for *mention* you would write [ˈmɛnʃən] or [mɛnʃn̩].
    a. *wounds*
    b. *grounds*

c. *psychologist*
d. *photograph*
e. *photography*
f. *drained*
g. *spine*
h. *thought*
i. *rather*
j. *doughy*

2. Transcribe passage (a) into IPA using your own pronunciation, and translate passage (b) into standard English orthography:
   a. If life hands you lemons, make lemonade.
   b. [ˈdɪfr̩nt stroks fr̩ ˈdɪfr̩nt foks]

3. Render this Early Modern English passage into current English orthography. Then retranscribe it to reflect your own pronunciation. Summarize any differences, listing them by type.

ɪf əɪ proˈfɛːn wɪθ məɪ ʊnˈwʊrðiɪst hand
ðɪs ˈhoːli frəɪn, ði dʒɛntl̩ fəɪn ɪz ðɪs
məɪ lɪps, tuː ˈblʊʃɪŋ ˈpɪlgrɪmz ˈrɛdi stand
tu smuːð ðat rʊf tʊtʃ wɪθ ə ˈtɛndɪr kɪs

4. Describe fully each of the sounds represented by the phonetic symbols. The first is given as an example. For each vowel indicate whether it is
   - high, mid, or low
   - front, central, or back
   - rounded or unrounded
   - tense or lax

   For each consonant indicate whether it is
   - voiced or voiceless
   - labial, labiodental, dental, alveolar, postalveolar, palatal, velar, or glottal
   - oral stop, fricative, affricate, nasal, or approximant

   a. [ʒ] voiced postalveolar fricative
   b. [ə]

c. [dʒ]
d. [ð]
e. [e]
f. [ŋ]
g. [ɪ]
h. [ɒ]
i. [æ]
j. [r]
k. [b]
l. [ʊ]
m. [h]

5. Give the phonetic symbol represented by each of the following articulatory descriptions, as in the example.
    a. voiceless alveolar fricative ([s])
    b. high back tense rounded vowel
    c. voiceless dental fricative
    d. voiced velar oral stop
    e. low front lax unrounded vowel
    f. alveolar nasal
    g. voiced labiodental fricative
    h. voiceless postalveolar affricate
    i. mid central unrounded vowel
    j. voiceless postalveolar fricative

6. Vowel exercise: As noted in the text, English vowels can differ quite a bit across dialects. If your speech differs from the types described in the text, this may have made it difficult to follow some of the points in the chapter.

    Using the vowel chart provided as a guide, where the terms *front*, *central*, and *back* correspond to tongue position on the horizontal axis and *high*, *mid*, and *low* refer to tongue or jaw position, plot the position of the vowels in the words below *as you yourself pronounce them*, and don't be surprised if they deviate from their position in the chart.

Transcribe the vowels in these words, and then place the corresponding example letter in the appropriate place in the chart. Your vowel may or may not belong in the positions sketched in the chart.

a. *pen*
b. *pain*
c. *pin*
d. *born*
e. *barn*
f. *bone*
g. *pull*
h. *pool*

Six

Regular Allomorphy; Numeric Elements

REGULAR ALLOMORPHY IN GENERAL

In the overview of allomorphy in chapter 4, we discussed a set of variations that simply have to be memorized on a morpheme-by-morpheme or a word-by-word basis. But some allomorphy is **regular**—that is, generally predictable—because it follows some simple phonetic principles. Regular allomorphy that applies to all native English words, such as the variation in the pronunciation of the plural morpheme in *cats*, *dogs*, and *finches*, comes to English speakers so naturally that they may be completely unaware of it. But some regular allomorphy is more challenging because it applies only to Latinate vocabulary. Such alternations result from changes due to classical Latin and Greek phonology, and they require study before we moderns can apply them fluently.

Latin Letters and Sounds

Mastering regular allomorphy in Latinate vocabulary is straightforward if we understand two things: what sounds the letters stand for in Latin, and what rules apply to each set of sounds. The bulk of this chapter deals with the rules, but first we consider the letter sounds.

As table 6.1 shows, the great majority of letters were pronounced in classical Latin the same way they are in English today, for all practical purposes. One difference is that the letters *c* and *g* always represent velar sounds in Latin: [k] and [g], never ˣ[s] or ˣ[dʒ]. The oddest classical letter-consonant correspondences could be for the letters *j* and *v*. In English these represent obstruents, but in classical Latin they were approximants. The vowels have approximately the same value as the corresponding IPA symbol: *a* is a low vowel, *e* and *o* are mid vowels, and *i* and *u* are high vowels. Most sounds in Latin can be pronounced either short or long. For the consonants, a long pronunciation is indicated in the orthography by writing the consonant twice, for example, *mitt* 'send' has a long consonant. Latin didn't indicate vowel length in the spelling, nor do we here, since Latin vowel length is reflected in English only in a few cases dealt with in this chapter.

The Greek elements pose few problems, because they are always romanized—rendered in Latin spellings—before being adopted into English. The only unusual letter sound you will encounter is [y], a front rounded vowel like the *u* in French or the *ü* in German; in English this Greek sound is pronounced in the same way as the letter *i*.

We hasten to add that the pronunciations just described are essentially those of classical Rome. These can help you understand Latin and Greek spellings and allophonic rules despite two thousand years of sound changes that have obscured some patterns. The most common differences between Latin and English pronunciations are listed in table 6.1. Additionally, most of the vowels are pronounced as [ə] when unstressed in English. Let yourself be guided by your feel for the spoken language—or a trusted authority.

Assimilation

Sometimes a consonant changes its place of articulation to match that of another consonant. This assimilation is almost always **anticipatory** in English and the classical languages: the consonant changes to match the place of articulation of the consonant immediately following it. In short,

Regular Allomorphy; Numeric Elements

Table 6.1 MOST COMMON PRONUNCIATIONS OF THE LATIN LETTERS IN CLASSICAL LATIN AND IN MODERN ENGLISH.

Letter	Latin pronunciation	English pronunciation
a	[a], [aː]	[æ] *static*, [e] *stadium*
ae	[ae]	[ɛ] *Daedalus*, [i] *Caesar*
au	[aʊ]	[ɒ] *autumn*
b	[b]	[b] *bubonic*
c	[k]	[k] *clinic*, [s] *cite*
ch	[kʰ]	[k] *chord*
d	[d]	[d] *divine*
e	[ɛ], [eː]	[ɛ] *epic*, [i] *femur*
eu	[eu]	[ju] *euphoria*
f	[f]	[f] *fission*
g	[g]	[g] *galaxy*, [dʒ] *general*
h	[h]	[h] *hero*
i	[ɪ], [iː]	[ɪ] *image*, [aɪ] *item*
j	[j]	[dʒ] *joke*
k	[k]	[k] *kinetic*
l	[l]	[l] *lily*
m	[m]	[m] *matrix*
n	[n], [ŋ] before velars	[n] *note*, [ŋ] *sanctify*
o	[ɔ], [oː]	[a] *obvious*, [o] *oval*
oe	[ɔe]	[ɛ] *Oedipus*, [i] *amoeba*
p	[p]	[p] *paternal*
ph	[pʰ]	[f] *phone*
qu	[kw]	[kw] *quantum*
r	[r]	[r] *rose*
rh	[hr]	[r] *rhythm*
s	[s]	[s] *sponge*, [z] *misery*
t	[t]	[t] *tuba*
th	[tʰ]	[θ] *thermal*
u	[ʊ], [uː]	[ə] *ultimate*, [ju] *utopia*

(*continued*)

Table 6.1 Continued

Letter	Latin pronunciation	English pronunciation
v	[w]	[v] *vacuum*
x	[ks]	[ks] *sex*, [gz] *example*, [z] *xenon*
y	[y], [y]	[ɪ] *hypocrite*, [aɪ] *hypothesis*
z	[dz]	[z] *zone*

we say the consonant assimilates in place to the consonant to its right. A common example is the nasal consonant [n]. Before a component beginning with a bilabial consonant, [n] becomes [m]. We see this when the Latin prefixes *con-* 'with', *in-* 'not', and *in-* 'in' and the Greek prefix *syn-* 'with' appear before a bilabial consonant:

con- + *pose*   *compose*
con- + *bine*   *combine*
con- + *mute*   *commute*

in- + *possible*   *impossible*
in- + *balance*   *imbalance*
in- + *mutable*   *immutable*

in- + *pose*   *impose*
in- + *bibe*   *imbibe*
in- + *merse*   *immerse*

syn- + *path* + *-y*   *sympathy*
syn- + *phon* + *-y*   *symphony*
syn- + *bol*   *symbol*
syn- + *metr* + *-y*   *symmetry*

Although we are discussing the allomorphy rules from the standpoint of Latin and Greek pronunciation, in this chapter we present the words in their anglicized forms. While the very ends of some of these words have nonclassical forms, the parts of the words that are involved in the phonological processes are spelled the same way in both languages.

Note that this rule works before ‹ph› in *symphony* even though the sound of ‹ph› is [f] in English—a labiodental, not a bilabial. In classical Greek, ‹ph› represented a bilabial sound, aspirated [p^h], and so the rule applies.

Place assimilation also applies to the nasal infixes of chapter 4. This is why we find *n* in the allomorph *fund* 'pour', but *m* in *cumb* 'lie'. The assimilation rule can be expressed formally as follows:

Place Assimilation of [n]

n → m / ___ {p, b, m}

This notation is not as daunting as it may look. The part to the left of the diagonal slash describes a phonological change, and the part to the right shows where that change occurs. The arrow says that the sound to its left, [n], changes into the sound to its right, [m]. The low line after the slash stands for the sound in question: it says that [n] must change its pronunciation before any of the sounds in the set {p, b, m}.

You may wonder why this rule is labeled in such general terms. Why is it called *Place Assimilation* and not simply *Labial Assimilation*? In fact, other types of place are assimilated as well. Before a velar consonant, [n] becomes the velar nasal [ŋ]. But because [ŋ] is spelled ‹n› in Latin, the assimilation leaves no mark on the spelling—*congregate*, *synchronize*, *incur* with nasal infix—and so we tend to gloss over that part of the rule.

When the [n] assimilates to a following [m], the result is the letter sequence ‹mm›, which stands for a long [m:] in Latin and Greek. Because the [n] has become totally like the following consonant, the process is called a **total assimilation**. Before the other consonants, [n] is still a separate sound, changing just its place of articulation, so by contrast we can call the process **partial assimilation**. Its nasality remains.

Another type of assimilation involves phonation. In many cases, a voiced consonant like [b] becomes voiceless (i.e., [p]) before a voiceless consonant (often [t]).

Phonation Assimilation

[voiced obstruent] → [voiceless] / ___ [voiceless obstruent]

[voiceless obstruent] → [voiced] / ___ [nasal]

To take one example, the root *scrib* becomes *scrip* before *t*. This *t*, as noted in chapter 4, is frequently added to a Latinate root, creating a new allomorph. That is why *prescribe* changes its [b] to [p] in *prescription*. Here are a few more examples:

reg **t** + -or	*rec*tor (cf. *regular*)
frag **t** + -ion	*frac*tion (cf. *fragile*)
leg + -sis	*lex*is [-ks-] (cf. *prolegomenon*)

Note that *g* devoices to *c* [k] even though words like *regent* are pronounced with [dʒ] in English. This underscores the need to apply the rule to Latin rather than English sounds.

Phonation Assimilation does not generally apply between prefixes and roots, as shown by *sub-tract*, where the rule would wrongly devoice the [b]. Similar cases are o**b**-*tain* and e**c**-**b**olic. Instead, the next two rules below account for total assimilation of the final prefix consonant to the following one.

Usually, Phonation Assimilation winds up converting voiced consonants into voiceless ones. But here are some examples in which a voiceless consonant assimilates to a voiced one:

do**c** + -ma	do**g**ma (cf. *orthodox*)
se**c** + -ment	se**g**ment (cf. *secant*)

Some sounds undergo total assimilation before the liquid sounds, [l] and [r]. The most important cases of liquid assimilation involve [n] and [r].

Liquid Assimilation
{n, r} → l / ___ l
{n} → r / ___ r

Here are some examples:

con- + lude	collude
con- + rupt	corrupt
in- + leg + -al	illegal

in- + *ration* + *-al*	*irrational*
inter- + *lig* + *-ent*	*intelligent*
per- + *lucid*	*pellucid*
coron + *-la*	*corolla* (cf. *corona*)

Technically [d] is subject to the same rule of Liquid Assimilation (e.g., *alleviate* from *ad-levi-ate*), but it undergoes total assimilation in so many additional environments as well that it is useful to make a special rule for it:

Total Assimilation of *ad-*

ad- → aC$_1$ / ___ C$_1$ (not [m] or glides)

The notation C$_1$ is for matching consonants. That is, whatever consonant follows the [d], that's the consonant it becomes. Recall that Latinate roots may add an extra *t*, as happens here with *accept* and *affect*.

ad- + *liter* + *-ation*	*alliteration*
ad- + *rog* + *-ant*	*arrogant*
ad- + *brevi* + *-ate*	*abbreviate*
ad- + *greg* + *-ate*	*aggregate*
ad- + *pet* + *-ite*	*appetite*
ad- + *cep t*	*accept*
ad- + *fec t*	*affect*
ad- + *not* + *-ate*	*annotate*
ad- + *simil* + *-ate*	*assimilate*

In addition, [b] undergoes total assimilation before Latin velars, but in order to witness this change, we need to restore some Latin-derived roots to their original form. The English roots *cipit* and *ges* in the following examples began with velar stops in Latin: [k] in *cipit* and [g] in *ges*. These stops shifted their articulations to the [s] and [dʒ] we hear in English, thus obscuring the assimilatory nature of the change in the final consonant of the prefixes illustrated here:

ob- + *cipit* + *-al*   *occipital*
sub- + *gest*   *suggest*

This shows why the rules work best if applied to the classical Latin pronunciations rather than to the later English ones. Interestingly, for many speakers *suggest* can undergo yet other assimilation whereby the *gg* is pronounced as a single consonant [dʒ].

English owes many of its double letters to total assimilations. If you are having difficulty parsing a word that contains a double letter, do not forget to consider the possibility that the first of the pair may have come from a different sound that was changed by total assimilation. By far the most frequent cases of total assimilation involve the assimilation of the final consonant of a prefix to the first consonant of a root. What are the basic forms of the prefixes in the following words: *syllogism, irradiate*?

Deletion

A vowel at the end of a morpheme is frequently **deleted** before another vowel. In Greek, that second vowel can be preceded by an [h], which is often deleted itself. In the following rule, **V** stands for any vowel, and the symbol ∅ ("zero") stands for the absence of a sound.

Vowel Deletion
V → ∅ / ___ (h) V

This rule works on the final vowel of a fairly large number of prefixes.
It also works on the final vowel of the root before a variety of suffixes:

anti- + *agon* + *-ize*   *antagonize*
ana- + *hode*   *anode*
cata- + *hode*   *cathode*
cello + *-ist*   *cellist*
America + *-an*   *American*

Vowel Deletion should not be confused with the spelling rule that leaves off the silent vowel ‹e› when certain suffixes are attached: *nude~nudist*, and so on. Instead, Vowel Deletion applies to vowels with an actual pronunciation in some allomorphs, for example, to *ana-*, whose final vowel is found in *analyze*, and to the *o* that we hear in *cello*.

Consonants also undergo deletion. The consonant [s] is generally deleted before voiced consonants:

[s] Deletion
s → ∅ / ___ [voiced C]

Here are some examples:

dis- + *lig* 'gather' + *-ent*	*diligent*
dis- + *vulg* 'crowd'	*divulge*
jus 'law' + *dic* 'say' + *-ious*	*judicious*
bis 'twice' + *-n* + *-ary*$_A$	*binary*

In the last example, *-n* is a suffix found in numbers, with the meaning '(number) at a time'.

When combining morphemes would bring together three consonants, often one or two of them is deleted. The rules for Cluster Simplification are complicated and do not need to be learned in detail; the important thing is that long runs of consonants may lose one or more consonant.

Cluster Simplification
C → ∅ / ___ s C
C → ∅ / C ___ C

among other variants.

sub- + *spic* 'look' + *-ious*	*suspicious*
ex- [ɛks] + *vade*	*evade*
ex- + *mitt* 'send' + *-ing*	*emitting*
ad- + *scribe*	*ascribe*
ad- + *scend*	*ascend*

amb- 'around' + *put* 'cut' + *-ate*	*amputate*
con- + *gn* + *-ate*	*cognate*
in- + *gnore*	*ignore*
trans- + *jec t* + *-ory*	*trajectory*
syn + *ste* + *-mat*	*system*
syn + *stol* + *-ic*	*systolic*
torqu t 'twist' + *-ure*	*torture*

Cluster Simplification rules ordinarily don't apply when the cluster is due to prefixation, except when the prefix is *ex-*. Note how the [s]-Deletion rule applies as well: *ex-vade* → **esvade* → *evade*. Now consider cases where *ex-* appears before [s], as when prefixed to *spec* 'look, see', *secr* 'holy', and *cess* 'go, let go':

ex- + *spect*	*expect*
ex- + *secr* + *-able*	*execrable*
ex- + cess	excess

For words like *expect*, without Cluster Simplification, we would predict the [s] of [eks-] to combine with adjacent root-initial [s] to form a long consonant. The first clause of Cluster Simplification explains why the first [s] is absent. The second clause of Cluster Simplification comes into play in the remaining two preceding examples, where the [s] of [eks-] fails to be realized before the initial [s] sound of the roots *secr* and *cess*.

Another case where expected consonants go missing arises from the fact that Greek did not allow a word to end in an oral stop. So Greek morphemes that end in stops often lose them, even in English, when used alone or at the end of a word:

Greek Final Stop Deletion

[stop] → ∅ / ___ at the end of a word

Many examples involve the sequence *-mat*, but there are a few other examples as well. (An additional loss of a final vowel in some of these examples is not due to Greek phonology but is part of a much later process of getting words to conform better to French and English word patterns.)

traumat	*trauma* (cf. *traumatic*)
dramat	*drama* (cf. *dramaturge*)
symptomat	*symptom* (cf. *symptomatology*)
themat	*theme* (cf. *thematic*)
schemat	*scheme* (cf. *schematic*)
mastodont	*mastodon* (cf. *orth-odont-ist*)

Insertion

A small set of one-syllable prefixes ending in a vowel add a [d] before a root that begins with a vowel.

[d] Insertion

Ø → d / V ___ V after some prefixes

re- + *und* + *-ant*	*redundant*
se- + *it* + *-ion*	*sedition*
pro- + *ig* + *-y*	*prodigy*

This rule may have come about because otherwise Vowel Deletion would result in a very short prefix. For example, in *sedition* the *d* at the end of prefix allomorph *sed-* prevents the loss of *e* before the root *it* 'go'; without it, hypothetical ˣ*se-it-ion* would become ˣ*sition*.

Another insertion rule applying only to prefixes has no such obvious motivation:

[s] Insertion

Ø → s / b ___ {p, t, c} after prefixes

This rule is surprising because all it does is produce big consonant clusters. In some words these clusters are tolerated, but in others they are subjected to the consonant simplification rules:

ab- + tract	abstract
ab- + cess	abscess
ab- + cond	abscond
ob- + tens + -ible	ostensible
sub- + tent + -ation	sustentation

PRACTICE

Analyze the following words, using the preceding rules to guide your analysis:

correct
tiger
illicit
Antarctic
aspect
intellect

Rhotacism

Rhotacism is the process of turning [s] into [r]. Latin morphemes with a final [s] change this to [r] in words where it appears between two vowels.

Rhotacism
s → r / V ___ V

Here are some examples:

rus + -al	rural (cf. rustic)
jus + -y	jury (cf. justice)
mus + -ine	murine (cf. muscle)
genus + -ic	generic

Vowel Changes

Latin Vowel Weakening occurs when a morpheme appears in a syllable other than the first syllable of a word. It affects only short vowels. It is actually a series of rules, as follows:

Latin [a] Weakening

a → e / [syllable] ___

That is, [a] regularly becomes [e] when it is not in the first syllable of the word:

de- + fact	defect (cf. fact)
re- + capt + -ive	receptive (cf. captive)
in- + apt	inept

Latin [e] Weakening

e → i / [syllable] ___ C V

Short [e] becomes [i] when it is followed by a single consonant and a vowel. Latin [e] Weakening affects not only the [e] in a morpheme's basic allomorph but also the [e] that derives from Latin [a] Weakening.

de- + fac + -ient	*defecient → deficient
re- + cap + -ient	*recepient → recipient
con- + ten + -ent	*contenent → continent

Latin Vowel Weakening includes several other minor rules as well. The consonant following the vowel can influence the outcome of the weakening. For instance, vowels tend to become [e] before [r] (*experiment* not ˣ*expiriment*) and [i] before [ŋ] (*infringe* from *frang*). When consonants affect the quality of vowels, we speak of **vowel coloring**.

Vowel coloring also occasionally occurs independently of vowel weakening, even in word-initial syllables. This is especially common before [l]:

[l] Coloring

{e, o} → u / ___ l in a closed syllable

Here are some examples:

com- + *pell* + *-sive*	c*u*lpulsive (cf. *compel*)
col t + *iv* + *-ate*	c*u*ltivate (cf. *colony*)
in- + *salt* 'jump'	**inselt* → *insult*
ad- + *olt*	ad*u*lt

Note how in the example of *insult*, the [e] that undergoes this rule came from Latin [a] Weakening.

Other Consonant Changes

Many Latin roots have an allomorph ending in [t], so it is especially important to understand changes that roots undergo before this consonant. We have already seen that [t] can trigger Phonation Assimilation (*rect-or* from *reg*), and [l] Coloring (*cult-ivate* from *col*), or prevent rules like Rhotacism (*justice* vs. *jury*) and Latin [e] Weakening (*recept-ive* vs. *recipient*) from applying. An additional rule applies when this *t* forms an allomorph of a root already ending in a dental stop, [d] or [t]. Because [d] in this environment would become [t] anyway by Phonation Assimilation, our rule simply needs to apply to the sequence [t] + [t], where the plus sign separates the added [t] from the root-final [t] or [d].

[t][t] to [ss]

tt → ss when roots are combined with suffixes

Here are some examples:

pat t+ -ion	*passion* (cf. *patient*)
mitt t+ -ive	**mittive → missive* (cf. *transmitter*)
fid t + -ion	**fittion → fission* (cf. *pinnatifid*)
con- + ced t + ion	**concettion → concession* (cf. *concede*)
sent t + -ual	**senssual → sensual*
sent t	**senss → sense*
dis- + grad t	**digratt → *digrass → digress* (cf. *grade*)
ex- + lūd t + -ive	**elūttive → *elūssive → elusive*

In many cases, Cluster Simplification applies after the change of *tt* to *ss*, resulting in just a single *s*. This happens whenever another consonant precedes the *ss*, or even a long vowel. Because we are not memorizing whether a root like *lud* 'play' has a long vowel or not, these shortenings of *ss* may appear unpredictable. When you see a word whose root form ends in [s], recall that it might be an allomorph of a root ending in a *t* or *d*.

NUMERAL MORPHEMES: DISTINGUISHING BETWEEN LATIN AND GREEK MORPHEMES

Many of our number terms derive from Latin and Greek, and they are among the commonest English words directly formed from classical morphemes. Often they reflect the tendency to combine Latin morphemes with other Latin morphemes and Greek morphemes with other Greek morphemes. For example, in *pentagon* 'a five-sided geometrical figure' the roots *penta* 'five' and *gon* 'angle' both come from Greek. But with the root *later* 'side', which comes from Latin, we use the Latin numeral morpheme *quadr* 'four' in *quadrilateral* 'a four-sided geometrical figure'. Morphemes often occur with others from the same source language simply because the entire word was borrowed from that language. The word *pentagon*, for example, originated in Greek; it wasn't first coined in English from Greek roots. Some words coined anew in English follow the old pattern, but there's no requirement that all morphemes in a word be monolingual in origin. The word *monolingual* is a case in point, as it is composed of *mon* "one" (G) and *lingu* 'tongue' (L). Other examples of morpheme mixing are *neonate* (G, L), *amoral* (G, L), *dysfunction* (G, L), and *posthypnotic* (L, G).

Despite such cases, words with roots from a given language often contain other elements from that language. Here are some clues to the presence of Greek elements in a word:

- One of the letters that were borrowed into Latin just for spelling Greek words: ‹y› as in *hyper-, hypo-, myc, cryph, my, onym, pachy*; ‹z› as in *zo, zyg, zym*.
- An initial ‹k› as in *kilo, kerat, kin*. (This is an alternative transcription of what is usually spelled ‹c›.)
- Any of the combinations ‹rh›, ‹ph›, ‹th›, and ‹ch› (pronounced [k], not [tʃ]) as in *rhin; pher, troph, taph; the, esth, sthen, path; arch, chrom, chrys*.
- A spelling that represents an initial cluster not pronounceable in English, such as ‹ps› (*psych, psittac, pseud*), ‹pt› (*pter, pto, pty*), ‹pn› (*pneum*), ‹mn› (*mne*), ‹x› (*xyl, xen, xer*). (Note that <x> is the spelling of the cluster [ks].)

Latinate elements provide a few clues to their origin as well. Generally, a word element in complex scholarly or scientific vocabulary cannot be Greek (and hence is probably Latinate) if it contains

- ‹f› as in *fer, fa, ferr*
- ‹j› as in *jus, juven*
- ‹v› as in *voc, cav, ven, ov, vin, ver, vid*
- ‹qu› as in *quart, quadr, squam, equ, loqu*

The numeral elements are widely used. They precede the root they modify (or count or order) as in *unicycle* (literally 'one wheel') and *millennium* 'one thousand years'. But most of them are not, strictly speaking, prefixes, because they can function as the sole root in a word, as in *dual* and *monad*, in which *-al* and *-ad* are suffixes.

Listed in table 6.2 are the elements most commonly used in traditional numeric compounds. Other important variants are Latin *du* 'two' (*dual, duplex*) and Greek *dy* 'two' (*dyad*), *dich* '(split) in two' (*dichotomy*), and *trich* '(split) in three' (*trichotomy*).

English ordinal numbers are mostly formed from cardinal numbers by suffixing *-th* (e.g., *tenth*), but some ordinals are irregular (e.g., *third* from *three*) and the words *first* and *second* are totally unrelated to the corresponding cardinal. A very similar situation existed in Latin and Greek.

Table 6.2 CLASSICAL NUMERIC ELEMENTS.

Meaning	Latin	Greek	Examples
1	un	mon	*uniform, monologue*
2	bi	di	*bisexual, dichloride*
3	tri	tri	*triple, tricycle, triptych*
4	quadr	tetra	*quadrangle, tetrahedron*
5	quinque	penta	*quinquennium, pentagon*
6	sex	hexa	*sextet, hexagon, hexameter*
7	septem	hepta	*semptemvirate, heptagon*
8	octo	octa	*octane, octopus, octahedron*
9	novem	ennea	*November, enneastyle*
10	decem	deca	*decemvirate, decagon, decade*
20	viginti	icosa	*vigintillion, icosahedron*
100	cent	hecaton	*century, hecatomb*
1000	mille	chili	*millennium, chiliasm, chiliarch*
10,000	—	myri	*myriad, myriarch*
½	semi-	hemi-	*semiconductor, hemisphere*
1½	sesqui-	—	*sesquicentennial, sesquipedalian*
both	ambi-	amphi-	*ambidextrous, amphiploid*
few	pauc	olig	*paucity, paucifolious, oligarchy*
many	mult, plur	poly	*multiple, plurality, polygon*
all	omn, tot	pan-~pant-	*omniscient, total, Pantheon, pantomime*

The Latin ordinals are particularly frequent and should be learned by heart: *prim* (*primary, primogeniture*), *secund* (*second*), *terti* (*tertiary*), *quart* (*quart, quarter, quartet*), *quint* (*quintet, quintessence*), *sext* (*sextet, sextuplets*), *septim* (*septimal*), *octav* (*octave*), *non* (*nones, nonagenarian*), *decim* (*decimal, decimate*). Higher numbers use the suffix *-esim*, as in *centesimal*. Greek ordinals are also used, and the first three, *prot* (*prototype, protozoa, protopathic, protoplasm*), *deuter* (*deuterium, Deuteronomy*), and *trit* (*tritium*), are worth learning. Latin also had a series called the distributive numbers. In principle, these were formed by adding the suffix *-n* or *-en* to the basic form of the number, but so many unusual sound changes ensued as to mask their origin. From 'two', these numbers are *bin* (*binary, binaural*), *tern* (*ternary*), *quatern* (*quaternary*), *quin* (*quinate*), *sen, septen, octon, noven,* and *den* (*denarius*).

The basic English numbers up to *thousand* are native, while those for *million* and above are constructed with classical morphemes. *Million* itself was derived from *mille* 'thousand' to mean a thousand thousands (1,000 × 1,000). New terms were invented in the modern period for every power of 1,000 above that: *billion, trillion, quadrillion,* and so on. The *-illion* was clipped from *million* and reinterpreted as a suffix for indicating large numbers. The prefix *bi-* 'two' in *billion* indicates that it multiplies 1,000 by 1,000 **twice** (i.e., 1,000 × 1,000 × 1,000, or 1,000,000,000), and similarly for *trillion* on up. An easy way to think of this is that the numeric element counts how many groups of 000 there are in addition to the first group.

A slight problem is that an older alternative system interprets the prefixes *bi-*, *tri-*, and so forth as referring to powers of a million. In this system, a billion is $1,000,000^2$ or 1,000,000,000,000; a trillion is $1,000,000^3$ or 1,000,000,000,000,000,000. This has been called the *long scale*, because the numbers get big fast. The English-speaking world has converged on the *short scale* in recent decades, but you may easily run into examples of long scale usage without any warning as to which scale was intended.

Confusion about the meaning of a term like *billion* can be very annoying, but nowhere is it potentially more caustic than in science. For this reason, scientists prefer to use scientific notation and the International System of Units (SI), both of which obviate the need for special words for large numbers. The SI has endorsed a set of prefixes for extremely large and extremely small measurements, such as *gigawatt* for a billion watts. These are listed in table 6.3, which is arranged by magnitude. This is also the chronological order in which the prefixes were standardized.

The first metric prefixes, as standardized during the French Revolution, drew on Greek and Latin roots for 'ten', 'hundred', and 'thousand': Greek roots for the large numbers, Latin roots for the corresponding fractions. But contrast these forms with the more traditional, classical formations: Greek *deca* 'ten' (as in English *decade*), *hecaton* 'hundred' (*hecatombe*), *chili-* 'thousand' (*chiliad*); Latin *decim-* 'tenth' (*decimal*), *centesim-* 'hundredth' (*centesimal*), *millesim-* 'thousandth' (*millesimal*). Most of the metric forms are somewhat different. In classical Greek, in fact, *hecto-* actually meant 'sixth'. Clearly, liberties were taken to make the prefixes fit a regular two-syllable pattern that is easy to pronounce and spell.

When prefixes were added for expressing even larger and smaller numbers, only prefixes that represent powers of a thousand were sanctioned.

Table 6.3 PREFIXES OF THE INTERNATIONAL SYSTEM OF UNITS.

Big numbers		Small numbers	
Number	SI prefix	Number	SI prefix
10^1	deca-	10^{-1}	deci-
10^2	hecto-	10^{-2}	centi-
10^3	kilo-	10^{-3}	milli-
10^6	mega-	10^{-6}	micro-
10^9	giga-	10^{-9}	nano-
10^{12}	tera-	10^{-12}	pico-
10^{15}	peta-	10^{-15}	femto-
10^{18}	exa-	10^{-18}	atto-
10^{21}	zetta-	10^{-21}	zepto-
10^{24}	yotta-	10^{-24}	yocto-

Classical Greek and Latin did not have terms for such large numbers, creating an opening for imaginative prefixes making mnemonic nods to real words. *Mega-* and *micro-* are based on the Greek elements for 'big' and 'small'. *Giga-* and *nano-* are based on Greek elements for 'giant' and 'dwarf'. *Tera-* is from a Greek word for 'marvel' or 'monster'—either a marvelously big number or one that is Godzilla-sized. *Pico-* is often claimed to be based on the Spanish word for 'beak', but Italian *piccolo* 'small' is more apposite.

For increasingly big and small things, the next strategy was to allude to the exponents of the numbers. For example, when a prefix for 1,000,000,000,000,000 was needed, people looked at it as $1,000^5$—base 1,000 because prefixes were defined only for whole powers of 1,000. But if they selected a classical word element like the Greek *penta-*, readers could very well think that it literally meant '5'; measurements like *12 pentagrams* or *100 pentameters* would be very ambiguous. One way out was to drop or change a letter or two in the classical word element. *Peta-* is *penta* '5' without the ‹n›, and *exa-* is *hexa* '6' without the ‹h› ($1,000^6$). *Zetta-* and *zepto-* are obscured forms of words for 'seven' like Greek *hepta*, Latin *septem*, and Italian *sette*. *Yotta-* and *yocto-* make one think of words for 'eight' like Greek *octo*, Latin *octo*, and Italian *otto*. Another obscurantist technique was to adopt words from a language not ordinarily used for international scientific vocabulary. *Femto-* and *atto-* are from Danish words for 'fifteen' and 'eighteen', referencing their power of ten—not their power of a thousand.

SUMMARY

Much of the allomorphy in Latin- and Greek-derived elements is best seen as the product of phonological rules applying to the original, classical pronunciation of the elements. Partial assimilation involves a consonant acquiring some of the phonetic features of the following consonant; in total assimilation, the two consonants merge into one consonant, usually long. The nasal [n] assimilates place features, obstruents assimilate voice, [n] and [r] assimilate totally to [l], and [d] assimilates to most consonants. Deletion processes may efface a vowel before another vowel or [h], [s] before a voiced consonant, a consonant from a large cluster, or stops at the end of Greek words. The shortening of long consonants not between vowels is another type of deletion. The less common opposite process, insertion or epenthesis, may insert [e] between a consonant and [r] at the end of a word, [d] between vowels during prefixation, or [s] before a voiceless stop after the [b] of a prefix. Rhotacism turns [s] into [r] between vowels. Latin Vowel Weakening affects syllables that are not at the start of a word: in general, [a] becomes [e], [e] becomes [i] in an open syllable. Latin also has vowel colorings, such as mid vowels becoming [u] before [l] in closed syllables. The combination of root-final [d] or [t] to a suffix that begins with [t], a common event in Latin, results in [ss] or [s].

There is a general, but violable, tendency for roots in the same compound to be drawn from the same language. This rule is easily obeyed for number morphemes, because large sets of numbers have been borrowed from both Latin and Greek. English uses Latin number morphemes to build names for very large numbers, but the current preference is to use scientific notation and the SI prefixes.

RULES FROM THIS CHAPTER

(1) **Place Assimilation of [n]** (e.g., *inert* vs. *imperfect*)
  n → m / ___ {p, b, m}

(2) **Phonation Assimilation** (e.g., *regular* vs. *rector*; *doctrine* vs. *dogma*)
  [voiced obstruent] → [voiceless] / ___ [voiceless obstruent]
  [voiceless obstruent] → [voiced] / ___ [nasal]

(3) **Liquid Assimilation** (e.g., *inert* vs. *illegal, irregular*)
  {n, r} → l / ___ l
  {n} → r / ___ r

(4) **Total Assimilation of** *ad-* (e.g., *adept* vs. *attend*)
ad- → aC₁ / ___ C₁ (not [m] or glides)

(5) **Vowel Deletion** (e.g., *cello* vs. *cellist*)
V → ∅ / ___ (h) V

(6) **[s] Deletion** (e.g., *dispel* vs. *diverge*)
s → ∅ / ___ [voiced C]

(7) **Cluster Simplification** (e.g., *adept* vs. *adscribe*; *torque* vs. *torture*)
C → ∅ / ___ s C
C → ∅ / C ___ C

(8) **Greek Final Stop Deletion** (e.g., *dramatize* vs. *drama*)
[stop] → ∅ / ___ at the end of a word

(9) **[d] Insertion** (e.g., *abundant* vs. *redundant*)
∅ → d / V ___ V after some prefixes

(10) **[s] Insertion** (e.g., *retention* vs. *abstention*)
∅ → s / b ___ {p, t, c} after prefixes

(11) **Rhotacism** (e.g., *justice* vs. *jury*)
s → r / V ___ V

(12) **Latin [a] Weakening** (e.g., *apt* vs. *inept*)
a → e / [syllable] ___

(13) **Latin [e] Weakening** (e.g., *content* vs. *continent*)
e → i / [syllable] ___ C V

(14) **[l] Coloring** (e.g., *adolescent* vs. *adult*)
{e, o} → u / ___ l in a closed syllable

(15) **[t][t] to [ss]** (e.g., *transmit* vs. *transmission*)
tt → ss when roots are combined with suffixes

WORD ELEMENTS

Element	Gloss	Source	Examples
bell	war	L	*belligerent, bellicose, antebellum, rebellion*
cens	judge	L	*censor, censorious, censure, census*

Element	Gloss	Source	Examples
cephal	head	G	*cephalic, cephalopod, acephalous, encephalitis, microcephaly*
crat~crac	govern	G	*democratic, plutocracy, autocratic, meritocracy, aristocrat*
cur	care	L	*cure, curate, manicure, secure, sinecure*
dem	people	G	*democracy, demographic, demiurge, endemic, epidemic, pandemic*
fla	blow	L	*conflate, inflate, flatulent, flavor, flabellum*
loc	place	L	*local, locus, allocate, collocation*
lumen~lumin	light	L	*lumen, luminary, luminous, illuminati*
man	hand	L	*manicure, emancipate, manual, manumission, manipulate*
pl~plec~plic	times, fold, entwine	L	*triple, quadruple, complex, duplex, complicated, explicate*
son	sound	L	*sonic, assonant, dissonant, sonnet, sonority*

ELEMENT STUDY

1. Guess the meanings of the following words based on the numeral morphemes in this chapter. Then look them up and in a few words explain the connection between the meaning of the numeral morpheme and the meaning of the word it appears in.
    a. *sesquiduple*
    b. *ambiguous*
    c. *monandry*
    d. *omnivore*
    e. *pandemic*
    f. *semitrailer*, or *semi*

g. *quinquagenarian*
h. *octuplet*
i. *novena*
j. *December*

2. Coin adjectives for the following definitions using the numeral morphemes in this chapter and other roots you have learned up to this point. Some of the words you create may be found in the dictionary; others may not. Don't try to capture every bit of the meaning of the definition in the actual morphemes of the term you coin; a prefix and a root or two should be sufficient. In each answer, aim for a word using all Latin or all Greek roots.

a. having the head of a human	___ic
b. having six heads	___ic
c. occurring every twenty years	___ial
d. governed by a two-member group	___ic
e. having a hundred angles	___al
f. having three gods	___istic
g. having three letters	___al
h. having two feet	___al

3. Parse and gloss, and then separately for each morpheme give all allomorphs you have learned. Give your parses in the standard format we've been using: prefix- root -suffix, with a hyphen after the prefix and another hyphen before the suffix but no hyphen for the root. Remember to follow this with a list of all allomorphs for each element.
   a. *hectoliter* (gloss *liter* as 'liter')
   b. *meritocracy* (gloss *merit* as 'deserve')
   c. *tetralogy*
   d. *inflationary* (*in-* isn't 'not')
   e. *perambulate* (*per-* isn't *peri-*)

EXERCISES

1. a. In all but two of the following words, the last letter of the prefix has been assimilated to the first sound of the root. What is the original (i.e., unassimilated) form of the prefix in each word? Use a dictionary to check your answers.
   b. For each word, indicate whether the final consonant of the prefix has been completely assimilated to the initial consonant of the next morph or only partially. In each case, say what phonetic characteristics of the final consonant of the prefix have changed as a result of assimilation to the consonant that follows it.
   a. *impossible*
   b. *corrupt*
   c. *effect*
   d. *infect*
   e. *suffer*
   f. *irrelevant*
   g. *embolism*
   h. *immemorial*
   i. *annotate*
   j. *opposition*
   k. *commit*
   l. *illegible*
   m. *occlude*
   n. *assimilate*
   o. *submit*

2. What is the root in these words? For a root with several allomorphs, give the one that most closely matches the morph in the word in question. Look up each word, and include a brief sentence about the relation between the root's literal meaning and its meaning in this word.
   Part 1: Chapter 6 elements:
   a. replica

b. *manner*
   c. *deflate*
   d. *luminescent*

   Part 2: Cumulative elements. Identify both roots in each word:
   a. *specific* [Note: the suffix *-fic* goes back to a Latin root element.]
   b. *philander*
   c. *manufacture*
   d. *tetrarch*
   e. *tetracephalic*
   f. *pandemic*

3. Give a word with a different allomorph of the root. For your answer, see if you can find a related word in which the change is triggered by adding an ending or changing the ending. Examples: *divide > divisive; deciduous > decisive.*
   a. *direct*
   b. *dialect*
   c. *ingredient*
   d. *process*
   e. *aroma*

4. The following examples were used in this chapter to illustrate the loss of ‹s› after *ex-*:

   ex- + *spire* → *expire*
   ex- + *secr* + *-able* → *execrable*
   ex- + *secut* + *-ive* → *executive*

   For each root *spir*, *secr*, and *secu*, give an example of a word in which the root appears with its initial ‹s›. What is the meaning of each root in your examples?

5. Analyze the following words, using the rules in this and preceding chapters to guide your analysis:
   a. *erect*
   b. *expect*
   c. *suspect*

d. *passive*
e. *abrasion*
f. *navigate*
g. *deceptive*
h. *explosion*
i. *rectitude*
j. *abscond*

6. What are the meanings of the boldface morphemes in these words, which appeared as examples in this chapter? For each word, find another word in which this boldface morpheme occurs. The morpheme may or may not have a different allomorph.
   a. *re**und**ant*
   b. *i**mmut**able*
   c. *co**nvent**ion*
   d. *co**llud**e*
   e. *an**od**e*
   f. ***naut**ical*
   g. ***cult**ivate*

7. For each of these words, change the boldface morpheme into one that takes a different allomorph of the prefix. For example, (a) could change by replacing *und* with *lev*, to give *relevant*.
   a. *re**und**ant*
   b. *i**mmut**able*
   c. *co**llud**e*
   d. *an**od**e*
   e. *sy**llog**ism*
   f. *i**rrad**iate*
   g. *co**nvent**ion*

8. English vocabulary borrowed directly or indirectly from Latin and Greek reflects a widespread rule of Velar Softening, which changes [k] to [s] and [g] to [dʒ] before Latin and Greek nonlow front vowels. These changes are not reflected in the spelling of

the consonants, and the vowels that trigger the changes can be spelled in a variety of ways in English: ‹i, e, y, ae, oe›.

In each of the following cases, Velar Softening has applied, and in most cases other allomorphy is involved as well. Identify the sounds (not the letters) that have changed due to Velar Softening along with any other changes that may contribute to the allomorphy in these word pairs. For example, in *agent—active*, the consonant of the element *ag* is pronounced [dʒ] in *agent* due to Velar Softening, while the [g] of *ag* devoices to [k] by Phonation Assimilation before [t].

   a. *legend, lectern*
   b. *fragment, fragile*
   c. *factor, deficit*
   d. *organ, energy*
   e. *cadence, incident*
   f. *gonad, gene*
   g. *critic, criticize*
   h. *captive, except*
   i. *matrix, matrices*

9. Number exercise: Identify and gloss the element in each word representing a quantity or number, and then give a very brief definition of each word.

   a. *pauciloquy*
   b. *oligandrous*
   c. *annul*
   d. *polychromatic*
   e. *decade*
   f. *duplicate*
   g. *hectogram*
   h. *monotype*
   i. *myriameter*
   j. *nonagenarian*
   k. *octet*

      l. *primer*
    m. *prototype*
     n. *quart*
     o. *quinquennial*
     p. *semilunar*
     q. *septimal*
     r. *sextillion*
     s. *trilogy*
     t. *unanimous*
     u. *vicennial*

10. The word *semester* contains two roots, both of which are heavily disguised, idiosyncratic allomorphs of entries in the element list. (Hint: The first root is a numeral, but it is not *semi-*.) What word elements from our list are these allomorphs of? Consult an etymological source if you are not certain.

11. What do the numeral morphemes in the words *Pentateuch*, *Decalogue*, and *Deuteronomy* count? For example, in the word *tritium*, the *tri* 'three' counts isotopes: tritium is the third isotope of hydrogen. Use the dictionary entry on the origins and definitions of these words for the answer.

Seven

Meaning Change

MEANING SHIFTS

So far, we have been mostly concerned with changes in form. Here we turn to shifts in meaning. If our goal is to understand a word's meaning by recognizing its components, then mastering **polysemy**—variation in meaning—is just as important as mastering allomorphy, variation in form.

As a culture evolves, it develops new concepts and changes old ones. Language responds to novel cultural, technological, and practical situations by adding new words and by modifying the meanings of existing ones. This chapter looks at the ways language adjusts meanings to fit new conditions.

We have already had to deal with the multiplicity of meanings for morphemes like *path* 'feel' or 'illness'. The connection between feeling and feeling ill is natural enough, and a study of meaning change points up many similar developments from a very general meaning to a more specific one. Another example is our word *deer*, which in Shakespeare's time referred to an animal of any sort ("Mice, and Rats, and such small Deare"). In fact, this word's German cognate *Tier* still has the broader meaning. Words and morphemes can just as readily acquire more general meanings from more specific ones. The Old English ancestor of Modern English *bird* meant 'young bird', the more general term, applicable to young as well as old, being *fowl*. Only later did *bird* become the general term for any feathered creature, regardless of age.

New meanings grow out of existing ones in many other ways. Though we haven't commented on it yet, even suffixes have a kind of rudimentary polysemy. We have seen suffixes, like *-ion* and *-ary*, that mainly dictate the part of speech of the host word. But consider *-oid*, which signifies something that resembles—usually imperfectly—the thing described by the root element. For example, a spheroid resembles a sphere. Planets are typically spheroids rather than spheres, because they are not perfectly round but slightly flattened at the poles. Similarly, a humanoid in science fiction resembles a human without being human biologically.

Other suffixes contribute more significantly to meaning. In fact, polysemous suffixes are the rule, not the exception, in English. The word *polysemous* itself contains one. Table 7.1 gives an idea of the range of meanings of *-ous*. A list of other *-ous* adjectives would present many other meanings as well. The adjective suffix *-ic* also has a wide range of senses, as shown in table 7.2. Other senses of *-ic* include 'with ROOT', 'connected with ROOT', 'characteristic of ROOT', 'of ROOT', and 'belonging to ROOT'.

Table 7.1 MEANINGS OF THE SUFFIX *-OUS*.

Word	Meaning	Root
aqueous	'**of, relating to, or resembling** water'	*aqu*
envious	'**feeling or showing** envy'	*envy*
gracious	'**characterized by** grace'	*grat*
libelous	'**constituting or including** a libel'	*libel*
polysemous	'**having** many meanings'	*poly, sem*

Table 7.2 MEANINGS OF THE SUFFIX *-IC*.

Word	Meaning	Base word
alphabetic	'**of or pertaining to** an alphabet'	*alphabet*
angelic	'**like** an angel'	*angel*
panoramic	'**characterized by** a panorama'	*panorama*
runic	'**consisting of** runes'	*rune*

Meaning Change

Differences in shades of meaning can be difficult to express, but a word's context helps to narrow down the possibilities. Use the following six examples to test your ability to infer the meaning of a suffix, as well as to explore differences in pronunciation when a suffix is used to form adjectives, nouns, and verbs. What is the part of speech of the word with the suffix *-ate* in each of these sentences? How does the part of speech affect the pronunciation of the suffix?

a. I **advocate** the abolition of television.
b. I am an **advocate** of equal rights for women.
c. He will **delegate** authority to his subordinates.
d. She was a **delegate** to the convention.
e. Jake was **desolate** when Pat left us.
f. The enemy will **desolate** the city.

As you can gather, adjectives and nouns in *-ate* are generally pronounced [ət] or [ɪt], while verbs in *-ate* usually are pronounced [et]. In prefixes and roots, polysemy is no less extensive than in suffixes. Here are a few examples:

nom	'law' or 'system'
path	'feel' or 'illness'
extra-	'outside' or 'additional'

Semantic change is just as frequent and natural as the sound changes from earlier chapters and, if anything, can shift meanings even more drastically than sounds are altered. For example, *infant* and *infantry* come from the same source, ultimately Latin, where the etymon of both words meant 'baby'. Later, in Italian, the meaning expanded to include servants ('footmen') and foot soldiers. The root of *infant* is *fa*, which means 'speak', so that an infant is literally someone who doesn't speak. What is really surprising is the semantic distance that *fa* has traveled over the ages, since it is also the etymological root of *fable*, *fame*, and *preface*.

An even more dramatic example is *cosm*, which can mean 'universe' (as in *cosmos* and *microcosm*) or 'adorn' (as in *cosmetic*). Those two meanings are so distant it raises the question whether we should list two distinct morphemes *cosm*, each with a different meaning, despite having the same form. For the most satisfying answer, we need to pursue the general distinction between polysemy and **homonymy**.

POLYSEMY VERSUS HOMONYMY

In both polysemy and homonymy, the same spelling or pronunciation has two or more different meanings, but in homonymy those meanings are not related except by accident. The homonymous words *ring* 'circular band' and *ring* 'to make a bell sound' are completely unconnected except by the coincidence of sharing a single form. Indeed, in Old English these two words were not even pronounced the same. Another pair of homonymous morphs from an earlier chapter are *in-* (one of two allomorphs) 'in, into' and *in-* 'not'. There are even triplets of homonymous morphs in English, such as *bat* 'club', 'flying mammal', and 'wink'. In this book we list homonyms as separate items in the word element lists and appendices, while polysemy is indicated by giving more than one meaning beside a single form. Our concern here is polysemy, which is much more common than homonymy and more revealing about the special expressive powers of English vocabulary.

Distinguishing the two formally identical prefixes *in-* 'in' and *in-* 'not' clearly is the right approach, since they are semantically totally distinct. By contrast, it is arguably more useful to regard *cosm* as a single polysemous morpheme, because the historical process that gave rise to this polysemy resembles a development we know about from many other cases. In ancient Greek, the word *cosmos* originally meant 'order'. The word came to refer to the world or universe because of its perfect order, at least in the Greek worldview. On a more mundane level, the Greeks applied the word to the aesthetic arrangement of clothing and ornamentation. This is really no different from what happened when *path* 'feel' came to include the notion of feeling ill. Another case of polysemy that arose in ancient times is

Meaning Change

troch, which appears in *trochee*, a poetic foot consisting of a long and short syllable, and in *trochoid* "wheel-like". The original meaning in both cases was 'run': a trochee is a short and fast poetic foot, and wheels permit fast motion.

Turning now to Latin, consider the root *fac*, glossed as 'do' or 'make'. This meaning is clear enough in words like *factor*, *fact*, *effect*, and *efficient*, but now consider *face*, *facial*, *deface*, *efface*, and so on. Are we dealing with a single morpheme *fac* with as broad a range of meanings as 'do', 'make', and 'face'? In etymological terms, we definitely are. *Face* and *efface* are historically related to *fact* and *effect*. The semantic connection is a series of associations: 'make' ↔ 'form' ↔ 'appearance' ↔ 'face'. The key to unraveling polysemy is to be alert to connections like these. Awareness of semantic connections among a morpheme's meanings makes parsing words easier and can be very revealing as well. Take the word *revealing*, for example. The prefix *re-* means 'back', and the root *vel* is the same root that appears in *velum*. In both words, *vel* means 'curtain'. Anatomists see the velum as a type of membranous curtain that hangs down from the hard palate, and revealing pulls back a figurative curtain. Another colorful example is *depend*, where *de-* means 'from' and *pend* means 'hang', providing a simple but graphic illustration of dependence. Whether a word is familiar or unfamiliar, chances are that it has undergone extensive meaning shifts over time.

REASONS FOR SEMANTIC CHANGE

To understand the kind of semantic change that leads to polysemy, consider first why meaning should change at all.

Errors and Misinterpretation

In certain situations, a speaker may be unable to communicate an idea perfectly. A case in point is the history of the word *bead*. Originally, *bead* meant 'prayer'. The shift in meaning came from the practice of using a string of beads to keep track of the sequence of prayers. Since counting prayers in this way is connected with counting the beads themselves, the word *bead* shifted to its current meaning. Similarly, the word *since* originally meant 'after', but because effects follow causes in time (as in *Since winter has arrived, we need to bundle up*), we came to use the word to mean 'because' as well.

Creative Variation

In many realms of language use, creativity is at a premium, and hackneyed phrases or clichés are avoided. Literature, folk speech, and slang are among the language styles that put a premium on linguistic innovation as a way of maintaining lively discourse and displaying verbal skill. Words like *cool*, *slick*, and *tight*, for example, have been extended to cover not just physical attributes but also aspects of personality, mood, and aesthetics.

Abbreviation

The desire to express ourselves quickly and efficiently often leads us to use a single word to carry the burden of a longer phrase. **Ellipsis** or 'dropping out' of the word *doma* 'house' from the longer Greek phrase *cyriacon doma* 'Lord's house' led ultimately to the English word *church*. The same has happened with *microwave* (*oven*), *cell* and *telephone* (*phone*), and *email* (*address*).

The Finite Word Stock

Ultimately, our main reason for multiplying word meanings is that the supply of vocabulary items is too small to convey the infinite variety of things we have to say. We have three choices: make new words, use longer phrases, or extend the duties of existing words. We do all three, but most

Meaning Change

often it's easier to extend the meaning of a word than to invent a totally new one, and speaking in ever-longer phrases quickly moves from cumbersome to impractical.

PATHS IN THE DEVELOPMENT OF MEANING

In the simplest cases, it is easy to discern a word's original basic meaning despite polysemy. For example, table 7.3 shows some developments of meaning for the word *horse* over roughly a thousand years.

In each case when the meaning was extended, the oldest meaning was retained. For example, when we speak of a car as having three hundred horses under the hood, that meaning is an extension of the basic meaning of *horse*, '*Equus caballus*', not of the meaning 'four-legged support' or 'cavalry'. We can think of the development of the meanings of *horse* as represented in figure 7.1, where the paths of development are shown by the arrows pointing from the older meaning to the one derived from it.

As new meanings accumulate, chances of confusion rise. If you walk into a Home Depot and ask for a horse, you might be met with stares, even though the store sells only one object that is called a horse. Anticipating that, you're likely to ask instead for a *sawhorse*. If the sawhorse is in plain sight, however, it would be fine to ask an attendant, "How much does this horse go for?"

Table 7.3 STAGES IN THE HISTORY OF THE WORD *HORSE*.

Time period	Meaning
Proto-Germanic times to present	'a member of the animal species *Equus caballus*'
Fifteenth century to present	'four-legged structure on which something is supported (e.g., for sawing)'
Sixteenth century to present	'cavalry soldiers'
Twentieth century to present	'the pulling power of one horse'

For some words, however, the original basic meaning is lost, leaving only extended meanings that are harder to trace to the original sense. This is the case with the word *hysterical*, whose Greek source *hystericos* originally meant 'uterine', which shouldn't be surprising in light of the meanings of its component morphemes, *hyster* 'womb' and *-ic(al)*$_A$. After time, however—in Greek, Latin, French, and after it was borrowed, English—this word took on a broad range of other senses, many of which disguise the original one. At one time doctors attributed various severe psychiatric disorders to uterine problems, so the word *hysterical* came to be used to describe such problems. Subsequently people used the word to describe strong emotional reactions even if perfectly normal and transient, such as hysterical anger or laughter. Nowadays, *hysterical* is often used simply to mean 'very funny', as in a hysterical joke.

Figure 7.2 shows that *hysterical* has evolved semantically in ways very different from the path of *horse*. A borrowing from Greek, *hysterical* literally meant 'uterine' in Early Modern English and became tied to particular

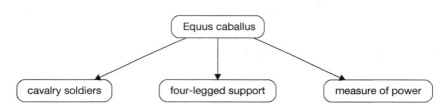

Figure 7.1 Development of the meaning of *horse*.

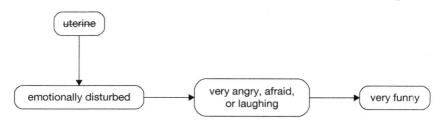

Figure 7.2 Development of the meanings of *hysterical*.

medical assumptions of that era linking the uterus to behavior. The more recent meaning shifts in *hysterical* take it successively further from the original Greek meaning—so far, in fact, that current medical dictionaries no longer include the original meaning 'uterine', as shown in figure 7.2, where that meaning is crossed out.

Fortunately, most meaning shifts follow more predictable paths. Indeed, many shifts are so obvious that they scarcely have to be mentioned.

CATEGORIES OF SEMANTIC CHANGE

Generally speaking, every semantic change involves an **association** of some kind. The associations between the different meanings of *path*—'feel' and 'illness'—are easy enough to see. Associations tend to fall into two categories. First, the range of things a word refers to can be extended to include an additional set of things that resemble the original set. The resemblance can be based on either form or function. Changes based on resemblance involve **metaphor**, a notion already encountered a few times in this book and probably familiar to you from literature or poetry. Using *bright* as a synonym for *intelligent* is a case of metaphoric shift. Another category of associations is based on a different type of connection, often in physical space, time, or the relationship of cause and effect. This type of association is called **metonymy**. The change of the meaning of *bead* from 'prayer' to 'prayer bead' to any type of bead was a series of metonymic shifts. When we say we admire Shakespeare, we could literally be referring to the author himself or to his work. Using the term *Shakespeare* to refer to the work of Shakespeare is an example of a metonymic shift.

Metaphor

Metaphor is so common in vocabulary we hardly notice it. Dozens of words in the previous paragraph are used in ways that can be traced to metaphor, as is apparent in just the first few words of the sentence *First,*

Figure 7.3 A real horse.

the range of things a word refers to can be extended to include an additional set of things that resemble the original set. Range 'extent' derives from an Old French word originally designating a row of soldiers. *Refer* has the root *fer*, whose original meaning was 'carry'. In *extend*, the root *tend* literally means 'stretch', and so on.

Metaphor is most often based on resemblance, as when the word *leaf* refers to a page in a book. We can reasonably conjecture that the meaning 'page' is derived from the botanical meaning and not the other way around because books are more recent, and less basic in nature, than leaves of plants. Metaphor is also clearly involved in applying *horse* to a four-legged support (compare figures 7.3 and 7.4).

Because humans often base their understanding of intangible and conceptual entities on physical ones, metaphor also involves a shift from the concrete to the abstract. A good example is the very word *understand*, which should literally mean 'stand below'. Compare the colloquial expression *to get behind* meaning 'to support or agree with'. Likewise, the words *comprehend*, *apprehend*, and *grasp* are all extended metaphorically to

Meaning Change

Figure 7.4 A metaphorical horse.

express the 'seizing' of something intellectually. Similarly, when we speak of *shelving* an old idea, we are using the metaphor of setting aside a useless physical object (like an out-of-date book) in reference to an idea, an abstract thing.

Spatial metaphor is a fundamental tool for developing new meanings. Most of the prefixes taught in this book are spatial in their basic sense but metaphorically extended to nonspatial concepts. Table 7.4 provides examples. In each case, the meaning has been extended in at least one way, but generally in a manner that still allows us to see the original meaning as well.

Metaphor is used so frequently that in case we are not speaking metaphorically, we may have to qualify what we are saying to indicate that a metaphor is not intended. When we say something like *I rolled on the floor laughing*, people are likely to think we're speaking metaphorically, and we might try to cancel out this expectation by adding the word *literally* as a way to communicate that we were actually rolling about. Unfortunately, the term *literally* itself has become extended, so that saying *I literally rolled on the floor laughing* still leaves open the question of whether we are speaking literally or figuratively.

Table 7.4 METAPHORIC EXTENSIONS OF MEANING OF SPATIAL PREFIXES.

Prefix	Spatial sense	Use in extended sense
de-	'away from'	negative: *desperate* 'lacking hope' (*sper* 'hope')
		intensive: *declare* 'make totally clear'
		reverse an action: *de-emphasize* 'reduce emphasis upon'
ex-	'out'	'open, visible': *expose* 'render visible or open' (*pon~pos* 'put')
		'not included': *except* 'exclude, bar' (*cep~cap* 'take')
extra-	'outside'	'beyond, not': *extraordinary* 'unusual'
ob-	'against'	negative, 'destructive': *obloquy* 'abusive language' (*loqu* 'speak')
per-	'through'	'thorough, strong': *pertinacious* 'holding on thoroughly' (*tin~ten* 'hold')
pre-	'in front of'	'before, early': *precocious* 'matured early' (*coc* 'ripen')
sub-	'under'	as part: *subsume* 'take in as member of a larger unit' (*sum* 'take in')
		'open or exposed to': *subject* 'bring into sphere of influence' (*jec~jac* 'throw')
		'inferior': *subhuman*

Metonymy

Metonymy is a shift in meaning from some object to something connected with it in some way other than by resemblance. For example, in the 1990s some of our undergraduates referred to their fathers as *the wallet*. A more lasting example is the use of the word *pulp* to refer to a variety of lurid literature, as in *pulp fiction*. In this shift, the material on which the literature was originally printed came to refer to the printed matter itself. Wheat, as its sounds subtly suggest, was named after the word *white*, because of its lightness of color. The connection involved in a metonymic change can be of almost any kind other than resemblance, including such associations as **source ↔ product** and **thing ↔ characteristic** and **person ↔ possession**.

Metonymy can work through the association not only between an object and a completely different one but also between a part of an object and the whole object itself, or between one type of thing and a more specific type of thing. Two clear examples appear in the sentence *The ranch hands herded a thousand longhorns*, where *hands* must be referring to entire workers and *longhorns* to entire cattle. When we use *plastic* to refer to a credit card, we use one aspect of that object to refer to the entire object. A *bite* of food may well contain several bites. This kind of metonymy can be subtle: it may be difficult to decide whether a particular usage is meant figuratively, literally, or perhaps both at once. In *Get your butt over here*, does the word *butt* refer to a body part or a whole person? Cases like *bite* and *butt*, where the word for a part can refer to a whole, or vice versa, are often given a special name, *synecdoche*, but here we group these uses under a single term *metonymy*.

Metaphor versus metonymy

Metaphor and metonymy both work by associating one concept with a related one, and it can be hard to distinguish the devices. A few clear comparisons may help. Take the word *head*. Metaphorically, *head* designates a protuberance at one end of things like pins, hammers, beer, and pimples; the top or most important part of something long, like a bed, column, or parade; something roughly spherical, like a head of cabbage; and so on. How about a metonymic use of *head*? When we refer to people or animals as *heads* (*charge ten dollars a head, a hundred head of cattle*), that is a type of metonymy associating the whole with the part. When we refer to the obverse side of coins as *heads*, it is not because that side itself looks like a head but because that side is often used for—metonymically associated with—portraits; we still say *heads* even if that side contains something other than a portrait. If we say someone loses their head, we are using *head* as a metonym for self-control, a faculty we associate with literal heads as the seat of rational thought.

Next consider the word *table*. There are several things called *tables* because they somehow resemble the piece of furniture, such as a geological feature (plateau) and a constellation (Mensa). But the word is also used to refer to things associated with a table, such as the food eaten from it (*He sets a good table*) or the people sitting around it (*That table ordered champagne*). To test your ability to distinguish metaphors from metonyms, determine whether *table* is used metaphorically or metonymically in these expressions:

The data are laid out in table 3.
That grape makes an excellent table wine.

Metaphors and metonyms are so frequent in language that it is not unusual for the two to be combined in a single expression. If a person refers to a toilet as *the head*, it is a metaphorical association with the primitive toilets on old sailing vessels. In turn, those heads were so called because they were located at the front, the head, of a ship—a metonymical association. And why was the front of the ship called its head? By metaphorical association with the front part of animals.

When talking about reading the *press*, we are again combining metaphors with metonyms. The term *press* for a printing press is metaphor, likening the modern printing process to Gutenberg's invention, which actually involved using a heavy screw to press the printing block against the paper. Calling a newspaper by the means used to print it is a metonym. If that is clear, test your ability to recognize metaphors and metonyms with this question. Note that *the press* has a general meaning, as when one refers to a member of the press in a sentence like, "I was interviewed by the press yesterday." Also, in talking about articles in the press, we normally are referring at most to a handful of newspapers. What term would you give to the relationship between the two uses of *press* in the last two sentences?

OUTCOMES OF SEMANTIC SHIFT

Metaphor and metonymy easily lead to what is sometimes called **narrowing** or **widening** of a word's range of reference. Narrowing (also called **specialization**) is the restriction of the meaning of a word to a subset of what it originally denoted. We mentioned earlier the example *deer*, which used to refer to any four-legged animal. Similarly, the word *adder*, which meant 'snake' in Old English and in Middle English, now refers only to a few varieties of snake.

The opposite change is also common. In widening (also called **generalization**), a word's meaning extends to include cases beyond the original ones. The Old French ancestor of the word *arrive* comes from the Latin prefix *ad-* and the root *rip* > *rive* 'shore', as in *river*. This original word, meaning 'to come ashore', widened its reference to the reaching of any destination. A much-cited example is *decimate*, which originally referred to the killing of every tenth soldier found guilty of a serious crime but now is often used to describe any killing or vanquishing on a large scale. This makes perfect sense. The original notion *decimate* had two key meaning components: the arbitrary selection of victims to be killed and the choice of every tenth soldier as a victim. Of the two concepts, clearly the most horrifying is the first. Furthermore, if *decimate* had clung to its literal meaning, we'd have had very few opportunities to ever use the word. Such generalization happens so naturally, sometimes there doesn't even need to be a literal use to widen. A dilapidated building is literally one whose stones are falling apart, yet there is no sign even from the original Latin that the term was applied only to stone buildings. Widening comes so naturally to us that—to the dismay of companies whose future is tied up with their brand names—we frequently use words like *Xerox* and *Google* as generic nouns and verbs to describe the actions of photocopying and web search. And, having extended to the meaning of *literally* as noted above to include *figuratively*, we have made this once meaningful word literally useless.

Not every semantic change results in widening or narrowing. Sometimes one specific meaning ousts another. The word *car* once meant 'wagon' or 'chariot' but instead is used today for automobiles, and there would be something bizarre about calling wagons or chariots cars.

Meaning shift can be relatively value neutral, as in most of the examples we've seen up to this point. But there are also surprising shifts from positive meanings to negative meanings and the reverse. An example of

melioration (shift from negative to positive) is seen in the word *nice*. Its Latin forebear was *nescius* 'ignorant' (*ne* 'not' + *sci* 'know'). A chain of shifts shows how it improved its lot: 'ignorant' > 'foolish' > 'fussy' > 'proper' > 'pleasant' > 'kind'. Some would say that is losing its positive value and is now almost neutral—'not disagreeable'. *Smart*, which originally meant 'causing pain', is another ordinary adjective whose meaning has been meliorated. The opposite of melioration, **pejoration**, is more common. *Silly* has had a history almost the opposite of *nice*: it originally meant 'blessed'.

Pejoration often goes hand in hand with **euphemism**, the process of substituting a new word for one that has acquired unpleasant associations—for example, *encore presentation* for a TV rerun. Once a euphemism is well accepted, the original term becomes even less acceptable, undergoing pejoration. And since the euphemism still refers to the same thing as the original term, the euphemism is itself subject to pejoration. For instance, the word *cripple* is now virtually taboo as a noun, being replaced by *handicapped person* or *disabled person*. In turn, some people advocate replacing these words with terms such as *person with a disability*, *handicapable*, and *differently abled*, while others have strong aversion to such euphemisms. Is *disabled* now a pejorative term? In the end, evaluative terms such as *melioration* and *pejoration* are subjective ways of looking at semantic changes, many of which can be described just as well by other terms. For instance, *notorious*, which originally meant simply 'widely known' but now means 'widely known for something scandalous', can be described as having undergone a narrowing.

Even though morphemes are our basic meaningful units, it is whole words and not morphemes per se that undergo semantic shifts. For example, many American English speakers now use *reticent* 'reluctant to speak' to mean simply 'reluctant', as in, "I'm reticent to break up with my best friend." Meanwhile, the root morpheme *tac~tec~tic* itself has not altered its meaning 'silent', and this morpheme does not cease to refer to speech in other words, such as *tacit*. Similarly, between *ostensible* and *ostentatious*, only *ostentatious* has a pejorative sense even though both begin with the morphemes *ob-* 'toward, against' and *ten~tend~tens*.

IMPACT OF SEMANTIC CHANGE ON WORD ANALYSIS

After a morpheme in a given word has lost its original sense, we need some ingenuity to relate the morpheme's gloss to the meaning of the word as a whole. The verb *insist* has parts meaning 'in, into' and 'stand' (*sist* is an allomorph of *st~sta*). Yet its meanings today have migrated to 'strongly demand' and 'strongly assert something'. This shows how futile it would be to give it a superficial interpretation like 'stand in'. Instead, it helps to immediately think metaphorically, because metaphor is by far the commonest kind of semantic change. In fact, even the native English word *stand* has many different meanings beyond the literal one. Examples in everyday English show this, as in, *Kim won't stand for it* or *The mayor stands up for the little guy* or *Pat has to take a stand*. In each case, we see subtle shadings that include 'tolerate', 'support', and 'be steadfast'. Now compare a few other words with the root *sist*: *persist, resist, desist, subsist, persist,* and *exist*. All have senses overlapping with the above uses of *stand* and, for that matter, *insist*. In the end, while there may be much more to the semantic development of *insist*, we can retrace at least a couple of major steps:

'stand on' (something) >
'stay planted on one spot' >
'firmly maintain one position in a disagreement'

This set of shifts employs processes described in this chapter and evident in element lists throughout the book. First is the flexibility of spatial prefixes: here, *in-* doesn't literally mean 'in' but something similar: 'on'. Second, a concrete, physical phenomenon becomes increasingly abstract. A single aspect of being *on*—that is, remaining firmly in position and thus continuing what one is doing—comes via metonymy to be the primary meaning. We also see a narrowing or specialization of meaning to include a resistance to opposition. The next-to-last step persists today in phrases like *insist on getting your own way*. We see a shift that appears to involve a metonymy between doing something continually and doing something strongly, possibly a matter of connection between cause and effect, because doing almost anything continually requires effort—in other words, doing it 'strongly'. Finally, in phrases like *insists that war is bad for the economy*, we see a subtle shift to a completely mental arena: the insister isn't doing anything but strongly stating an opinion.

You may wonder about the utility of applying these principles to *insist*, a term you recognize and are unlikely to ever have to analyze in a sentence. But the same principles also apply to less familiar words, such as *perspicacity*, which literally translates as 'through' + 'look' + A + N. In a context like, "Medicine is not a science of souls. Physicians lack the perspicacity to find the world-weary patient's real illness," you wouldn't need to do much more than take the literal reading—roughly, 'through looking-ness'—and interpret it in some plausible and straightforward, but not simplistic, way. You likely would arrive at a meaning for *perspicacity* like 'insight', 'vision', or 'deeper wisdom', rather than 'x-ray vision' or some whimsical alternative along these lines. And your interpretation would be supported by a dictionary definition 'acuteness of perception, discernment, or understanding', all good synonyms for your educated guesses.

SUMMARY

Polysemy is the term for multiple historically or semantically connected meanings in a word or morpheme. It contrasts with homonymy, when unrelated words or morphemes just happen to be spelled or pronounced alike. Polysemy comes about when semantic changes add new meanings without taking away the old one. Changes can arise through misinterpretation but are often the result of a desire to be creative, succinct (through abbreviation or ellipsis), and up to date (when things in the world change). Changes can be challenging to analyze when they occur in long chains. Any given change is the result of some kind of mental association, usually involving metaphor (resemblance) or metonymy (other incidental connection). Changes can also be characterized in terms of their outcomes. Narrowing or specialization happens when the meaning becomes more specific, and widening or generalization is the opposite. Melioration

Meaning Change

happens when a word takes on more positive connotations, and pejoration is the opposite.

EXERCISES

1. What are some differences between clipping (from chapter 3) and ellipsis?
2. Adding a prefix or suffix can alter the meaning of the root itself along with the meaning of the word. For example, *fiss* in *fissure* and *fission* comes from the Latin root for 'split', but a fissure and fission involve very different types of splitting. For each of the following pairs of words, what is the logic behind the development in meaning? Terms like narrowing and melioration may play a role in your answers, but see if you can get beyond these general terms and focus on the specific meaning differences involved in each pair.
   a. *exposure* versus *exposition*
   b. *containment* versus *content*
   c. *cure* > *curator*
   d. *censor* > *censure*
   e. *complication* > *complicit* (compare *implication* vs. *implicit*, where the root meaning is more constant)
   f. *sensitive* > *sensational*
3. Describe the meaning change in the **root element** (as opposed to the word as a whole) in the following word pairs over time. It's possible to complete this exercise without a dictionary, but a good etymological dictionary provides a fuller view of the stages the change went through.
   a. *species* > *spice*
   b. *regal* > *regular*
   c. *legible* > *legendary*
   d. *tendency* > *attendant*

Table 7.5 BUILDING WORDS WITH LATIN SPATIAL PREFIXES.

Prefix	duc	pos	port	jac~jec	sist	cap~cep~cip~cup
ab-	×			×		
ad-	×	×	×	×	×	×
circum-		×				
con-~co-	×	×	×	×	×	×
de-	×	×	×	×	×	×
dis-		×	×	×		
ex-	×	×	×	×	×	×
in-	×	×	×	×	×	×
inter-				×		×
intro-	×					
ob-		×		×		×
per-					×	×
pre-		×				×
pro-	×	×		×		
re-	×	×	×	×	×	×
se-	×					
sub-		×	×	×	×	×
trans-~tra-	×	×	×	×	×	

4. Many English words begin with Latin spatial prefixes. Table 7.5 indicates (with ×) words combining spatial prefixes with roots *duc* 'lead', *pos* 'place, put', *port* 'carry', *jac~jec* 'lay, lie', *sist* 'stand', *cap~cep~cip~cup* 'take'. Here are some words combining spatial prefixes with these roots:

abducent 'drawing apart', said of a muscle when it moves a limb away from the center axis of the body (lit. 'pulling away')

abduct 'to carry off by force' (lit. 'pull away')

adduce 'to present or bring forward a point for consideration in a discussion or analysis' (lit. 'draw toward')

adductor 'a muscle that pulls a body part in the direction of the center axis of the body' (lit. 'that which draws toward') *apport* 'the moving or producing of a physical object by a spiritualist medium (e.g., at a séance) without any apparent physical activity', or 'any object produced in this way' (lit. 'carry toward' or 'bring')

Others include *circumduction, conducive, conduct, comportment, deduce,* and *deduction.*

Choose five interesting or unfamiliar combinations from this list that form words whose meaning has shifted from the literal reading of their glosses. Using an etymological source like the Oxford English Dictionary or the Online Etymological Dictionary, describe the changes.

It may be enough to simply identify each shift with the appropriate term from this chapter, but feel free to explain further if needed. Keep in mind that when a spatial prefix is metaphorical, the meaning is not often accessible to us. When it's really indicating a direction, as so often in modern formations, then it is very useful to know the literal meaning of the prefix. Don't forget that allomorphy, especially partial or total assimilation, may disguise some morphemes in certain combinations.

5. Table 7.6 indicates (with 'x') English words combining Greek spatial prefixes with roots *leg~log* 'speak, study', *pher~phor* 'carry', *the* 'put', *tom~tm* 'cut', *bol~bl* 'throw', *sta* 'stand, state'. Here are some words combining Greek spatial prefixes with these roots:

anaphoric (grammatical term) 'referring to a preceding word or phrase' (lit. 'carrying back')

analogy 'similarity of properties, ratios, etc.' (lit. '[the act of] speaking upward')

anathema 'something banned or cursed' (lit. 'thing put up')

Others include *diathesis, epitome, epilog, anabolic, prosthetic,* and *synthesis.*

Choose five interesting or unfamiliar combinations from this list that form words whose meaning has shifted from the literal

Table 7.6 BUILDING WORDS WITH GREEK SPATIAL PREFIXES.

Root Prefixes	pher~phor	the	leg~log	tom~tm	bol~bl	sta~ste
ana-	×	×	×	×	×	×
anti-		×				
apo-			×			×
cata-	×		×		×	×
dia-	×	×	×	×	×	×
ec-			×			×
en-				×	×	
epi-	×		×	×	×	×	×
hyper-					×	×
hypo-		×				
meso-			×			
meta-	×	×			×	×
para-			×		×	
peri-	×				×	
pro-		×	×		×	×
pros-		×				
syn-		×	×		×	

reading of their glosses. For example, look for words combining *hypo-* and *sta* or *syn-* and *log*. Using an etymological dictionary like the *Oxford English Dictionary* or the Online Etymological Dictionary, describe the changes.

It may be enough to simply identify each shift with the appropriate term from this chapter, but feel free to explain further if needed. Don't forget that allomorphy, especially partial or total assimilation, may disguise some morphemes in certain combinations.

6. Which of the two meanings given for each of the words below is earlier? What knowledge about semantic shift or other factors leads you to this conclusion? (Use an etymological dictionary

like the *Oxford English Dictionary* or https://www.etymonline.com/ to check your answer.)
   a. *text* 'weave' as in *textile* or *text* 'writing' as in *textual*
   b. *ex-* as in *expose, extend* or *ex-* as in *ex-wife, ex-doctor*
   c. *divine* 'godly' or *divine* 'wonderful'
7. Analyze *perambulator*. This word is the source of the word *pram*, a baby carriage.
   a. Parse *perambulator*. What is the literal meaning of the component elements? What changes in meaning do the component elements undergo in this word?
   b. Originally, *perambulator* meant 'pedestrian, traveler'. The word acquired the meaning 'baby carriage' two hundred years later, in the nineteenth century, while retaining the original one (e.g., "Dickens was a determined perambulator of London," from the *Daily Telegraph*, 1971). How would you describe the meaning change?
8. Following the example of *insist* from the last section of this chapter, detail the major developments along the paths (such as metaphor or metonymy) and outcomes (such as narrowing or widening) of semantic shift involved in the history of the word *inaugurate* from its beginnings in ancient Rome to the present. Be sure to propose a plausible path for every step you can.
'take omens from the flight of birds' >
'consecrate by taking omens from the flight of birds' >
'consecrate an installation into office by taking omens from the flight of birds' >
'install in office'
9. Identify whether a word has undergone either a metaphoric or metonymic shift or both from an earlier meaning (on the left of the arrow). Use a dictionary if it helps. Explain your answer in a sentence or two.
   a. *vermicelli* 'small or thin worms' > 'a kind of thin macaroni not unlike spaghetti'

b. *red eye* 'an eye that is red' > *redeye* 'a minnow that has red eyes'
c. *seminary* 'a place where seeds are sprouted and nurtured' > 'school of religion'
d. *convince* 'to physically overcome' > 'to intellectually persuade'
e. *urbane* 'pertaining to cities; urban' > 'sophisticated'
f. *muscle* 'a little mouse' > 'an organ such as the biceps'
g. *sandwich* (capitalized) 'name of earl said to have dined on finger food rather than leave the gambling table' > 'food consisting of two slices of bread and a filling'
h. *moxie* (capitalized) 'American soft drink originally hyped to 'build up your nerve' > 'audacity, daring'

10. The following expressions use words figuratively. In most cases, metaphor or metonymy is involved. In addition, some of these expressions narrow or widen the literal meanings of the words they use. What term or terms from this chapter describe the change in the italicized word(s) from their literal meaning? Explain your answer. To make the task more straightforward, focus just on the figurative meaning of the italicized word.
    a. on the *wagon* 'no longer abusing alcohol'
    b. *weed* 'marijuana'
    c. over the *hill* 'way past one's prime, on the way out'
    d. *pop the question* 'propose marriage'
    e. *strike out* 'fail'
    f. *soft*ware 'computer app'
    g. *crap*ware 'useless computer app'
    h. *breath* of fresh air 'welcome new idea'
    i. *finger*food 'type of snack'
    j. these shoes are *killing* me 'these shoes really hurt'
    k. *harbor* resentment 'feel resentment'
    l. *knuckle* under pressure 'give way to pressure'

11. Choose a few of the following words discussed in Amanda Montell's book *Wordslut: A Feminist Guide to Taking Back the English Language* (New York: Harper Wave, 2019) and trace their

semantic development from their original English meaning to their present one(s). Use an etymological source such as the Online Etymological Dictionary https://etymonline.com or the more complete *Oxford English Dictionary*. Pay attention to whether any shades of the original meaning have remained up to the present day, and consider whether the terms typically used for males have behaved differently over time than the ones for females.
  a. *master*
  b. *mister*
  c. *mistress*
  d. *madam*
  e. *knight*
  f. *stud*
  g. *hussy*
  h. *tart*
  i. *slut*
  j. *sissy*
9. Political discussion has introduced a number of changes into our vocabulary. The estate tax is sometimes referred to as a *death tax*; antiabortion people refer to their position as *pro-life*, and so on. How do such examples compare to the types of change discussed in this chapter?

Eight

Usage and Variation

MANY ENGLISHES

Up to now, we have been considering English to be a language. As reasonable as that may seem, it is not totally accurate. What goes by the single name *English* is not a single language. Instead, it is a large set of varieties from different parts of the globe, used in a wide assortment of social situations.

Earlier chapters have mentioned variation in style. Some usages are more appropriate for formal contexts than for informal ones, while usages out of place in formal contexts may be perfectly fine in informal ones. Still, this doesn't begin to capture the range and complexity of the choices we're called to make in writing and in speech. Doctors, farmers, social workers, bakers, biologists, carpenters, philosophers, exterminators, psychologists, actors, educators, lawyers, gardeners, and physicists all either work with a set of special terms or use more general terms in special ways. A major goal of this book is to provide access to such specialized vocabularies and in particular to the words associated with more formal and scholarly styles.

At the same time, we need to consider whether formal styles deserve a privileged status over other styles. Innovations in our language come from many places on the social and professional spectrum. Consider the disparate recent origins of the words *latte, locavore, captcha, nimby, humint,* and *incent*. Clearly, English speakers are not looking just to one source for models to follow in their speech. As we have already seen, our rich and varied linguistic past has been built on constant changes to suit new conditions. Obviously, this process continues. The ongoing reshaping comes from the most and least educated speakers, from communities all over the country and the world. Our focus continues to be words, but let us keep in mind that variation also involves pronunciation, spelling, and other aspects of language.

ROOTS OF VARIATION AND CHANGE

Chapter 2 traced profound effects on the language to **external** forces, including war, invasion, geography, migration, commerce, and both social and technological change. Likewise, **internal** factors, including phonetic and semantic changes, have led to major and minor differences in pronunciation, meaning, word formation, and language use, as described in chapters 5 through 7. Every so often, a set of changes may unify a language; in the Old English period King Alfred the Great is credited with reforms that made the dialect of his court the literary standard for all of England. However, internal and external forces more often have the opposite effect: They create new, divergent varieties. Over the spans of decades and even centuries, language varieties and their individual usages may coexist, leading to competing vocabulary and grammar, along with competing pronunciations and spellings. In the end, some variants may win out over others. We owe *goodbye* to an earlier expression *God be with ye*, as shown by spellings *Godbwye* and *godbwye* (with variations in internal punctuation) from around the sixteenth century. By the eighteenth century, the greeting had stabilized as *good bye*, leaving only the choice of whether to spell it as two words, a single hyphenated word, or a single word. As we noted in chapter 3, that choice is still being worked out.

Variant forms can also lead to innovation. *Oblige* and *obligate* both came into the language with fine etymological credentials, the first from French and the second a few centuries later from Latin. The two verbs have very similar meanings, yet in use they have diverged enough to create a separate space in the language for each, so that "I'm much obliged" is an expression of gratitude, while "I'm much obliged" isn't. In the previous century, some British writers dismissed the word *obligate* as a crass Americanism, an attitude that still appears in the occasional language blog. Yet the two verbs have diverged in meaning, even while sharing the identical nominal form *obligation*. *Oblige* has lost much of its original legal connotation, while *obligate* has taken up the legal slack.

The accretion of variants that define distinct language varieties can ultimately result in different languages that are incomprehensible to one another's speakers. That is exactly what happened with the West Germanic tongue that was the source of both Modern German and Modern English.

SEEDS OF DIALECTAL DIVISION

The truth is that English has never been a single, unified speech form. In northern and southwestern England to this day, there are rural English folk whose speech is nearly incomprehensible to Americans and quite difficult to understand even for speakers from other parts of England. Elsewhere in Britain, too, distinct types of English survive and in some cases thrive among the modern Scots, Irish, and Welsh. Beyond the British Isles, new varieties of English have sprung up in Australia, New Zealand, the United States, and South Africa.

Farther from the heart of the world settled by English speakers, even more linguistic differentiation has occurred. In the former British colonies of India, Sri Lanka, Nigeria, Singapore, and many others, contact with local languages and other factors have created what have been referred to as **new Englishes**. The English used in these countries has official status and is taught in schools at various grade levels. It serves as an important language of mass communication and business, functioning in these nations as a **lingua franca**, a common language for groups that share no other language. Such local English was once modeled on the speech and writing of the educated upper classes of England, but today the population at large in these countries often speaks a rather un-British kind of English. In English-speaking countries of Asia and Africa, where national ties with

Britain have weakened since independence, the model for English is increasingly a local one. As a result, these national varieties are moving ever further from their historical roots in England. In time, they may come to differ as much from our English as Dutch differs from German today. In a sense, then, the very status of English as a world language contains the seeds for its eventual diversification and division.

WHERE DO STANDARDS COME FROM?

A **standard language** is a set of linguistic norms established by some generally accepted political or social authority. Unfortunately, the term *standard* is sometimes taken to imply that a single standard will suffice for every speaker of the language in every situation in which the language is used. Of course, there's no factual basis for that notion. English speakers around the country and around the world have different standards. Furthermore, as you're probably aware, each of us adjusts our language depending on a variety of factors, including whether we are writing or speaking and who we're communicating with. In a sense, then, each English speaker becomes conversant with a variety of standards.

In the extreme case, a standard may be shaped by the practice of a single respected speaker or writer or group of speakers or writers. In many countries, the standard is whatever the ruling classes in the capital city speak. The situation is not too different in England, where the language of London and environs has been setting the standard since the late Middle Ages. The standard in American English is more elusive, prompting the *American Heritage Dictionary* to caution that what is considered standard varies from region to region. With that caveat, the dictionary still comments on usages that fall outside the standard.

The one thing that standard languages have in common is that all are based on the way people spoke at one time. Apart from that, it's hard to generalize further, since the factors that go into adopting a standard vary widely, depending on politics, societal patterns, and linguistic considerations. On occasion, the authority is a grammarian's or lexicographer's description. For English this was the case with the dictionary of Samuel Johnson, who aimed to exhaustively enumerate the words and meanings of the language of the well educated in England. His American counterpart, Noah Webster, sought to promote national unity and independence by recording the vocabulary of the new American variety of English.

Internationally, national governments often play a role in setting language standards. Along with designating a particular language or set of languages as the official language of their country, they may also get into the act of language standardization. Dozens of countries have language boards or language academies that prescribe correct usages and spellings. The most famous is the Académie Française, whose mandate is to select preferred standards for grammar, vocabulary, and usage in France. Many countries have laws restricting to some extent the names (first or last) that parents can give to a child.

A lexicographer once said that the printing press froze English spelling in time. While not literally true, books profit from a certain amount of consistency, notably in spelling but also in punctuation, vocabulary, grammar, and usage. Inconsistencies may crop up here and there, but too many will puzzle and annoy readers and especially learners. In England at the end of the fifteenth century, the introduction of printing led to many decisions that crossed lines of regional linguistic variation in Britain. Even today we are living with results of decisions made back then. At the same time, old standards are being revised by new ones based on Internet communication, which is putting a premium on brevity and revising the rules of spelling and punctuation we learned in school.

Speaking versus Writing

We distinguish between spoken and written standards, for these are not the same. All of us normally acquire the spoken language of our community before receiving any formal education. But in school we are introduced to a new standard: a literary one. After many years of immersion in the new standard in school, we may come to write very differently from the way we speak. This is true even if our community speaks the standard language, and it is truer still if our community does not.

Spoken varieties continue to change even when a written language or accepted literary form doesn't budge. Writing is generally conservative, as we can see from the number of letters no longer pronounced in the word *knight*. Over time, writing tries to come into line with speech. Some languages—for example, Spanish, Norwegian, and Russian—have reformed their spelling to reduce inconsistencies. Over the years, English has witnessed quite a number of attempts by individuals and groups to reform its spelling system. Most successful of these was lexicographer Noah Webster, who argued for the common US alternatives like *color, center, defense, draft*, and *jail* to British *colour, centre, defence, draught,* and *gaol*, but failed to change *soup, tongue, steady, daughter*, and *island* to *soop, tung, steddy, dawter,* and *iland*. Among the worst issues is the sequence ‹ough›, famously pronounced differently in each of the following words: *bough, hiccough, rough, though, thought, through,* and *trough*. The sound [ʃ] can be spelled as in *fish, motion, passion, sugar,* and *facial*. Such inconsistencies are often bemoaned, but at the same time there is resistance to such modest innovations as *lite* and *thru* for *light* and *through*.

Changing Standards

We need only compare the literary usages of Shakespeare's time with our own to see that standards themselves can and must change. Such flexibility can strengthen a language. To the extent that the standard has vitality and wide usage, it may serve to unite a nation and facilitate communication, thereby serving the common good. But this is not to say that the only valid language is a standard one. Let us explore some cases where the standard language is actually inappropriate.

Where the Standard Fails

A standard serves many purposes, but no standard in any language is the appropriate medium for all communication. After Latin had evolved into the distinct Romance languages, it remained the written and spoken standard for members of the European priestly and scholarly community. Yet they, like their associates and neighbors, spoke local Old French, Old Spanish, and Old Italian varieties in many nonofficial contexts. Today, although government, business, and other authorities support the use of a single written standard, large numbers of people in France, Italy, and Germany grow up speaking a distinct regional variety of their languages. Regional dialects are often sources of great pride, bolstered by rich oral traditions and sometimes a written literature. Although the level of literacy in the standard is very high in these countries and all students study it in school, regional varieties are still often preferred for talk between relatives and friends, traditional folk customs, and a range of other activities.

CAN OUR TUNG BE CLEANE AND PURE?

Some experts are tolerant of regional dialects yet very protective of the standard language they command. Since the time of the earliest English standard, critics have seen fit to regard certain differences in usage as corruptions, barbarisms, and marks of intellectual and even moral decline. In England in the sixteenth century Sir John Cheke responded to those who used lots of words borrowed from French, Latin, and other foreign sources by writing, "I am of this opinion that our own tung should be written cleane and pure, vnmixt and vnmangeled with borowing of other tunges." He should have reconsidered his own choice of words before writing, because the words *opinion, mix, mangle,* and *pure* are themselves borrowed.

Gripes about innovative usages come from many quarters, including some of our most distinguished authors. Jonathan Swift despised the use of *rep* for *reputation* that was common in his day and condemned the practice of clipping words in general. An author writing in 1872 labeled the word *belittle* "incurably vulgar." In their 1908 *Dictionary of Modern English Usage,* Fowler and Fowler took the position that Americanisms should be treated as foreign words in British English. Straining to give

American English its due, these authors concluded, "The English and the American language and literature are both good things; but they are better apart than mixed." French law imposes fines on public authorities and some government-run companies for using foreign words in the media when a French equivalent exists.

It's perfectly conceivable that authors and governments have good reasons for opposing certain linguistic practices, which need to be evaluated in the broader societal contexts in which they occur, and we may or may not sympathize with one or another of these, but what unites attempts to control linguistic change is their failure. No language has ever really been frozen, and there is no good reason to expect that any ever will. Few prescriptivists seem to understand this fact, and many seem unaware that essentially all their linguistic battles are lost over time. Extraordinary efforts were made to convince speakers to never split an infinitive, and yet the previous phrase will not strike most readers as being odd, despite the fact that the infinitive *to split* has the adverb *never* interrupting it. In school we are taught to use the subjunctive in contrary-to-fact expressions like *as if he were the devil himself*. Yet we may not have learned that *as if he was the devil himself*, which is heard at least as often, also contains a more recent form of the subjunctive—*was*. (The indicative would be *is*.) Another example is the use of *hopefully* as a sentence modifier, as in *Hopefully it will rain today*. Critics see this use as illogical, because *hopeful* as an adjective should modify a word referring to a person, as in *we are hopeful*. The fact that no person is referred to in *Hopefully it will rain today* may still raise powerful objections among purists, but without much effect on the rest of the linguistic community, as one can easily gather from listening or reading.

A common justification used by purists is the desire to uphold clarity and precision in language. Clarity and precision are key, but sometimes they are invoked as a flimsy, pseudo-scholarly excuse for preferring the old to the new. In none of the three new but highly criticized developments cited in the previous paragraph does clarity seem to suffer.

Logic is another type of justification offered for resisting language change. Samuel Taylor Coleridge equated rules of grammar with rules of logic. But this can't be right. Experts want us to say *It is I* rather than *It is me*, allegedly because the word *is* (due to its equational meaning) logically takes the same case, nominative, on both sides. But this is not logic; it was merely a rule of Latin. In French, it is the opposite. It is totally ungrammatical to say ˣ*C'est je* (literally "It's I"), with the pronoun in the nominative case. The correct thing to say is *C'est moi* (literally "It's me"), with the pronoun in an objective case. What is grammatically correct does not always coincide with what strikes experts as logical. The basic reason is that language reflects its human origins, and humans are sometimes more opportunistic than logical, seizing on solutions that are convenient or clever but not necessarily logical.

We do not mean to imply that purists are totally unjustified in wanting to preserve the language. In many instances, their love for the language and for clarity point up features that deserve to be savored rather than forgotten or taken for granted. And we are firmly on the side of those who remind us that the richness of language is there to help us communicate freshly and without resorting to cliché. As this book was being written, Oxford University Press unveiled its choice for Word of the Year 2018: *toxic*. To the present authors, this came as a double message: recognition that the term had become very useful in today's culture but also as a warning not to overuse the term. Words like *toxic* and *iconic* were once powerful descriptors, but frequent use has robbed them of a lot of their expressive potential, just as we have seen happen with *awesome*, whose meaning has become noticeably depleted from the original 'inspiring awe'. But while advocating thoughtful use of language, we take objection to the belief, however sincere, that without continuing efforts to preserve the language in its present state it will disintegrate. The history of language change offers ample reassurances.

CORRECTNESS IS RELATIVE

The real problem with prescriptivism arises from putting it forth as an absolute. Experts sometimes act as if there is only one standard—theirs. This is so far from the truth that it is silly. The varieties of English that they habitually ignore (regional dialects, ethnic dialects, local variants) are just as valid, useful, and appropriate in their contexts as standard formal English is in its contexts. Consider this analogy. We all go by different names at different times. Our friends know us by a first name or by a nickname. Our family may know us by a different nickname. In other settings, our first name may not be appropriate, and our last name will be used. There is nothing wrong with this. Language use in general follows the same principle: a usage appropriate in some situations may be wildly out of place in others.

Language serves a multitude of needs determined by our nature and our surroundings. As long as language remains flexible it remains alive. If the primary purpose of speech and writing is the expression and communication of thought, we can evaluate any particular language or variety of language on the basis of its usefulness for these purposes. This is what we are really asking when we question whether it is "right" to use *lite* or *light*, *irregardless* or *regardless*, *hopefully* or *I hope that*, [æsk] or [æks] for *ask*, or *contact your senator* for *make contact with your senator*. Because no choice in these pairs is inherently superior to its partner, the question must be, which communicates better in a particular setting?

Our choice of language usage is a lot like our choice of other symbols, like the clothes we wear. If we want our symbolic behavior to be interpreted as we intend it, we need to be sensitive to the norms of the community and to the fact that no single set of norms is right for all occasions. For this very practical reason we all become adept at multiple varieties of language over time, just as an international traveler learns different languages or customs to function effectively in different lands.

Surely it is possible to learn and apply the rules of standard formal English without imposing them on other dialects. And surely it is possible to master the rules of standard English without concluding that anything is wrong with nonstandard dialects. Imposing homogeneity risks robbing the language of its expressive resources and robbing many speakers of the pride that they take in their speech. This, to us, is the real danger in prescriptivism.

WORD CHOICE AND CLARITY

Because this book is concerned with expanding vocabulary, we ought to address some deeper purposes of word study. Gaining access to the vocabulary of a scholarly or specialist group gives us a share of that group's power. Becoming familiar with a group's specialized language is one step toward membership in that group. While the intent of specialized vocabulary is to allow experts to communicate effectively, we all encounter occasions when language is used to mystify and bedazzle us, leaving us feeling like outsiders. English legal language, for example, has caused centuries of confusion and consternation to the average citizen. In a growing number of countries, efforts are underway to encourage clearer language in government documents, and in a few instances established laws have been redrafted in language more comprehensible to the layperson. In 1970s America, locales began passing laws requiring legal documents to be written in "plain English," leading up to the US Plain Writing Act of 2010, which requires federal agencies to use "clear Government communication that the public can understand and use." Specifics can be found at the US government website https://plainlanguage.gov/resources/articles/elements-of-plain-language.

Control of advanced vocabulary includes recognizing the danger that it can be used to obfuscate or disguise rather than clarify meaning. An enhanced vocabulary brings the ability to decode the sometimes unnecessarily altiloquent, arcane words of the initiated. We are certainly better off with this knowledge than without it. Otherwise, to learn from your physician that you are suffering from *otitis externa* may appear more significant, perhaps even more upsetting, than hearing that you have a simple inflammation of the outer ear. Similarly, we don't want to be too impressed, put off, or confused by the use of a phrase like *longitudinal extent* for the more straightforward *length*. Other kinds of example include the empty phrases known as bureaucratese (e.g., *We explored a comprehensive set of options before the finalization process*) and euphemistic circumlocutions (e.g., *vertically challenged* to mean 'short').

This is not to belittle the technical use of language but only the pretentious or manipulative use of it. In fact, technical terminology serves a very important function in every discipline as a means of communicating unambiguously. And multiple stylistic levels of vocabulary offer advantages even to the nonspecialist, who may wish to manipulate different connotations, such as degrees of formality, as well as fine distinctions in denotational meaning that often come with different word choices. In all such cases, clarity may require turns of phrase one might not use in ordinary conversation.

Written language in particular suffers some big disadvantages. Compared to speech, written language has limited ways of expressing emphasis, emotion, and other important aspects of communication. For example, it lacks the devices of intonation, pauses, and other subtleties that spoken language affords, not to mention the expressiveness that face and body movement provide in face-to-face interaction. Speech usually affords immediate feedback from the listener, so that one can quickly detect and correct miscommunication, whereas mistakes in writing often endure. So choosing the right word can be more critical to writing than to speech.

Ultimately, an enhanced and enlarged vocabulary, like any part of the complex phenomenon called language, is a multipurpose tool. Like a hammer, it can be used either to build or to injure. The choice is ours.

RELATED READING

The *American Heritage Dictionary*, which for decades has had a usage panel of noteworthy writers and language experts, publishes the A*merican Heritage Guide to Contemporary Usage and Style*, with over five hundred pages and fifteen hundred entries on usage, grammar, and style.

WORD ELEMENTS

Element	Gloss	Source	Examples
aden	gland	G	*adenoids, adenoma, adenomyoma, adenopathy*
alg	pain	G	*nostalgic, analgesic, neuralgia, algogenic, algolagnia*
aur	ear	L	*aural, auricle, aurilave, auris, auristillae*
axill	armpit	L	*axilla, axillar, axillary*
caud~cod	tail	L	*caudate, caudal, caudiform, longicaudate, coda*
cervic	neck	L	*cervical, cervix, cervicoaxillary, cervicodynia*
cut	skin	L	*subcutaneous, cuticle, cuticula, cutis*
dermat~derm	skin	G	*dermatitis, dermopterous, hypodermic, taxidermy, pachyderm*
galact	milk	G	*galactic, galaxy*
gastr	stomach	G	*gastric, gastritis, gastrointestinal, gastronome, gastropod*
gravid	pregnant	L	*gravid, gravidity, multigravida, primigravida*
hem~haem~em	blood	G	*hemophilia, hemoglobin, hemostat, hematology, hematoma, haemochrome, anemia, methemoglobin*
hepat	liver	G	*hepatitis, hepatolysis, hepatoma, hepatotomy*
hist	body tissue	G	*histamine, histogenesis, histology, histoma, histoteliosis*
hyster	womb, neurotic disorder	G	*hysterectomy, hysteria, hysterical, hysterolysis, hysteropathy*

Element	Gloss	Source	Examples
-ia	land, state, medical condition	G, L	*Albania, utopia, aphasia, neuralgia, exophthalmia, pneumonia*
-itis	inflammation	G	*hepatitis, endocarditis, neuritis, phlebitis, pleuritis*
lab	lip	L	*labial, labia, labiocervical, labiomancy, labiomental, labret*
lacrim~lachrym	tear	L	*lachrymose, lacrimase, lacrimatory*
lact	milk	L	*lactate, lactein, lactiferous, lactose*
laryng	voice box	G	*laryngitis, laryngectomy, laryngophony, larynx*
mamm	breast	L	*mammary, mammae, mammal, mammogram, mammoplasty*
nas~nar	nose	L	*nasal, nasopharynx, nasturtium, nares, narial, nariform*
nephr	kidney	G	*nephritis, nephron, nephrostomy, epinephrine, nephrocele*
-oma	tumor, growth	G	*carcinoma, fibroma, glaucoma, melanoma*
op	see	G	*optic, autopsy, biopsy, isometropia, myopic*
ophthalm	eye	G	*ophthalmology, exophthalmic*
os~or	mouth	L	*oscitation, osculant, osculate, oral, oratory, oracle*
oss	bone	L	*ossify, osseous, ossuary*
oste	bone	G	*osteoporosis, osteophagia*
phleb	vein	G	*phlebitis, phlebosclerosis, phlebostasis, phlebotomy*
phob	fear	G	*phobia, phobic, agoraphobia, claustrophobia, hydrophobia, Russophobia*

Element	Gloss	Source	Examples
phylac	guard	G	*prophylactic, phylactery, anaphylaxis, phylaxin*
pne~pneum	breathe, lung	G	*apnea, dyspnea, pneumatic, pneumonia, pneumothorax*
pulm~pulmon	lung	L	*pulmocardiac, pulmometer, pulmonary*
rhin	nose	G	*rhinoceros, rhinitis, rhinoplasty, oxyrhine*
sarc	flesh	G	*sarcophagus, sarcoma, sarcopoietic, sarcosome, sarcasm*
scler	hard	G	*sclerosis, arteriosclerosis, sclera, sclerosant, sclerotic*
sep	putrid, infected	G	*sepsis, sepsometer, septicemia, antiseptic*
stom~stomat	mouth	G	*stomatitis, stoma, stomach, colostomy, cyclostome*
thromb	clot	G	*thrombosis, thrombus, thrombocyte, thromboembolism, prothrombin*
vas	vessel, duct	L	*vascular, vasectomy, vas, vasodilator*
ven	vein	L	*intravenous, vena, venomotor, venose, venostasis*

ELEMENT STUDY

1. What is the root in these words? Look up each word and include a brief sentence about the relation between the root's literal meaning and its meaning in this word (Part 1: Chapter 8 elements):

a. *tracheostomy*
b. *cervicitis*
c. *scleroderma* (two roots)
d. *thrombophlebitis* (two roots)
(Part 2: Cumulative elements):
e. *sclerotomy*
f. *hyperemia*
g. *cutisection*
h. *binaural*
i. *hematochrome*
j. *hysteria*

2. Your surgeon offers you a choice between a *nephrotomy*, *nephrectomy*, and *nephrostomy*. Parse the three words and explain the difference in their meaning. Give your parses in the standard format: prefix- root -suffix.

3. Note that *sarcasm* contains the root for 'flesh'. What is the connection between the literal and figurative meanings?

4. Here are some disease names derived from the Greek. The prefix *dys-* normally means 'bad, improper'. Parse all four words, using the standard format "prefix- root -suffix". Based on their structure, what sorts of disorder do you think these words involve?
   a. *dysemia*
   b. *dysphemia*
   c. *dyspnea*
   d. *dystopia*

5. Here are descriptions of some diseases whose names are derived from Greek. What do you think they are called?
   a. inflammation of the liver
   b. inflammation of the stomach
   c. inflammation of the larynx
   d. inflammation of a gland
   e. inflammation of the nose

6. The following words from the field of medicine contain a number of morphemes you have not yet encountered. With

the help of an unabridged dictionary—or, better yet, a large dictionary of medical terms plus a glossary or dictionary of roots—briefly define, parse, and gloss each term. For example,

nephr	*o*	*tom*	*-y*
'kidney'		'cut'	N

nephrolithotomy: 'surgical removal of kidney stones'

Dorland's Illustrated Medical Dictionary (32nd ed., Philadelphia, PA: Saunders, 2011, https://www.dorlandsonline.com) is one of several good larger medical dictionaries generally available. If you cannot find a particular term in the dictionary you use, you may still find portions of it or similar words that allow you to make an educated guess at the meaning of your word. For example, with *antixerophthalmic*, you might only find *xerophthalmic* or *xerophthalmia*, which should suggest that *antixerophthalmic* means 'against xerophthalmia'.

a. *leukocytotaxis*
b. *achromotrichia*
c. *brachymetacarpia*
d. *aphonogelia*
e. *retrocalcaneobursitis*
f. *antixerophthalmic*
g. *endosteoma*
h. *lithotroph*
i. *paraplegia*
j. *hemostasis*
k. *chromaffinoblastoma*
l. *paronychia*

EXERCISES

1. Some people draw a distinction between the vowels [a] and [ɒ], and others do not. Determine whether you make this distinction in your own speech. A good test for this is to pronounce word

pairs like *cot~caught*, *Don~Dawn*, and *knotty~naughty* and see if there is any difference. Then survey eight to ten people from different parts of the United States or Canada to see if they distinguish such words. Paying attention to the geographical backgrounds of the individuals as far as you can ascertain them, can you make any generalization about who makes the distinction? Besides the speaker's geographical background, does any other factor seem to play a role in the pronunciation of this word?

2. Look up the following words in a large dictionary, paying attention to any variation in spelling and pronunciation as well as to notes on etymology or word history and standard versus nonstandard usage. Describe, explain, and evaluate the indications of variation and any usage arguments in light of the discussion found in this and earlier chapters as well as your own knowledge of variation in their pronunciation and spelling and your sense of usage. It may help to consult multiple dictionaries and, perhaps, to check for differences between British and American usage.

a. *hopefully*
b. *irregardless*
c. *either*
d. *ask*
e. *which*
f. *nuclear*
g. *shall, will*
h. *ain't*
i. *anxious*
j. *hectic*
k. *prodigious*
l. *process*
m. *fair*
n. *host*

o. *disinterested*
p. *every*
q. *cohort*
r. *convince*
s. *balding*
t. *contact*$_v$

3. Pick a trendy expression (at the time of writing, "woke," "turnt," and "chill" are good choices, but you are the best judge of what's currently a good choice) and examine its use in different contexts, written and oral.

    For written contexts, choose different types of publications that you can consult online. Among these might be national newspapers, alternative newspapers, and blogs. For oral contexts, select a variety of contexts that you have easy access to: television, class lectures, and informal conversations, for example.

    What differences do you notice in how the expression functions in the different contexts you studied? Does it function differently in written versus oral contexts? In informal versus formal writing or speech? Does the expression mean something different in the different contexts?

4. English lecturer Anne Merrit wrote in the *Daily Telegraph*, "Text-speak . . . is creeping beyond . . . smartphones and into pupils' everyday language," "looks like a simple decline in proper language skills, born out of a digitally literate culture that has grown too comfortable in an age of abbreviations and spellchecks."

    Examine recent text messages you have sent or received. In what ways and to what extent does the language in them depart from the standards of written language in the media? Give several examples, and if possible, suggest whether text messaging is merely adding some new usages to English or actually replacing existing usages.

5. Comment on this quote from the Queen's English Society, which worked for several decades to preserve English in the United Kingdom from declining standards:

"We do not want the language to lose its fine or major distinctions. Some changes would be wholly unacceptable as they would cause confusion and the language would lose shades of meaning."

The dividing line between acceptable and unacceptable changes often differs for different speakers. Using your own speech as the model, help to make the distinction clear by giving one or two examples each of an acceptable change versus an unacceptable one.

6. British broadcaster John Humphrys has warned that "our laziness and imprecision are leading to unnecessary bloating of the language—'language obesity.' We talk of future plans and past history; of live survivors and safe havens. Children have temper tantrums and politicians announce 'new initiatives.'" We can easily agree that excess verbiage should generally be avoided, but how well do Humphrys's examples hold up? Test their validity by seeing whether you can develop contexts in which *future plans, past history, temper tantrums,* and *new initiatives* make good sense and are clearer and preferable to stripping these expressions of their modifying adjectives.

Nine

Latin and Greek Affixes in English

European science, technology, and arts long drew their inspiration from the enduring scientific discoveries and technological innovations of the Ancient Greeks and Romans, and exactly the same applies to philosophy and the arts. Thus, it's no surprise to find that our language draws so many words—and with them, much of word structure itself—from the ancient classical languages. The connection is evident from the very terms *science*, *technology*, *philosophy*, and *arts*. Chapter 2 briefly mentioned some early classical loanwords in the Germanic languages that gave rise to English in the fifth century. Later, our Latin- and Greek-derived vocabulary stock increased dramatically. In the Middle English period, words that French had acquired from Latin and Greek poured into our language. During the Renaissance, our language looked directly to Latin and Greek for vocabulary to express contemporary advances as well as renewed knowledge from the past. Even now, much of our new technical vocabulary is sourced from these ancient languages, as we gather from names of fields that only came into existence in the twentieth century, like *biotechnology*, *psychometrics*, and *cinemicrography*. What's more, we draw from the same classical stock for new everyday terms like *megavitamin*, *telecommute*, and *polyunsaturated*.

A good portion of the allomorphy from earlier chapters came about not from English phonetics but from changes required by the inflectional and derivational systems of Latin and Greek. In this chapter we trace these changes to basic aspects of Latin and Greek morphology. Learning these should make English words easier to parse.

NOUN INFLECTION

Chapter 3 briefly mentioned inflection, a device to express such attributes as the number of nouns. Inflection is almost always indicated by adding endings to **stems**. Stems are simply roots along with any derivational affixes; by this definition, *book*, *bookish*, and *bookishness* all qualify as stems. When representing stems, we attach with a final hyphen to indicate that inflections are to follow. Thus, to the English stem *book-* we may add the plural ending *-s* to form *books*. For the singular, *book*, we add nothing, though many other languages do. In short, English nouns inflect for number, contrasting singular and plural. You may have run across languages that also mark case (e.g. nominative, accusative) with inflections, but the sole inflection on English nouns indicates the genitive form (*book's*, *books'*).

Latin and Greek are more challenging. Like English, they inflect for number, contrasting singular and plural. They also inflect for case, but way more enthusiastically than English does: English nouns have just two forms in the singular and two in the plural, while a Latin noun can appear with up to five different endings in the singular and four in the plural. For example, the word for 'bull' may appear in a Latin sentence in any of the forms *taurus*, *taurī*, *taurō*, *taurum*, or *taure*, and in the plural as *taurī*, *taurōrum*, *taurīs*, or *taurōs*.

When English borrows a Latin or Greek noun whole—without stripping off its endings—it almost always borrows the word in the nominative case. The nominative case is the one used for the subject of a sentence: **Taurus** *vidit agricolam* '**The bull** saw the farmer'. It is also the form used when citing, or talking about, a word. If someone asked you what the Latin word for 'bull' is, you would answer *taurus*, rather than picking one of the other case-inflected forms like *taurum*. Widescale adoption of the nominative form means that we don't need to master the other cases for our purposes.

You will appreciate this free pass all the more when you consider that different nouns form their case endings differently; the genitive singular, for example, can be expressed by any of five different endings, depending on the word.

However, the nominative case is not devoid of complications of its own. Different words form the singular and plural with different inflectional endings. For English speakers this can be a lot to keep straight, and this in turn has led to an extra complication. For some words—but not all—an additional option is to replace the classical ending with the regular English plural suffix. *Memorandum* has two accepted plurals, *memoranda* and *memorandums*, as does *millennium*: *millennia*, *millenniums*. Yet some other words in *-um* take only the Latin plural ending. The plurals of *bacterium* and *quantum* are *bacteria* and *quanta*, never, as far as we can find, ^x*bacteriums* or ^x*quantums*. Words with two plurals sometimes develop distinct meanings for each plural form. The plural of *medium* is either *media* or *mediums*. The first refers to sources of mass communication, such as newspapers and broadcast companies, as well as to physical objects in science and technology, including devices for storing data. The meaning of the second is more general; we'd choose *mediums* over *media* as the plural of expression *happy medium*, whether referring to a convenient middle position or to a contented clairvoyant. *Media* and *mediums* have diverged even further from one another now that *media* has come to be treated as singular as well as plural, as when *social media* is followed by *is* or by *are*. Another common word that has been moving from its original Latin plural form to a singular is *agenda*, which functions as the subject of a singular verb in *The agenda is up in the air* and which can take the plural ending *s* to denote a set of agendas.

Latin words in *-us* also vary in the preferred plural ending in English. The situation is so chaotic, English speakers have understandably given up on following any rule. Latin *alumnus* is a singular word whose plural was *alumni*, and Greek singular *criterion* had the plural *criteria*, yet it's not uncommon nowadays to see *alumni* and *criteria* used in English as singulars. Whatever one's tolerance level for such innovations, it's good to be aware of the classical singulars and plurals, especially in scholarly contexts. Table 9.1 lists singular-plural pairs of some of the most commonly used endings.

In general, the plural ending regularly replaces the corresponding singular ending. Because *scapula* ends in an *-a* in the singular, you can infer that the plural is *scapulae*. But what about *apparatus*? Table 9.1 lists two possible plural endings for words ending in *-us*. Most take *-i* in the plural, so people often guess that the plural of *apparatus* is ˣ*apparati*. Unfortunately, that turns out to be the wrong guess: *apparatus* is actually one of a minority of words that take *-us* in the plural, so the correct answer is *apparatus*. Other Latin and Greek words that are sometimes used with the Latin or Greek plural shown in table 9.1 are *antenna, larva, hippopotamus, radius, sarcophagus, syllabus, basis, analysis, series, cranium, memorandum, millennium, symposium, phenomenon*, and *polyhedron*.

Memorizing table 9.1 can take you a long way toward handling Latin and Greek plurals, but we must still address one important class of nouns: words that have *-s* in the singular and *-es* in the plural. In a few words this works in a straightforward way: *stirps*, plural *stirpes*. But usually some complications arise. In Latin, as we have seen, [ks] is spelled *x*, so we get words like *appendix*, plural *appendices*. These words are straightforward from a phonological point of view, but the additional spelling rule makes the singular and plural look more different from each other when written than when pronounced.

Table 9.1 Nominative plural endings in Latin and Greek.

Singular	Plural	Example
-a	*-ae*	*alumna*
-es	*-es*	*species*
-is	*-es*	*crisis*
-on	*-a*	*criterion*
-um	*-a*	*memorandum*
-us	*-i*	*alumnus*
-us	*-us*	*hiatus*

Very often, though, there are pronunciation changes as well. Some of them result from phonological changes described in chapter 6. Consider, for example, *larynx*, plural *larynges*. If we work backward from the plural form, we can see that the stem is *laryng-*. Adding *-s* to that stem, to form the singular, would give ˣ*laryngs*. But the Phonation Assimilation rule would lead us to expect the [g] to devoice to [k] before the voiceless consonant [s]. That plus the spelling rule for *x* gets us to the expected singular spelling.

In *index*, yet another phonological rule comes into play. If we start off with a stem form *indec-*, with the *c* pronounced as [k], the singular form makes immediate sense. Adding the plural ending *-es* to the stem would give a plural ˣ*indeces*, pronouncing the *c* as [s] by Velar Softening. The rule of Latin [e] Weakening takes us the rest of the way. Recall that this rule does not apply in a closed syllable, and so the singular form retains the stem vowel [e]. A final case we might mention are words where Cluster Simplification comes into play. We might expect the singular of *glandes* to be ˣ*glants*, but Cluster Simplification reduces it to *glans*. Cluster Simplification is particularly common in Latin and Greek at the end of words, with many stem consonants being lost in the nominative singular.

This set of rules works for a great number of singular and plural forms that don't quite match, but other cases call for simply memorizing the plural. Rote memorization of plurals pays off in two ways. First, the Latin or Greek plurals are often used in English. Second, the plural form tends to have the more basic stem used for building new words. If you knew only the singular forms *appendix* and *larynx*, you would not know how to add *-itis* to make the medical name for an inflammation of those organs: ˣ*appendixitis*? ˣ*laryncitis*? But knowing the plural forms *appendices* and *larynges* immediately leads to the correct derivation: remove the plural ending and add the suffix to get *appendicitis* and *laryngitis*. Similarly, the irregular plural *genera* ties in better with derivatives like *generic* than does the singular form *genus*.

You are now in a position to understand a great deal about how plurals work in words borrowed from Latin and Greek. Just remain aware of the several exceptions; it is never a bad idea to consult a dictionary before using a Latin plural ending on an unfamiliar word. A blind use of table 9.1 can lead to strange plurals like ˣ*octopi* from *octopus* or ˣ*pentaga* from *pentagon*. Worse yet, some words only look like they come from a Latin noun. Despite its final *-us*, *caucus* does not have a Latin origin and so takes the regular English plural form, *caucuses*. *Ignoramus* actually derives from Latin but not from a Latin noun. The source is a verb meaning 'we don't know'. Accordingly, the plural is *ignoramuses*, not ˣ*ignorami*. Although such overgeneralizations find their way into print often enough, many of your readers and listeners would be sure to object to them.

Clearly the regular singular-plural pairs of Latin and Greek in table 9.1 have given way to a variety of patterns in English, and a dictionary is really the only way to be sure we have the right plural form. A final note of caution is that Latin plurals often mark a word as scholarly or technical. Sometimes that is appropriate; sometimes it can be annoyingly pedantic. When in doubt, take your cue from your intended audience. As our distance from classical culture continues to widen, we expect fewer words to take Latin and Greek endings.

Practice

The plural pair *appendixes* and *appendices* show that nouns from a classical source can take either the original ending or the regular English one. But not all such nouns behave like this. What are the proper plural forms for the following words? Don't feel bad if you have to look them up.

quantum
tantrum
compendium
bacterium
moratorium

datum
stimulus
Stradivarius
electron
automaton
etymon
pharynx

DERIVATION

Now that we have surveyed the inflectional patterns of Latin and Greek, let's take a look at some of the most common derivational patterns.

Nouns

The kernel of all lexical words is the root, which almost always takes the form of a simple syllable—for example, *oss* 'bone', *caud* 'tail', *hom* 'human', *ped* 'foot'. Some roots can form words by attaching inflectional endings directly to the root. For example, from the root *caud* comes the noun *cauda* 'tail'. There are also several suffixes that can be inserted between the root and the inflectional endings to make nouns. Table 9.2 lists some of the more common of these. All the words given as examples have been borrowed into English with little or no change, so we leave the translations as an exercise for the reader. We do, however, occasionally note in parentheses the root or base form the example word was derived from.

A few of these suffixes have some useful semantic content. The suffix *-arium* designates a place, *-or* designates a person or thing that does something, and the suffixes that begin with [l] are diminutives: they often name something that is smaller than usual.

Table 9.2 Noun-forming suffixes.

Nominative singular	Examples
Latin	
-arium	*librarium, sanctuarium, dispensarium, aquarium*
-ia	*miseria, constantia, agentia, scientia, abundantia*
-la	*molecula* (*mole* 'mass'), *capsula* (*caps* 'box')
-lum	*granulum* (*grano-*)
-lus	*alveolus* (*alveo-* 'hollow'), *circulus* (*circo-*)
-mentum	*tormentum* (*torqu*), *momentum* (*mov*), *complementum*
-monia	*acrimonia, alimonia, hegemonia*
-monium	*matrimonium, patrimonium*
-tas (stem *-tat-*)	*gravitas, fidelitas, sobrietas, aequalitas*
-tio (stem *-tion-*)	*electio* (*leg*), *fissio* (*fid*), *captio* (*cap*), *illuminatio* (*luc*)
-tor	*actor* (*ag*), *successor* (*ced*), *doctor* (*doc*)
-tura	*lectura* (*leg*), *fissura* (*fid*), *captura* (*cap*), *pictura* (*pig*), *natura* (*gena* 'birth')
-tus (plural *-tus*)	*adventus* (*ven*), *rictus* (*rig* 'gape'), *coitus* (*ī*)
Greek	
-ma (stem *-mat-*)	*pragma* (*prac*), *schema, thema, epigramma* (*graph*)
-sis	*praxis* (*prac*), *analysis, stasis*
-tor	*rhetor* 'orator', *chiropractor* (*prac* 'do')

Adjectives

Like nouns, adjectives are formed by adding at least one suffix to the root, as shown in table 9.3. Adjectives take various forms in the Latin and Greek nominative singular. They are listed here in their masculine form, but that detail is unimportant, because adjectives are rarely borrowed into English without dropping the inflectional ending or replacing it with a silent ‹e›.

The clearest semantics can be found here with *-(i)or*, which forms comparative adjectives. The suffixes *-ilis* and *-bilis*, when applied to a verbal root, often describe things that are readily affected or produced by the

Table 9.3 ADJECTIVE-FORMING SUFFIXES.

Suffix	Examples
-acos	cardiacos
-alis	regalis (reges 'kings')
-bilis	capabilis, tangibilis, affabilis
-icos	polemicos, anarchicos
-ilis	facilis, fragilis; puerilis (puer 'boy')
-(i)or	inferior, superior, posterior, junior
-osus	verbosus (verbum 'word'), bellicosus (bellum 'war')
-tivus	captivus, fugitivus

state or activity named by the root; for example, a *fragilis* thing (English *fragile*) is something easily or readily broken. Quite often, though, the most accurate thing we can say about suffixes like these is simply that they form adjectives.

Verbs

Verbs, too, are formed by adding a suffix to a root. In the simplest cases, the suffix is a single vowel, which may get lost or replaced by silent ‹e› when borrowed by English. For example, the root *err* 'wander' adds *-a-* to form a verb. This *-a-* was discarded from the English verb *err*, but we still see it in derivatives like *erratic* and *inerrant*. Often other elements are added as well. The nasal infix mentioned in chapters 4 and 6 was originally a way of making a present-tense verb from a root. And a few words add the suffix *-sc-*, which often has the meaning 'begin to', as in *candesce-* 'begin to glow' (cf. English *incandescent*). Several verbs add a *-ta-* or *-ita-*, which originally was meant to intensify the meaning of the verb. For example, English *agitator* comes from the same root as *actor* (*ag*).

Beyond these basic facts, the most important thing to know about verbs is how they form participles. A **participle** is derived from a verb and is used as an adjective or noun. The **present participle** stem in Latin ends in *-ent*. Thus, we get the present participle stems *docent-*, *agent-*, *sapient-*, and *sentient-*. If the verb ends in *a*, the *e* of *-ent-* is deleted, giving adjective forms like *errant-* and along the way providing evidence for tracing our verb *err* back to the Latin stem *erra*. These Latin present participles end here in a hyphen, our notation for showing that they were borrowed into English in their stem form, without any inflectional ending. When used as nouns, present participles commonly denote a doer. For example, an *agent* is one who *acts* on another's behalf. For slightly more abstract nouns, *-ia* is often added to the participial stem in Latin: *agentia*, *sapientia*, and *sentientia*. These were usually borrowed into English with *-ce* or *-cy* in place of the Latin *-tia*: *agency*, *sapience*, and *sentience*.

The **perfect participle** is the other highly important participle in Latin. Its function is to modify a noun, expressing that the noun is in a state indicated by the participle's verb stem. It often has a passive feeling, in contrast to the active feel of the present participle. For example, the perfect participle stem of *dissolv-* 'loosen, break up' is *dissolut-*, which can be translated as 'loosened, broken up', or, metaphorically, 'morally lax'. Something that breaks things up, actively acting on other objects, is denoted by the present participle *dissolvent-*; something that has been passively broken up is *dissolut-*.

The form of the perfect participle stem can differ quite a bit from verb to verb. Usually it simply adds *-t-* to the root. Thus, from the root *doc* comes the perfect participle stem *doct-*; from *fac* comes *fact-*. Above we saw that the Latin verb for *err* carried the suffix *-a-*, giving Latin *err-a-*. From this form Latin derives the perfect participle *err-a-t-*, the source of the English noun *erratum*. Some of the phonological rules discussed in chapter 6 may apply. Especially common is Phonation Assimilation: the root *ag* forms the perfect participle stem *act-*. The rule [t][t] to [ss] also applies very frequently, sometimes with Cluster Simplification. Thus, the root *sent*, which forms the present participle *sentient-*, forms the perfect participle *sens-*. One can think of this as a sequential derivation: *sent + t > senss > sens*. Additional rules and irregularities make it difficult to predict exactly what form the perfect participle will take, but one hard and fast rule—observed in all of the examples just cited—is that its stem always ends in a ⟨t⟩ or an ⟨s⟩: *doct-, err-a-t-, sens*, and so on. When perfect participles are used in English, a silent ⟨e⟩ is often added to the end of the word: *dissolute, animate*. English uses quite a few Latin perfect participles in their original adjectival meaning. Thus, *dissolute* corresponds closely to the Latin perfect participle meaning of *dissolut-*. But, even more commonly, perfect participles function in English as nouns or verbs. Thus, English *fact* is always used as a noun, and *act* is used as a noun or a verb.

Another Latin participle worth knowing is the **gerundive**. This participle specifies that the named activity ought to be done. For example, *agenda* is a Latin plural gerundive re-interpreted as singular in English expressing a set of things to be done at a meeting; a *memorandum* is something that should be remembered. The gerundive is very similar in form to the present participle, except that it has *d* instead of *t*. Not rarely, gerundives appear in English with the Latin suffix *-um*, plural *-a*, in which case they denote things, as opposed to people. Perfect participles show up with these endings as well. For example, the English words *errata* and *data* were originally Latin plural perfect participles.

SUMMARY

Latin and Greek inflectional endings are found on many words that have been borrowed into English without any adaptation. Such words are mostly nouns, which are borrowed in the nominative case; some of these use the original Latin ending to express the plural. The correct plural to use with Latin nouns can frequently be predicted from the ending of the singular. For other words, the plural cannot be correctly formed unless one knows the stem, which appears in most derivative words.

Most Greek and Latin words are formed by adding derivational suffixes to roots, to form noun, adjective, or verb stems, as well as present, perfect, and gerundive participles.

WORD ELEMENTS

Element	Gloss	Source	Examples
ac	sharp	L	acid, acrid, acerbic, acuity, exacerbate
acr	height, tip	G	acrophobia, Acropolis, acromegaly
agr	field	G, L	agriculture, agrostology, agronomy
alb	white	L	albino, album, albumen, albescent, albedo, albumin
aster~astr	star	G	asteroid, asterism, astral, astronomy, astrolabe
aud	hear	L	auditory, audit, subaudition, audiology
auto~tauto	self	G	autonomy, tautology, autolysis, automaton, tautonym, tautophony, autodidact
bath~bathy	depth	G	bathos, bathysphere, bathyal, bathochrome
bene~bon	good	L	benediction, benefactive, bonus, bonhomie, debonair
brach~brachy	short	G	brachycephalic, brachylogy, brachydactylic, amphibrach
carn~car	flesh	L	carnal, carnelion, carnivorous, incarnation, carrion
cli	lean, lie	G, L	client, recline, proclivity, clinograph, declivity, cline
cred	believe	L	credible, credit, credo, credendum, incredulous
cryph~cryp	hide	G	apocryphal, crypt, cryptonym, cryptogenic, cryptogamic
damn~demn	loss, harm	L	damnation, condemn, indemnify, indemnity
dic	say	L	dictate, dictum, interdict, juridical, benediction, malediction, jurisdiction
do	give	G	anecdote, dosology, epidote
do~da~di	give	L	donor, condone, data, dative, addition, tradition, perdition, edit
dol	suffer	L	condolences, dolorous, condole, indolent

Element	Gloss	Source	Examples
flu~fluc~fluv	flow	L	*fluid, confluence, influence, flux, fluctuate, fluvial, effluvium*
gloss~glott	tongue	G	*gloss, glossary, glossolalia, bugloss, diglossia, polyglot, glottal, glottis, epiglottis*
gno	know	G	*diagnosis, agnostic, gnosis, gnostic*
gno~no~gni	know	L	*ignorant, prognosticate, cognition, notion, notorious*
gyn~gynec	woman	G	*gynecologist, polygyny, gynecocracy, androgyne*
hes~her	to stick	L	*adhesive, cohesive, coherent, hesitate, inhere*
hydr~hydat	water	G	*hydrate, dehydrate, hydrolysis, hydrography, hydatid*
jus	law	L	*justice, jury, jurisprudence, juridical, abjure, adjure, adjudicate*
lith~lit	stone	G	*megalith, neolithic, lithotomy, albolite, dendrolite*
mega~megal	great, million	G	*megalith, megabyte, megaton, megalomania*
misc~mix	mix	L	*miscellany, miscegenation, promiscuous, mixture, permixture*
nihil~nil	nothing	L	*annihilate, nihilism, nihil obstat, nil*
ocul	eye	L	*oculist, ocular, monocle*
pen~pun	punish	L	*penal, penitent, penology, punitive, impunity*
ple	full, many	L	*plenty, plenary, plethora, replenish, replete*
pon~pos	place, put	L	*postpone, impone, propose, interpose, apposite, opposite, postiche*
pug~pugn	fist, fight	L	*pugilist, pugnacious, impugn, oppugn, repugnance*
tac	arrange	G	*tactic, hypotactic, syntax, taxidermy, taxonomy, taxon, taxis*

Element	Gloss	Source	Examples
tach~tachy	fast	G	*tachometer, tachistoscope, tachygraphy, tachylite*
terr	earth	L	*extraterrestrial, terra cotta, Mediterranean, inter, disinter, terra incognita*
vac~van	empty	L	*vacuum, vacuity, evacuate, vanish, vanity, evanescent*
ver	turn	L	*convert, extrovert, verge, converge, divergence, converse, inverse, adverse, obverse, perversity*
viv~vit	live	L	*vivid, vivacious, viviparous, convivial, vital, vitamin, curriculum vitae*

ELEMENT STUDY

1. What is the root in these words? Look up each word, and include a brief sentence about the relation between the root's literal meaning and its meaning in this word.

    Part 1: Chapter 9 elements:

    a. *note*
    b. *fluent*
    c. *pardon*
    d. *adherent*
    e. *immiscibility*
    f. *expletive*

    Part 2: Cumulative elements:

    g. *animadversion*
    h. *brachygraphy*
    i. *monoculous*
    j. *lithovore*

2. False friends: **pen~pun** 'punish' vs. **pug~pugn** 'fist, fight'

Two roots in this chapter, **pen~pun** 'punish' and **pug~pugn** 'fist, fight' share some features and have similar meanings yet are distinct enough to be relatively easy to tell apart. They do go back to distinct PIE roots *k^wei for **pen~pun** 'punish' and *peuk for **pug~pugn** 'fist, fight'. However, some of their allomorphs, not listed in our textbook entries, may lead to confusing one with the other. In each of the following words, identify the root, using a dictionary if necessary.
   a. *expugnable*
   b. *oppugnation*
   c. *penalize*
   d. *punitive*
   e. *subpoena*
3. False friends:
   a. It would be tempting but incorrect to identify the element **dol** as the root in the word *redolent* 'aromatic'. Look up *redolent* and parse it correctly.
   b. A simple phonetic rule of thumb distinguishes the root *ver* 'turn' from the root *ver* 'true'. Put the following words with *ver* 'turn' in one column and words with *ver* 'true' in another. Then determine what it is about adjacent sounds that will almost always tell you which root is which. Finally, explain what makes *verdict* an exception to this rule.
   aver, inversion, perverse, revert, veracity, veritable, versatile, converge
4. The following words from the fields of biology and medicine contain several morphemes you have not yet encountered. With the help of an unabridged dictionary and specialized dictionaries of biological and medical terms and using a glossary or dictionary of roots (Donald J. Borror, *Dictionary of Word Roots and Combining Forms* [Palo Alto, CA: Mayfield, 1960], is recommended), briefly define, parse, and gloss each term. Give your parses in the standard format: prefix- root -suffix.
   a. *tectospondylic*

b. *endolymphangial*
   c. *Pithecanthropus*
   d. *insessorial*
5. Parse and gloss the following words:
   a. *viviparous*
   b. *occasion*
   c. *supplicant*
   d. *dolorific*
   e. *eclecticism* (root isn't 'law')
   f. *assonance*
6. Find the word in the following list that best matches the dictionary definition given. Do not refer to a dictionary at first; you may do so when you are finished. Some of the words are decoys. Use no word more than once. Work from definition to word. Avoid multiple answers, but if you can't decide between two choices, give both and explain the problem for a chance at partial credit.
    1. *heteronomous*
    2. *licentious*
    3. *polity*
    4. *telegamic*
    5. *probophily*
    6. *autocratic*
    7. *atmesis*
    8. *peristaltic*
    9. *parhomologous*
    10. *delectation*
    11. *inculpatory*
    12. *theurgy*
    13. *homotronic*
    14. *malocclusion*
    15. *gradiometric*
    16. *apandrous*

Latin and Greek Affixes in English   229

17. *paratomy*
18. *perigonium*
19. *mesophilic*
20. *dolorifuge*
21. *parergon*
22. *anatopism*
23. *thearchy*
24. *parachromoparous*
25. *appetent*
26. *hypidiomorphic*
27. *toparch*
28. *syntrurgious*
29. *illicitness*
30. *metachronism*
31. *alegonymy*
32. *homeostasis*

a. ___Marked by the absence of legal or moral constraints.
b. ___Improper closure of the teeth so that the cusps do not fit together.
c. ___Possessing functionless male organs.
d. ___Having only some constituents with distinct crystalline form (said, e.g., of a rock).
e. ___Civil order.
f. ___Desiring eagerly.
g. ___Thriving in an intermediate environment (e.g., of moderate temperature).
h. ___A subordinate activity or work.
i. ___A sac surrounding the reproductive organs in certain species.
j. ___Reproduction by fission along a special division zone.
k. ___The tendency in an organism to maintain a stable internal condition.
l. ___A human act, process, power, or state of supernatural efficacy or origin.
m. ___An error in a temporal sequence placing an event after its real date.
n. ___A minor ruler or prince.

o. ___ Of or pertaining to involvement or implication in a charge of misconduct.

p. ___ Subject to external controls.

q. ___ Something that banishes or mitigates grief.

7. Fill in the blanks in each string of morphemes and other elements, then write out the complete word formed.

a.

___ tic ___ -ia = _____
'putrid' A 'blood' 'condition' = 'illness resulting from toxins in the blood'

(Use the allomorph of the morpheme meaning 'blood' which lacks an initial consonant.)

b.

___ ___ = _____
'lung' 'inflammation' = 'alternative term for *pneumonia*'

(Do not use *pne~pneum* for 'lung'.)

c.

___ s = _____
'important [singular] = 'pivotal point in an
point'   argument or discussion'

(Apply a spelling rule.)

d.

___ ___ = _____
'gland' 'tumor' = 'tumor with glandular structure'

e.

sine ___ e = _____
'without' 'care' = 'paid job requiring no work'

8. Gloss the boldface morphemes in the space provided.
   a. **rhinolaryng**ology 'study of disease of ___ & ___'
   b. **lact**ation 'production of _____'

EXERCISES

1. Based on what you've learned in this chapter and the meanings of the roots, some of which you can find in the appendix and others in a dictionary, parse the following Latin and Greek expressions using the standard format: prefix- root -suffix. You're free to look up the meanings of the roots. Then give a short definition that reflects, at least in part, the meanings of the individual morphemes.
   a. Latin perfect participles: *desideratum, (terra) incognita, errata, invicta*
   b. Latin present participles: *parent, recumbent, errant*
   c. Latin gerundives: *addendum, explicandum, memorandum, corrigendum, referendum, agenda, pudenda, disputandum, disputanda*
   d. Greek: *schema, stigmata*
2. Following are a few words and phrases from the field of law. Briefly define, parse, and gloss each term. If a search engine doesn't lead to definitions, try a large dictionary or a legal dictionary (e.g., Bryan A. Garner, ed., *Black's Law Dictionary*, 11th ed. [Eagen, MN: Thomson Reuters, 2019]). Apply your knowledge of Latin morphology to parse and gloss the components.
   a. *probation*
   b. *logomachy*
   c. *jurisdiction*
   d. *impignoration*
   e. *defenestration*
   f. *mortuus sine prole*

3. The following terms from the field of botany contain several morphemes you have not yet encountered. Note that some consist of two words: the first for the genus and the second for the species. Most botanical terms take their endings from Latin. With the help of a large dictionary and a specialized dictionary of botanical terms and a glossary or dictionary of roots, briefly define, parse, and gloss each term. The use of Latin in botany is described in considerable detail by William T. Stearn (*Botanical Latin*, 4th ed. [Portland, OR: Timber Press, 2004]). This book also has a useful glossary.

An example:

Calochortus pulchellus: 'yellow globe tulip', a plant with delicate yellow flowers. Its bulbs are considered a delicacy in India.

cal (o)	*chort*	*us*	*pulch*	*ell*	*us*
'beautiful'	'feeding place, garden'	N [singular]	'beautiful'	[diminutive]	A [singular]

You can see from this example that the connection between the meaning of the morphemes and the characteristics of the thing being described can be quite a distant or tenuous one.

   a. *rhizocorm*
   b. *filiformis*
   c. *procumbens*
   d. *Oryza angustifolia*
   e. *caulocarpous*
   f. *Leucospermum*
   g. *involutus*
   h. *pleniflorus*

4. Loanwords from Greek and Latin: Of vocabulary that has been borrowed into English from Latin and Greek since the Renaissance, much but not all has been learned vocabulary, and many but not all borrowings were not full Latin and Greek words but rather morphemes—roots and affixes.

Choose two words of different types from each of the following six sets and parse each word. Comment on structure that appears to have been carried down from Latin or Greek, as described in this chapter, but also be aware of resemblances to the structure of native words like *unfriendliness*. Adapted from Robert Stockwell and Donka Minkova. *English Words: History and Structure* (Cambridge: Cambridge University Press, 2001).

Latin, 1500–1600

acumen, appendix, axis, caveat, circus, compendium, corona, folio, genius, genus, innuendo, medium, radius, regalia, stratum, vacuum, vertigo

Latin, 1600–1700

affidavit, agendum, apparatus, census, desideratum, dictum, fiat, imprimatur, momentum, specimen, status, stimulus, vertebra

Latin, 1700–1800

auditorium, bonus, deficit, habitat, inertia, prospectus, referendum, ultimatum

Greek via French, pre-1500

academy, atom, climate, ecstasy, emblem, idiot, logic, magic, mystery, plane, rhetoric, scandal, spasm, sphere, theater, tragedy

Greek via Latin, pre-1500

agony, allegory, crypt, history, mania, mechanic, paper, theme, thesis, thorax

Greek, 1500–

acrostic, amnesty, chorus, crisis, despot, dilemma, disaster, elegy, machine, pathos, skeptic, stigma, trophy

Ten

The Prehistory of English and the Other Indo-European Languages

THE DISCOVERY OF THE DEEPER LINGUISTIC PAST OF ENGLISH AND RELATED LANGUAGES

The origins of the languages of the world have intrigued humans throughout history. The story of the Tower of Babel in the Hebrew Bible expresses a widespread feeling that the diversity of languages is a remarkable state that needs to be explained: why aren't we all still speaking the original language of the first humans? As seen in previous chapters, we now understand that linguistic change is normal and universal. And given that change is unavoidable, languages of different groups are certain to diverge if the speakers are not in close contact with each other. But recognizing divergence as a linguistic generality is many steps from understanding the specifics of how our current languages diverged from common ancestors. Research into both the general patterns and the specific details of language history is the concern of **historical linguistics**.

The current tradition of scientific inquiry into historical linguistics began in the eighteenth century, when scholars proposed that Hungarian and Finnish, until then considered quite separate languages, were in fact related through descent from a single hypothetical ancestor, which

Table 10.1 COGNATE WORDS IN LATIN, GREEK, AND SANSKRIT.

Meaning	Latin	Greek	Sanskrit
'creeps'	serpit	herpei	sarpati
'family'	genus	genos	janas
'ten'	decem	deca	daśa
'three'	tres	treis	trayas

is now known as Proto-Finno-Ugric. In a 1786 address, the British jurist Sir William Jones hypothesized that most of the other languages of Europe and the ancient Indian language Sanskrit were part of another such family of related languages. Jones, who worked in India during the British colonial period, was one of the first Europeans ever to intensively study Sanskrit, which functions as the language of Hinduism, much as Latin has in Roman Catholicism. He proposed that Sanskrit, Latin, and Greek might have "sprung from some common source," which itself might no longer be spoken. Table 10.1 gives a few vocabulary correspondences among the three languages.

Jones's address kicked off a boom of historical linguistic scholarship in the nineteenth century. These investigations established the existence of the family of languages that came to be identified as *Indo-European*, so called because speakers of those languages occupied, at the dawn of the Western historical period, much of the Eurasian landmass stretching from the Indian subcontinent to the western boundaries of Europe.

THE INDO-EUROPEAN LANGUAGES

Divergent dialects arose as the Indo-Europeans migrated to far-flung areas of Europe and Asia and became isolated from each other. These dialects gave rise to the individual subgroups of the Indo-European family. There are perhaps thirteen branches of Indo-European. Eight branches have languages that are still spoken; a sampling of those languages includes

Germanic. English, German, Dutch, Yiddish (West Germanic); Norwegian, Swedish, Danish, Icelandic (North Germanic or Scandinavian)

Italic. Latin, with its descendants, the **Romance** languages: French, Italian, Spanish, Portuguese, Romanian

Hellenic. Greek

Celtic. Gaelic, Irish, Welsh, Breton

Balto-Slavic

  Baltic. Lithuanian, Latvian

  Slavic. Russian, Ukrainian, Czech, Polish, Serbian, Croatian, Bosnian, Bulgarian

Indo-Iranian

  Indic. Sanskrit and its descendants: Hindi, Bengali, Urdu, Romany (Gypsy), Punjabi, Gujarati

  Iranian. Farsi (Persian), Pashto

Armenian

Albanian

Some branches of Indo-European are known from written records but have no living descendant languages. The extinct languages of the Tocharian branch were once spoken in western China, and the Anatolian languages, which include Hittite, were spoken in Turkey. Among the branches of Indo-European still populated by living languages were others that have since died out. An example is Gothic, from the Germanic branch.

FROM PROTO-INDO-EUROPEAN TO GERMANIC

One of the fundamental discoveries about the Indo-European language family was the set of sound correspondences usually called *Grimm's law*, named for Jakob Grimm, also known as one of the two brothers who collected the famous folktales. In the early 1820s, he put the finishing touches on some observations about Germanic first noted by Rasmus Rask. As you can see from the word-initial consonants in table 10.2, English (viz. Germanic) words that descended from the original Indo-European

Table 10.2 SOME OBSTRUENT CORRESPONDENCES AND RECONSTRUCTED PIE.

English	Latin	Greek	Sanskrit	PIE
father	**p**ater	**p**atēr	**p**itā	*$*p$
three	**t**rēs	**t**reis	**t**rayas	*$*t$
hundred	**c**entum	**h**ecaton	**ś**atam	*$*\acute{k}$
where	**qu**is	**p**ou	**k**va	*$*k^w$
ten	**d**ecem	**d**eca	**d**aśa	*$*d$
kin	**g**enus	**g**enos	**j**anas	*$*\acute{g}$
quick	**v**īvus	**b**ios	—	*$*g^w$
be	**f**uit	**ph**ȳei	**bh**avati	*$*b^h$
do	**f**acit	**th**es	**dh**ātu	*$*d^h$
gold	**h**elvus	**ch**loē	**h**aris	*$*\acute{g}^h$

NOTE: Words in a given row all have the same root, but not always exactly the same meaning, as the English word. ^{h} means the consonant is pronounced in a breathy fashion. ^{w} means the consonant is pronounced with rounded lips. An acute accent ´ over a velar means it has a somewhat more front pronunciation than other velars.

language, Proto-Indo-European (PIE), usually have different obstruents than do the words of the same meaning in other Indo-European languages. Grimm's law showed, however, that underneath these differences was regularity. For example, if a word begins with [f] in English, the Latin word for the same meaning regularly begins with a [p]. This led to the hypothesis that Proto-Indo-European had a consonant that, by sound changes in Germanic or Italic or both, became [f] in one branch and [p] in the other.

The discovery of **recurrent sound correspondences** helped put historical linguistics on a firm scientific basis. We might even say more generally that this was a first step toward establishing linguistics as a discipline with a reliable methodology. Prescientifically, one could come by the idea that two languages are related by simply noting how similar they look to each other. But words can resemble other words to a greater or lesser degree, so it is hard to tell when resemblance is merely coincidental. In contrast, it is not at all likely that pairs of languages would have a large number of words with recurring sound correspondences. This makes recurring sound correspondences the ideal evidence for suggesting how closely languages are related to one another.

Historical linguists often take the further step of guessing what the original sound was that led, for example, to [f] in English but to [p] in Latin. This is known as **reconstruction**. Reconstructions are usually preceded by an asterisk (*) to show that the form is based on inference and not on any written record. Proto-Indo-European was spoken before the invention of writing, and so the only things we can say about the language are necessarily based on reconstructions. Following tradition, we spell PIE reconstructions in a way that is very similar to the IPA we have been using for English. The few differences will be pointed out when first encountered.

The last column in table 10.2 gives the commonly accepted reconstructions for the PIE consonants under consideration. Reconstructions are based, when possible, on the most likely changes that have been documented in other languages. For example, *p is reconstructed because linguists have observed [p] changing into [f] in more languages than [f] changing into [p].

The correspondences in Grimm's law make perfect sense if seen as the result of a sound shift in Proto-Germanic that regularly affected the phonation and manner of articulation of the stop consonants without substantially changing their place of articulation. Thus, we can see a shift in which

1. The **voiceless** stops changed their manner of articulation from that of stops to that of the similar fricatives:

    *p > [f]

    *t > [θ]

    *ḱ > [x], which later > [h] in English

    *kʷ > [xʷ], which later > [hw], now usually [w] in English

2. The unaspirated **voiced** oral stops lost their voicing:

*d > [t]

*ǵ > [k]

*gʷ > [kʷ]

3. The **breathy** aspirated stops lost their aspiration to become simple (unaspirated) voiced stops:

*bʰ > [b]

*dʰ > [d]

*ǵʰ > [g]

If *d^h > [d] and *d > [t] and *t > [θ], why didn't all three of these dental sounds eventually become [θ]? And one might ask the same question for the other places of articulation. The answer is that these changes must have happened in the order of enumeration (1–3), so that, for example, by the time *d changed to [t], *t had already changed to [θ] and that particular sound change had stopped operating. This makes Grimm's law a **chain shift** of sounds, not unlike the Great Vowel Shift, which was discussed in chapter 2.

Practice

The sound correspondences just presented show many cognates that you may not have recognized before, such as *father* and *paternal*. Use Grimm's law and the examples in table 10.2 to decide which of the following word pairs have cognate roots. In each pair, the first word is of Germanic origin, while the second is borrowed ultimately from Latin or Greek, sometimes through French. But not all are cognates!

break, fragile
take, capture
hundred, centipede
hearty, courageous
tale, fable

THE NATURE OF PROTO-INDO-EUROPEAN

Sounds

From examining a more complete set of recurrent correspondences, linguists have reconstructed the consonants of Proto-Indo-European as shown in table 10.3. Note carefully that *y spells the consonant in English *yes* (IPA [j]), not the rounded Greek vowel as in IPA [y].

Figuring out what a long-extinct language sounded like involves many educated guesses, and so it is no surprise that many controversies and unanswered questions remain. Consequently, you need not be intimidated about pronouncing these sounds correctly in class: you can always tell your teacher that you subscribe to a different theory. The pronunciation of three of the fricatives is so contentious that we did not even hazard a guess as to where to put them in the chart. Most often, writers prefer to simply assign them numbers: $*h_1$, $*h_2$, and $*h_3$; the symbol $*H$ is used when there is not enough evidence to distinguish among the three. They are known as **laryngeals**, for no good reason; they probably had no particular connection with the larynx.

Table 10.3 THE CONSONANTS OF PROTO-INDO-EUROPEAN.

	Labial	Dental	Velar Front	Velar Back	Velar Round
Obstruents					
Oral stops					
Voiceless	*p	*t	*ḱ	*k	*kʷ
Voiced	*b	*d	*ǵ	*g	*gʷ
Breathy	*bʰ	*dʰ	*ǵʰ	*gʰ	*gʷʰ
Fricative		*s			
Nasal	*m	*n			
Approximant		*r	*y		*w
Lateral		*l			

Proto-Indo-European had five vowels, both long and short, much like Latin; they are transcribed *a, *e, *i, *o, *u, with macrons when long: *ā, *ē, *ī, *ō, *ū. In addition, nasals and approximants were often used as **syllabic consonants**, that is, in place of a vowel. For example, the word for 'seven' was *septm̥, with the m serving as the vowel of the second syllable, much as in the contemplative exclamation hmm. It is traditional to draw a circle under syllabic consonants. In most words, there is a single vowel or syllabic consonant that is pronounced with a higher pitch than the rest of the word; this is denoted by an acute accent, as in á and ḿ̥.

Laryngeals have two interesting effects on vowels. One is **laryngeal vowel coloring**. When *h₂ appears next to an *e, the pronunciation of the *e becomes *a; for example, *h₂eǵr- 'field' gives us Latin agr- as in agriculture. Similarly, when *h₃ stands next to an *e, the latter becomes *o: *h₃ekʷ- 'eye' ends up as Latin oc- as in oculist. The other effect is **laryngeal lengthening**: when a laryngeal comes after a vowel or syllabic consonant in the same syllable, the effect in daughter languages is for the laryngeal to disappear but for the preceding sound to be lengthened. For example, *pléh₁dʰuh₁ 'crowd' ends up as Latin plēb-, the source of plebeian.

Grammar

In addition to the sounds, a great deal more is known about Proto-Indo-European. Much of its morphology has been reconstructed. It had heavily inflected nouns and verbs, like its descendants Latin and Greek, only more so. Proto-Indo-European seems to have had at least eight cases. Instead of distinguishing only singular and plural number, Proto-Indo-European had a third category, the dual, used for denoting exactly two things; for example, one *h₁éḱwos 'horse', two h₁éḱwoh₁, three or more h₁éḱwoes. Adding a huge complication, different words often expressed the same cases and numbers with different inflectional endings. Adjectives had to be inflected for the same case and number as the noun they modified, and also had to agree with their gender—a mostly arbitrary three-way contrast that we call masculine, feminine, and neuter, but which in fact had little to do with sex.

Some of the irregular allomorphy in chapter 4 has its origins in grammar rules that were more regular in Proto-Indo-European. For instance, the nasal infix in some allomorphs of roots like *frang* 'break' indicated present tense. The ablaut examples described in chapter 4 are relics of an extensive system of vowel alternations in Proto-Indo-European.

THE INDO-EUROPEAN WORLD

Indo-European was the first large language family on which Western scientists practiced **linguistic archaeology**. Vocabulary shared by disparate branches of the Indo-European diaspora shows that they once shared a substantial lexical and cultural base. By comparing words in the descendant languages and extrapolating from the regular correspondences observed in words like those noted earlier, linguists have been able to infer a great deal about the Indo-European language and the Indo-Europeans themselves as they lived five to six thousand years ago. The following aspects of the physical and conceptual universe are just a few of those represented by the Indo-European morphemes that have been reconstructed. Traditional transcription is used here; a useful exercise would be to read the Proto-Indo-European words aloud, using the phonetic values from the previous section. English words in italics are based ultimately on these words; translations are added only when not obvious from the English derivatives.

Names for things in the physical environment include **snóygʷʰos* (*snow*), **ǵʰéyōm* 'winter' (*hiemal, hibernate*); the plants **bʰeh₂ǵos* (*beech*) and **bʰerHǵós* (*birch*); and the animals **h₂ŕ̥tḱos* 'bear' (*arctic*), **wĺ̥kʷos* (*wolf, lupine*), **bʰébʰrus* (*beaver*), **ḱas-* (*hare*), **múh₂s* (*mouse*), **h₁éḱwos* 'horse' (*equine*), **gʷṓws* (*cow, bovine, bucolic*), **uksḗn* (*ox*), *h₂ówis* 'sheep' (*ewe, ovine*), **suHs* (*swine, sow*), **ḱwṓ* 'dog' (*hound, canine*), **h₃érō* 'eagle' (*erne, ornithology*), **ǵʰh₂éns* (*goose, anserine*), **gerh₂-* (*crane*), and **bʰey-* (*bee*). The overall pattern of such vocabulary suggests that the

Proto-Indo-Europeans lived in temperate woodlands, neither too hot for snow nor too cold for the attested flora and fauna.

The Proto-Indo-Europeans knew of *$ǵʰḷtóm$ (*gold*), *$h_2r̥ǵn̥tóm$ 'silver' (*argentine*), and *$h_2éyos$ 'bronze' (*aeneous*), but apparently not iron. They had the *$néh_2us$ 'ship' (*navy*), which they would *$h_1r̥h_1yéti$ (*row*), but apparently had no sails. Words like *$h_2melǵeti$ (*milks*), *suH (*sow*), and *$h_3éngʷn̥$ 'butter' (*unguent*) demonstrate knowledge of husbandry; *h_2erh_3- 'plow' (*arable*), and *$gʷérh_2nus$ (*quern*) demonstrate that they had agriculture. They must also have known how to *$wébʰeti$ (*weave*) *$h_2wl̥h_1neh_2$ (*wool*). Perhaps most important, they had the *$kʷékʷlos$ (*wheel*) and *$h_2eḱsis$ (*axle*). Some of these activities and culture items were not invented until around 4000 BCE, which suggests the Proto-Indo-Europeans must not have left their homeland before then. A popular theory proposes that all these details from linguistic archaeology are most compatible with what traditional archaeology has learned about the Kurgan culture that was situated in eastern Ukraine around that time. Conceivably the use of the horse and the wheel—hence war chariots—gave this culture the military edge to eventually spread through so much of Europe and southwestern Asia.

The Proto-Indo-Europeans appear to have worshipped at least one god, called *$dyḗws\ ph_2tḗr$, that is, *Father Zeus*, the Roman *Jupiter*. They were patrilocal and patriarchal. The *$déms\ pótis$ 'master of the house' (*despot*) would *$wedh$- 'lead away' a woman to live in his *$dṓm$ 'house' (*domicile*). This led eventually to an extended family, whose members would live together in a *$weyḱós$ 'village' (*vicinity*).

CHANGES LEADING TO LATIN AND GREEK

As the Proto-Indo-European speakers spread throughout Europe and Asia, the descendant languages underwent many independent changes, such as Grimm's law in Germanic. Most significant for our purposes are those that occurred in Latin and Greek. A few of the most important of these are listed next.

Greek

Proto-Indo-European vowels are well preserved, with only two important changes. Long and short *u moved forward in the mouth, becoming y. Thus *múh₂s 'mouse' > mȳs (the root my is used in English in the metaphorical sense 'muscle'). The other important vowel change is that long *ā became ē. Thus *méh₂tēr 'mother' > mātēr > mētēr (*metropolis*).

Most of the oral stops did not undergo anything as comprehensive as Grimm's law. But as you can see from table 10.2, the PIE breathy aspirates became voiceless aspirates.

The labialized oral stops (*kʷ, *gʷ, *gʷʰ) ordinarily became labials in Greek: *p, b, ph*. These are the changes shown in table 10.2. There are also conditioned changes: the labialized stops become dentals (*t, d, th*) before front vowels. Thus *kʷetwóres 'four' > tessares.

Word-initial *s became [h]. Thus *septḿ̥ > hepta.

Laryngeals (*h₁, *h₂, *h₃) either disappeared, perhaps leaving behind traces in the form of laryngeal vowel coloring or laryngeal lengthening (e.g., *deh₃- 'give' > dō-), or they turned into the vowels *e, a,* and *o,* respectively (e.g., *h₁régʷos > erebos 'darkness', *ph₂tḗr > patēr).

Syllabic consonants like *r̥ or *m̥ did not remain such in Greek. Instead, Greek usually added an *a* next to the consonant. Thus *k̑r̥d- 'heart' > card-. Often the syllabic nasals *m̥ and *n̥ simply became *a*, as in the aforementioned *septḿ̥ > hepta.

The glide [w] normally disappeared: *widéseh₂ > ideā.

Latin

Much of the regular allomorphy described in chapter 6 is due to changes that happened in the descent of Latin from Proto-Indo-European. In particular, Rhotacism, despite its Greek-derived name, is distinctively Latin: *swésōr 'sister' > soror. So is the change of *t + t* to *ss*.

Latin vowels preserved the Proto-Indo-European state of affairs pretty well in the first syllable, but in subsequent syllables the distinctively Latin vowel weakenings often make it difficult to tell what the original vowel was.

As table 10.2 shows, most of the oral stops are very similar to the original Proto-Indo-European ones—except that *g^w became the glide [w]—until we get to the breathy aspirated consonants. The single most useful rule to learn is that these usually became *f* in Latin.

Laryngeals either disappeared, behaving as in Greek, or they turned into the vowel *a*. Latin did not get different vowels for the three different laryngeals (e.g., *$d^h h_1 k$-* > *fac* 'do'; *$ph_2 t\acute{e}r$* > *pater*).

Syllabic consonants added a vowel next to the consonant. Thus *$k\acute{r}d$-* 'heart' > *cord-*; see table 10.4 for details.

APPLICATION TO WORD STUDY

We have been concentrating on how native English, Greek, and Latin words have changed since Proto-Indo-European times, but for us as students of English vocabulary, the bigger news is the remarkable amount of stability over the past six thousand years. Many Proto-Indo-European sounds have not changed at all in one or more of the three languages we are focusing on, and of those that have changed, many of the changes are minimal or show regular correspondences between the languages. The similarities and correspondences can help us to associate Latin and Greek morphemes with each other and with native English words. To apply this knowledge to recognizing and learning a new Latin or Greek morpheme, you can guess at its possible English cognates by applying the expected sound correspondences. Easier and more reliable would be to consult a list of Proto-Indo-European roots and their major English, Greek, and Latin descendants. You can find such a list on the web at https://www.ahdictionary.com/word/indoeurop.html.

The correspondences in table 10.4 are valid for most initial consonants and many medial and final consonants. The alternants enclosed in parentheses are for reference only and need not be memorized.

Table 10.4 Consonant correspondences for PIE, Greek, Latin, and English.

PIE	Greek	Latin	English
*p	p	p	f (v)
*t	t	t	th
*ḱ, k	c	c	h (gh)
*kʷ	p, t, c	qu	wh
*b	b	b	p
*d	d	d	t
*ǵ, g	g	g	c, k (ch)
*gʷ	b, d (g)	v (gu)	qu
*bʰ	ph	f (b)	b (v)
*dʰ	th	f (d)	d
*ǵʰ, gʰ	ch	h (g)	g (y)
*gʷʰ	ph, th (ch)	f (v)	w
*s	h, s	s, r	s
*h₁	e, —	a, —	a, —
*h₂	a, —	a, —	a, —
*h₃	o, —	a, —	a, —
*m	m	m	m
*m̥	a	em	um
*n	n	n	n
*n̥	a	en	un
*l	l	l	l
*l̥	al (la)	ul	ul
*r	r	r	r
*r̥	ar (ra)	or	ur
*w	— (h)	v	w
*y	z (h)	j	y

FURTHER READING

A brief, authoritative, and accessible account of Proto-Indo-European language and culture is Calvert Watkins's *Indo-European and the Indo-Europeans*. It can be found at the back of the third and fourth editions of the *American Heritage Dictionary of the English Language* as well as in Watkins's *The American Heritage Dictionary of Indo-European Roots* (2000). These are republished versions of an article dating back to 1969.

Two recommended books on the topic are B. W. Fortson IV, *Indo-European Language and Culture: An Introduction* (Wiley, 2011), and J. P. Mallory, *In Search of the Indo-Europeans: Language, Archaeology and Myth* (Thames & Hudson, 1989).

The guidelines used in the text for transcribing Proto-Indo-European forms are the ones supplied in the Wiktionary article "About Indo-European," https://en.wiktionary.org/wiki/Wiktionary:About_Proto-Indo-European.

WORD ELEMENTS

Element	Gloss	Source	Examples
al	other	L	*alias, alibi, alter*
all~allel	other	G	*allomorph, allogenic, allopathy, allele, allelocatalytic*
card	heart	G	*cardiac, electrocardiogram, endocardium*
cord	heart	L	*cordial, misericord, accord, discord*
cruc	cross, important point	L	*crucify, crucial, cruciform, crucible, cruciate, excruciating, crux*
dec	acceptable	L	*decent, decor, decorum, decorous, decorist*
ed~es	eat	L	*edible, edacious, obese, esurient, esculent, comestible*
fa	speak	L	*famous, fate, ineffable*

Element	Gloss	Source	Examples
fer	carry	L	*transfer, fertile, differ, refer*
fratr	brother	L	*fraternity, fraternal, fratricide*
ge	earth	G	*geology, geode, georgic, perigee, apogee, epigeal*
gemin	twin	L	*Gemini, geminate, gemellus, bigeminal, trigeminus*
ger	old person	G	*geriatric, gerontology, gerontogeous, gerontomorphosis*
graph~gramm	write	G	*graphic, graphite, telegraph, pantograph, digraph, telegram, epigram, diagram, tetragrammaton*
juven~jun	young	L	*juvenile, rejuvenate, junior*
lat	carry	L	*translate, collate, elate, prelate, ablation, illation, superlative, dilatory*
lig	tie	L	*ligament, ligate, ligature, oblige, alligation, colligate, religion*
lign	wood	L	*ligneous, lignify, lignite, lignescent*
loqu~locu	speak	L	*loquacious, colloquial, soliloquy, obloquy, grandiloquence, circumlocution. elocution, interlocutor*
magn	great, large	L	*magnify, magnanimous, magnum, magniloquent, magnitude*
matr	mother	L	*maternal, matrilineal, matrix, dura mater, material*
metr	mother, uterus	G	*metropolis, metritis, metrorrhagia, endometrium*
myc	fungus	G	*mycology, mycosis, streptomycin*
noct	night	L	*nocturnal, nocturn, noctule, equinox*
nomen~nomin	name	L	*nominate, nominal, nomenclature*

Element	Gloss	Source	Examples
nyct	night	G	*nyctophobia, nyctitropism*
onom~onomat~onym	name	G	*onomatopoeia, onomastic, pseudonym, synonym, antonym, eponym, patronymic*
orth	straight, correct	G	*orthodox, orthography, orthogonal, orthopedic, orthotic, anorthite*
pale~palae	old	G	*paleolithic, paleontology, paleobotany, paleoclimatic, palaeo-Christian*
patr	father, country	L, G	*paternal, patriarchal, patrilocal, expatriate, repatriate, sympatric, perpetrate, patron*
ped	foot	L	*pedal, centipede, expedite*
ped~paed	child, teach	G	*pediatric, encyclopedia, pedagogy, pedology, pedodontia, pedophilia, orthopedic, paedomorphism, paedogenic*
pha~phe	speak	G	*aphasia, phatic, emphasis, euphemism, blaspheme*
pher~phor	carry	G	*metaphor, peripheral, pheromone, hemapheresis, euphoria, phosphor, electrophoresis*
phyll	leaf	G	*chlorophyll, phylloid, phyllotaxis, heterophyllous, phyllophagous*
phyt	plant	G	*phytogenic, phytogenic, phytoplankton, neophyte*
pod~pus	foot	G	*podiatry, cephalopod, octopus, platypus*
pom	fruit	L	*pomegranate, pomade, pome, pomiferous, pomology, pomaceous*

Element	Gloss	Source	Examples
pred	preying	L	*predator, predacious, depredation, osprey*
rhiz	root	G	*rhizome, rhizopod, rhizophagous, mycorrhiza*
sal~sil	jump	L	*salient, salacious, saltitory, saltation, saltigrade, resilience*
salv~salu	safe, greet	L	*salvation, salvable, salvo, salubrious, salutary, salutatorian, salute*
soror	sister	L	*sorority, sororial, sororicide, sororate*
spor	scatter, seed	G	*sporadic, diaspora, sporogenesis, sporophyll, sporozoan*
the	put	G	*thesis, antithesis, prosthesis, anathema, epithet, parenthetical*
uxor	wife	L	*uxorious, uxorial, uxoricide, uxorilocal*
val	strong	L	*valor, valid, valence, valetudinarian, convalesce, prevalent*
voc	call, voice	L	*vocal, vociferous, vocation, invoke, convoke, evocative, revoke*

ELEMENT STUDY

1. Parse, gloss, and give allomorphs and brief dictionary definitions for the following words. Give your parses in the standard format: prefix- root -suffix.
    a. *effluent*
    b. *quincentennial*
    c. *interlocutor*

2. What is the root in these words? Look up each word and include a brief sentence about the relation between the root's literal meaning and its meaning in this word.
   Part 1: Chapter 10 elements:
   a. *value*
   b. *synthetic*
   c. *insult*
   d. *salacious*
   e. *infant*
   f. *latitude*
   g. *phratry*
   Part 2: Cumulative elements: Parse these words, identifying all the elements and their meaning.
   a. *astrobleme*
   b. *fratricide*
   c. *eloquent*
   d. *polygraph*
   e. *tachycardia*
3. False friends: **pl~plec~plic** 'fold, entwine, times' versus **ple** 'full, many'
   The elements **pl~plec~plic** 'fold, entwine, times' (chapter 6) and **ple** 'full, many' (chapter 9) look similar—even more so than their forms as represented here indicate, since along with being an allomorph of the element meaning 'fold, entwine, times', **pl** can also serve as an allomorph of the element **ple** 'full, many'. Using the simple glosses 'fold' and 'full' to identify the two elements, identify the root in each of these cases:
   i. *expletive*
   ii. *replica*
   iii. *apply*
   iv. *complement*
   v. *compliment*
4. False friends: **ped** 'foot' versus **paed~ped** 'child, teach':
   The element **ped** 'foot' shares an allomorph with **paed~ped** 'child, teach'. Which one is a root in the words below?

a. *pediatric*
   b. *pedonym*
   c. *impede*
   d. *pedestal*
   e. *pedarchy*
5. False friends: **metr** 'mother' versus **meter** 'measure'
   The element **metr** 'mother' is easy to confuse with another Greek root, **meter** 'measure', which has an allomorph **metr**, as in *metric*. Which of the two is a root element in the following? Note that the gloss 'mother' is extended to mean 'womb' as well.
   a. *symmetry*
   b. *clinometry*
   c. *metritis*
   d. *metrize*
   e. *metropathia*
6. It would be tempting but incorrect to consider the element **salv~salu** 'safe, greet' as the root in the word *salve*, meaning 'balm, ointment'. Look up the etymology of this word to find the correct origin.
7. With the help of dictionaries or a search engine, parse, gloss, and simply define the following electronics terms:
   a. *rheostat*
   b. *electrode*
   c. *anhysteresis*
   d. *fluorescent*
   e. *resistance*
   f. *impedance*
   g. *potentiometer*
   h. *superheterodyne*
   i. *commutator*
   j. *insulation*
8. Why do you think *cruciferous* vegetables such as broccoli, cabbage, and cauliflower are so called? The answer isn't obvious, but before looking it up, use your knowledge of word elements to make an educated guess.

EXERCISES

1. The members of each of the following pairs of words or boldface morphemes share a single Proto-Indo-European source. In each pair, one has been borrowed into English from Latin, French, or Greek while the other is an inherited, native Germanic word. On the basis of your knowledge of consonant correspondences, identify the word in each pair that is borrowed.
   a. *sediment, sitter*
   b. *float, pluvial*
   c. *cram, agora*
   d. *fantasy, beacon*
   e. *dough, figure*
   f. *spume, foam*
   g. *erode, rat*
   h. *farina, barn*
   i. *eaten, edible*
   j. *vehicle, wain*

2. Use Grimm's Law to identify a Latinate root that is cognate with the words *fill* and *full*, which are from the Germanic part of our vocabulary. Ignore the vowels. Hint: the Latinate root in question was in the element set from an earlier chapter.

3. Fill in the blanks using your knowledge of Grimm's law to complete the elements in this list of Greek and Latin root forms and their cognates in modern English. In your answers give the correspondences to the PIE consonants shown in **boldface** type. Leave empty the cells that are totally blank. Some cells in the rightmost column are intentionally left blank to avoid giving away the answer.

PIE	Greek	Latin	English word	PIE root meaning
a. *$\mathbf{d^h}$eu			_ew	'flow'
b. *$\mathbf{b^h}$eh₂	_a, _e	_a	_an	'speak'

PIE	Greek	Latin	English word	PIE root meaning
c. *bend			_en	'protruding point'
d. *bʰer	_er, _or	_er	_ear	'carry'
e. *pet	__er		_ea_er	'fly'
f. *ten	_on	_en(d)	_in	'stretch'
g. *ḱerd	_ard	_ord	_eart	
h. *bʰu	_yt		_e	'plant, grow'
i. *ḱer	_ran	_orn	_orn	'head'
j. *h₂eug	au_	au_	e_e	'increase'
k. *gel		_el	_ool	
l. *peh₂u	_ed	_auc	_ew	'little'
m. *terh₂		_rans	_rough	'cross over'
n. *kan		_an	_en	'sing'
o. *pah₂		_an 'bread'	_ood	
p. *sweh₂d	he_	sua_	swee_	'pleasant'
q. *treud		_rud 'push'	_rea_	'squeeze'
r. *dʰeh₁	_e	_ac 'make'	_o	'put, set'

Eleven

Later Changes

From Latin to French to English

Previous chapters made a direct link between current English vocabulary and Latin and Greek elements as they were spelled and pronounced in classical Roman times. This worked because the great bulk of our learned vocabulary was borrowed with the original Latin spelling. As a result, for all practical purposes English has incorporated much of the phonology and morphology of Latin into this higher vocabulary.

Nevertheless, classical Latin is not the end of the story. All languages change, even Latin. In this chapter we trace some of changes that Latin underwent since its classical period and show their impact on current English vocabulary.

LEARNED BORROWINGS

When words or morphemes are borrowed directly from written Latin, they are known as **learned**, or **scholarly**, **borrowings**. Learned borrowings present the fewest changes from classical Latin usage, but even they are by no means unchanged from the language of Cicero. When used in English, Latin words and word elements may have very different semantics, spelling, pronunciation, and endings.

Semantics

In chapter 7 we saw that words and elements change their meaning over time for many reasons. In the case of borrowings from Latin, the most important driver of change is the need to increase the word stock. Scholars and scientists have shown no reluctance to borrow Latin words in only their most technical meanings, or even to assign them meanings they never had in classical times. For example, in classical Latin, *continent-* meant 'continuous' or 'uninterrupted'. It could be applied to all sorts of objects, including land, in which case it meant 'mainland', as opposed to an island. The idea of reserving the word to apply specifically to one of the seven great landmasses of the world is a seventeenth-century invention that would have seemed quite foreign to the Romans.

Spelling

Since Roman times, spelling is what has changed the least. This is partly because earlier documents provide a model for later authors to follow—an especially attractive model for authors who as a group prided themselves on their knowledge of Latin. As a result, from the sixteenth century on, many words of Latin extraction are spelled as if they were still Latin. In the modern era, mass media and mass marketing have perhaps contributed to greater spelling conformity as well. In several cases, though, modern spelling departs from the classical norm. The ancient Romans did not distinguish uppercase from lowercase letters, nor did they distinguish the vowel *i* from the consonant *j* or the vowel *u* from the consonant *v*. These very useful distinctions were introduced in modern times, and we doubt that even the most classically inclined scholar believes that we should go back to spelling the Latin loanword *junior* as IVNIOR.

One prominent change in classical Latin spelling, however, is still a bit controversial. Classical Latin had two diphthongs, *ae* and *oe*, that eventually came to be pronounced the same as the letter *e*. It became so common to confuse these three forms that eventually people tended to give up and just write *e* in all cases, so that Latin *haesitation-* became *hesitation* and *poenal-* became *penal*. On the other hand, the diphthongal spelling is retained in proper names like *Caesar* and *Oedipus*, in the plural ending *-ae* as in *alumnae*, and in highly technical scientific terms like *paedomorphosis* or *coelacanth*. In between is a broad gray area. Is it *encyclopaedia* or *encyclopedia*? *Aesthete* or *esthete*? *Foetus* or *fetus*? Usage varies, with the United States often leading the way in abandoning the classical digraphs in favor of a single *e*.

Pronunciation

The third area of change in learned loans was in pronunciation. Classicists have been less successful at preserving Latin pronunciation than Latin spelling. Actually, until about a hundred years ago, even scholars tended to pronounce Latin—not just Latin loanwords in English but actual Latin text—with complicated rules far removed from the pronunciation of ancient Rome. Latin words have a surprisingly long history of phonetic changes. For example, *j* and *v*, which were approximants in classical Latin ([j] and [w]) but are obstruents in English ([dʒ] and [v]), are pronounced as obstruents in all the Romance languages—evidence of a sound change that must have occurred throughout Latin-speaking Europe before the Middle Ages. Recall from the Element Study in chapter 6 the Velar Softening rule, whereby Latin *c* and *g*, which were always velar [k] and [g] in classical Latin, are often pronounced [s] and [dʒ] in English. To be more precise, the sounds represented by these letters are pronounced more toward the front of the mouth before vowels that were front vowels in Late Latin. The English letters that correspond to these are ‹e, i, y, ae, oe›, as in *cell, gel, civics, gingival, cycle, gyrate, Caesar, algae, coelacanth*. But you will find lots of exceptions, especially if you look at words that are not Latinate, such as *kill, gill, Kyle*. Recently coined words can go either way, as attested by the fact that the GIF's inventor intended the pronunciation [dʒɪf], but many other speakers prefer the [g] of the source word *graphics*. It turns out that the Romance languages have a Velar Softening rule too, though the outcomes vary from language to language; this must also be a very old, though postclassical, sound change.

These changes entered English when English-speaking scholars imitated the pronunciation of continental European scholars—mostly from France—for whom these changes occurred throughout their language. French scholars pronounced the root *civ-* 'citizen' as [siv] instead of classical [kiːw] because "[w] > [v]" and "[k] > [s] before [i]" were regular sound changes in French. English speakers pronounced *civ-* as [siv] because they learned how to pronounce Latin words from the French. English speakers did not change [w] to [v] in native words like *wind*, nor did they change [k] to [s] in words like *kiss*.

Other changes are entirely the work of English speakers. Many of the vowels are pronounced quite differently from anything heard in ancient Rome. Most noteworthy is that many vowels were lengthened and subsequently raised or diphthongized, or both, during the Great Vowel Shift (chapter 2). As a consequence, Latin *a*, *e*, and *i* are often pronounced [e], [i], and [aɪ] in English.

These changes are by now hundreds of years old and well established in English. It is difficult to imagine that zealous reformers will ever convince English speakers to restore classical Latin pronunciations on any great scale, turning familiar words like *circus* into ancient forms like [kɪrkʊs]. However, we have noticed people undoing the Great Vowel Shift in several words and phrases like *re* (formerly [ri], now mostly [re]), *per diem* (older [daɪəm], now mostly [diəm]), and in *-i* plurals as in *stimuli* and *fungi* (older [aɪ], now often [i]). Even people who don't speak Latin seem to understand that the Great Vowel Shift is unique to English, and they seek to supply more authentic-sounding pronunciations to words they perceive as foreign in origin.

Endings

Many Latin and Greek words have been borrowed whole, in their original citation form. Thus, nouns from chapter 9 that take Latin plurals retain their Latin singular endings as well, as do many more words that take normal English plurals, like *camera*, *bonus*, and *senator*.

The more general pattern, however, is for words to change or drop their endings when they are borrowed into English. There are at least two reasons for this. The first is that Latin endings have many functions that do not carry over to English. For example, *citabar* 'I was being cited' is broken down into the root *cit*, the verb marker *-a-*, the imperfective suffix *-ba-*, and the passive suffix *-r*. It must have seemed more natural to get rid of that complexity by stripping off the ending entirely, leaving simply the stem *cit-*. By adding only a silent *e*, English wound up with a word that looked like and could be used like any native English word, with no unnecessary inflectional apparatus.

Sound change is a second factor in the loss or simplification of Latin endings. In French, syllables after the stressed one were generally lost or turned into *e*. This, naturally, got rid of many inflectional endings. Because Latin words that were inherited by French as a daughter language had reduced or lost their inflectional endings, it must have been natural to think of applying the same changes to words when scholars borrowed them directly from Latin. As in other matters related to Latinity, French precedent strongly influenced English usage. In most, though by no means all, Latin words borrowed into English, endings are discarded or replaced by silent *-e*. Very often we ended up with Latin words in their stem form. Words like *legislature*, *contradict*, *natal*, *nation*, *omnipotent*, and *procure* never appear in such guises in Latin, but such shortened, endingless words are the norm for Latin borrowings in English as in French.

The rest of the learned borrowing is normally spelled like the original Latin, sometimes with adjustments based on Old French sound changes. For example, *tabula*, whose Latin stem ends in a vowel plus [l], lost that vowel in French and added a final *e*, giving *table* in French and subsequently in English. The full original Latin stem is still visible in derivatives like *tabular*. The same applies to Latin *corpusculum*, *circulus*, and the suffix *-abilis*, which become *corpuscle*, *circle*, and *-able* in English. The Latin adjective-forming suffix *-os-*, which we find in English *bellicose*, more often appears in the Old French form *-ous*, as in English *laborious*.

Another common alteration from Old French replaces the root *fic* 'make' with *-fy* at the end of the word, as in *beautify* (cf. *beautification*).

It is hardly surprising that Latin words changed, especially considering that they were passed down through French over the course of a millennium or so. What is remarkable, though, is that, except for having a French ending, a huge number of these words look exactly like they did in Latin! The explanation for this in almost all cases is that after the word was borrowed into English from French, scholars went back and restored the original Latin stem. Possibly they wished to preserve the pattern noted back in chapter 1, whereby borrowings from French were more common words (like *chief* and *chef*), while the more learned borrowings (like *capital*) were based directly on Latin. They didn't restore the Latin endings, though, following the well-established precedent for dropping the original endings from words borrowed directly from Latin.

In their zeal to make English look more like Latin than like French, scholars occasionally went overboard. The root in our word *scissors* goes back to Latin *cis* 'cut' as in *incision* and *incisors*. But before coming into English, *scissors* passed into French, where it became *cisoires*. Late-fifteenth-century scholars, bent on restoring the root to its original Latin form, wrongly guessed that the Latin root was *scind* 'split' (as in *rescind*). An allomorph of *scind* is *sciss* (as in *rescission*), and that allomorph is the one that was "restored" in our word *scissors*, which by all rights ought to have come to us as *cisors*. According to the *Oxford English Dictionary*, the confusion may have been due to a postclassical Latin word *scissor* meaning 'tailor', among other things.

BORROWINGS FROM POPULAR FRENCH

In contrast to the learned borrowings we discussed in the previous section, many words that English borrowed from French don't look very much like the Latin words they descended from. For example, we saw in chapter 1 that the word *chief*, which was borrowed from Old French, descended from the Latin morpheme *cap*. Similarly, *friar* is not spelled like its ancestor *frater*, and *voyage* is not spelled like *viaticum*. In general, no attempt is made to spell words in a Latin fashion if they are not perceived as Latin words. This can happen if the original word was never written down in classical Latin texts. If *language* ever existed as a Latin word, something like **linguaticum*, it was no doubt coined long after the classical Latin period. Other words may date back to classical times but were not used in the standard literary style of Latin and so were never or only rarely written down. Such words are said to descend from popular Latin, which is often called Vulgar Latin. For example, English borrowed the word *river* from Old French, but the classical Latin words for 'river' were *amnis* and *flumen*. The word *river* must have come from a Vulgar Latin word like **riparia*.

Perhaps a more important reason why people didn't respell words like *voyage*, *chief*, and *friar* in a Latin fashion is that these words just don't seem like Latin. They had changed so much in the thousand years or so since the classical Latin period that their original Latin roots were unrecognizable. Words that descend naturally from Latin into French, accumulating changes over the centuries, without being affected by scholarly knowledge of Latin, are called **popular French** words. When they are borrowed into English, their relationship to the Latin morphemes we have been studying in this book may be irregular or flat-out obscure.

Explaining all the changes that took place between Latin and Old French would be a massive undertaking, but here are some useful highlights.

Deletions

French usually preserved, in one form or another, the beginning of the word and the stressed vowel (here underlined). Other vowels were often deleted.

periculosum	*perilous, parlous*
rotundum	*round*
cadentiam	*chance*

*foc**a**rium*   *foyer*
*rati**o**nem*   *reason*

Coronalizations

Besides the coronalization reflected even in scholarly loans, several more types affected popular words. As expected, Velar Softening turned c [k] into ch [tʃ] before Latin nonlow vowels. Various other changes also produced palatal or postalveolar sounds:

cap-	*chief*
cantum	*chant*
gaudium	*joy*
judicem	*judge*
diurnalem	*journal*
cambiat	*change*
fructum	*fruit*
legalem	*loyal*

Diphthongizations

Probably the changes most characteristic of Old French were the **diphthongizations**: simple Latin vowels turning into diphthongs. Many of these later turned back into simple vowels, so often the most explicit evidence for the diphthongization is in the spelling, which still has two vowel letters.

fidem	*faith*
manutenet	*maintain*
pictum	*paint*
sanctum	*saint*
punctum	*point*

Later Changes

WORD ELEMENTS

Element	Gloss	Source	Examples
al	wing	L	*aliform, ala, alar, alary, alate, aliferous, aliped, alula*
api	bee	L	*apiary, apiculture, apian, apiarist*
arachn	spider	G	*arachnid, arachnoid, arachnean, arachnodactyly, arachnophobia*
bov	cow	L	*bovine, bovate, bovid, Ovibos*
bu~bou	cow	G	*bucolic, bulimia, butyric, boustrophedon*
chir	hand	G	*chiropractor, chiropodist, chiromancy, Chiroptera, enchiridion*
clam~claim	call out	L	*clamor, clamant, conclamation, acclaim, declaim, reclaim*
clav	key	L	*clavier, clavichord, clavicle, claviger, autoclave, conclave, enclave, exclave*
col~cul	inhabit, grow	L	*colony, arboricole, saxicole, arenicolous, cultivate, culture, horticulture*
curs~curr	run	L	*cursor, cursory, cursive, discursive, excursive, incursion, precursor, curriculum, current, concur, recur*
dendr~dry	tree	G	*rhododendron, philodendron, dendriform, dendrite, dendrochronology, dryad*
dent	tooth	L	*dental, dentition, edentate, trident*
dyn	power	G	*dynamo, dyne, dynasty, dynamic, aerodyne*
en~oen	wine	G	*enology, oenophile, oenomel, oenotherapy*
ev	age	L	*medieval, coeval, primeval, longevity*

Element	Gloss	Source	Examples
formic	ant	L	*formic, formicary, formicivorous*
herp~herpet	to creep, reptile	G	*herpes, herpetology, herpetism*
hor	hour	G	*horoscope, horology, horologe, horometry*
ichthy	fish	G	*ichthyology, ichthyosis, ichthyism, Ichthyornis, Ichthyopsida*
lu~lv	dissolve	L	*solution, dissolute, solvent, dissolve*
ly	loosen	G	*analysis, dialysis, electrolyte, lyotropic*
mal	bad	L	*malice, malicious, malign, malefactor, maleficent, malevolent*
mant~manc	prophesy	G	*necromancy, ceromancy, mantic, chiromantic, praying mantis*
mun	public service, gift	L	*municipal, munificent, commune, communicate, immune, remunerate*
nau	boat	G	*nautical, astronaut, nautilus, Argonaut, nausea*
nav	boat	L	*naval, navigate, nave, navicular*
null	nothing	L	*null, nullify, nullity, annul*
odont	tooth	G	*periodontal, mastodon, odontoid, orthodonture*
oo	egg	G	*oocyte, oogamous, oology, oolite*
orn~ornith	bird	G	*ornithology, ornithomancy, ornithosis, notornis*
ov	egg	L	*ovum, ovary, ovule, ovulate, oval, ovate, ovoid*
ox~oxy	sharp	G	*oxymoron, oxygen, oxycephaly, paroxysm, oxytone, oxyacetylene, oxalic, amphioxus*
phag	eat	G	*sarcophagus, phagocyte, anthropophagy, bacteriophage, dysphagia*

Element	Gloss	Source	Examples
pithec	ape	G	*Pithecanthropus, pithecan, pithecological, Australopithecus, Dryopithecus*
plac	please	L	*placate, placid, placebo, implacable*
plac	flat	G	*placoid, placenta*
pter	wing	G	*pterodactyl, helicopter, pteridophyte, pteridology, apterous, archaeopteryx*
rog	ask	L	*interrogate, rogatory, supererogatory, abrogate, prerogative, subrogate, surrogate*
sen	old (person)	L	*senior, senile, senescent, senator, senectitude, senopia*
serp	to creep, snake	L	*serpent, serpentine, serpigo, serpolet, Serpula*
som~somat	body	G	*psychosomatic, soma, somatic, somatogenic, somatotype, acrosome, chromosome*
soph	wise	G	*sophisticated, sophist, sophistry, sophomore, philosophy, theosophy, gastrosoph*
strat	stretch, level, layer	L	*stratum, stratify, stratigraphy, stratus, prostrate, substrate*
tel~tele	end, complete	G	*teleology, teleorganic, telencephalon, telephase, telesis, telic*
trop	to turn	G	*heliotrope, trope, tropism, tropotaxis, entropy, phototropic*
verm	worm	L	*vermicelli, vermicular, vermiform, vermifuge, vermouth*
vin	wine	L	*vine, vinaceous, viniculture, vinegar*
xyl	wood	G	*xylophone, xylem, xylograph, xyloid, xylose, xylophagous*

ELEMENT STUDY

1. What is the root in these words? Look up each word and include a brief sentence about the relation between the root's literal meaning and its meaning in this word.

   Part 1: Chapter 11 elements:
   a. *curriculum*
   b. *indent*
   c. *lysis*
   d. *nave*
   e. *tropical*

   Part 2: Cumulative elements. Identify and gloss all the elements in these words:
   a. *expugnable*
   b. *mandate*
   c. *strategy*
   d. *navigate*
   e. *vociferous*

2. False friends: **plac** 'please' vs. **plac** 'flat':
   Chapter 11 has two identical elements **plac**. One comes from Latin and the other from Greek. Here are examples of each from the text: **plac** 'please' (L.) *placate, placid, placebo, implacable;* **plac** 'flat' (G.) *placoid, placenta.*
   Which form, the Latin-derived or the Greek-derived **plac**, is in these words? Use the Latin or Greek origins of the other elements in the word to guide your answer.
   a. *placable*
   b. *placoderm*
   c. *pleasant*
   d. *placebo*

3. False friends: **pl~plec~plic** 'fold, entwine, times' versus **ple** 'full, many' versus **plac** 'please' versus **plac** 'flat':
   In the following list of words, the root morpheme comes from the set **pl~plec~plic** 'fold, entwine, times' (chapter 6), **ple** 'full,

Later Changes 269

many' (chapter 9), **plac** 'please' (chapter 11), and **plac** 'flat' (chapter 11). Note that quite a few use allomorphs not listed here, so you may need to look them up. Identify which of these is the root in each of the following words:
   a. *plate*
   b. *place*
   c. *placque*
   d. *placoid*
   e. *replete*
   f. *reply*
   g. *ply*
   h. *platitude*
   i. *placenta*
   j. *polyplacophoran*
4. Here are some phobias using elements from our morpheme sets or roots that you may recognize. What do you think they mean? For the best guess, use both your knowledge of morphemes and your knowledge of conditions that affect humans.
   a. *aerophobia*
   b. *algophobia*
   c. *autophobia*
   d. *cryophobia*
   e. *dysmorphophobia*
   f. *gamophobia*
   g. *iatrophobia*
   h. *nyctophobia*
   i. *phobophobia*
   j. *scopophobia*
5. What would be appropriate terms for the following phobias and manias?
   a. abnormal fear of depths
   b. abnormal fear of spiders
   c. abnormal fear of dogs
   d. abnormal fear of animals

e. abnormal fear of snakes
f. obsession with males
g. obsession with wine
h. obsession with cutting (said of overeager surgeons)
i. obsession with solitude
j. obsession with foreign things

6. Use the literal meanings of the word elements to express these doctors' specialties:
    a. orthodontist
    b. periodontist
    c. chiropodist
    d. gerontologist
    e. ophthalmologist

7. Parse and gloss the following words, using their definitions as guides to associating their analyzed and actual current meanings.
    a. *myriapod* 'arthropod with long, segmented body'
    b. *senopia* 'changes in lenticular elasticity, due to sclerosis, at a stage following presbyopia'
    c. *ichthyosis* 'skin disorder characterized by rough, dry skin with platelike hardenings'
    d. *complacency* 'smugness' (*com-* is intensive)
    e. *communion* 1. 'a Christian religious denomination'; 2. 'the Eucharist'
    f. *coeval* 'isochronous' (*-al* = ADJECTIVE)
    g. *altiloquent* 'sesquipedalian'
    h. *entropy* 'total measure of energy (specifically, in the universe) not available for work'

8. The following words are taken from the field of philosophy. Using an unabridged dictionary and a glossary of morphemes, briefly define, parse, and gloss each term.
    a. *monothelitism*
    b. *encratism*
    c. *theophany*
    d. *metempsychosis*
    e. *panentheism*

Later Changes

9. Find the word in the following list that best matches each dictionary definition given. A search engine and a good dictionary should help identify enough unfamiliar morphemes to assist you. Some of the words are decoys. Use no word more than once. Work from definition to word. Avoid multiple answers, but if you can't decide between two choices, give both choices and explain the problem.
   1. *dynotrusion*
   2. *Cynodontia*
   3. *degramic*
   4. *metastasis*
   5. *hypergamy*
   6. *androgynous*
   7. *tmesis*
   8. *peristaltic*
   9. *protuse*
   10. *delectation*
   11. *inculpatory*
   12. *pantocrator*
   13. *homeoregion*
   14. *anthobrach*
   15. *ectropion*
   16. *ergatogyne*
   17. *nephropathy*
   18. *telegenic*
   19. *epiopticon*
   20. *mastobrach*
   21. *ambiplasty*
   22. *epipodium*
   23. *symplectic*
   24. *theurgy*
   25. *illative*
   26. *anthophyte*
   27. *epiphonema*

28. *epiphilious*

a. ___ An abnormal turning out of a part of the body (e.g., of an eyelid).
b. ___ Pertaining to the grammatical case denoting movement into a place or thing.
c. ___ Relating to or being an intergrowth of two different minerals.
d. ___ Marriage into a higher social class or caste.
e. ___ A division of Triassic Therapsida comprising a number of small carnivorous reptiles often with cusps on the teeth resembling those of certain mammals.
f. ___ A flowering plant.
g. ___ The omnipotent lord of the universe.
h. ___ An occult art by which one may evoke or utilize the aid of divine and beneficent spirits.
i. ___ A wingless queen ant resembling a worker.
j. ___ A summary argument concluding a discourse.
k. ___ A lateral ridge or fold along either side of the foot of various gastropods.
l. ___ The separation of the parts of a compound word by intervening words (e.g., of *another* in *a whole nother thing*).

EXERCISES

1. Using the meanings of Latin and Greek morphemes you've learned or can find in a glossary, and the information on typical changes in the forms of words in Romance languages illustrated in this chapter, give the English word borrowed from French that comes from the Latin word shown. The first two items are completed as examples. You may use a dictionary to confirm your answers.

Later Changes   273

	Latin	**French > English**
a.	*tractum*	____trait____
b.	*musculum*	___muscle___
c.	*diversitatem*	_____
d.	*lacte*	café au _____
e.	*planum*	_____
f.	*magister*	_____
g.	*catena*	_____

2. Based on your knowledge of sound changes in the development from Latin to French as well as plausible semantic changes, draw from the following list ten pairs of doublet words or phonemes, where one item is a learned Latin borrowing and the other item comes from the same word but was affected by popular French changes. Ignore parts in parentheses. Many of the words are decoys.

solid
fancy
fang
wide
capit(al)
capt(ure)
clam(or)
couch
emblem
chase
junct(ion)
cadence
employ
involve
choir
contin(ent)
chorus

rouge

fantasy

ruby

joint

claim

journey

char(coal)

calm

implic(ate)

chance

rouse

contain

isle

view

insul(ate)

video

APPENDIX 1

Elements to Glosses

Element	Gloss	Chapter	Source
a-~an-	not, without	3, 4	G
-a	[plural]	9	L, G
ab-~abs-	from, away	3, 6	L
-able~-ible~-ble	A	3, 11	L
abs-~ab-	from, away	3, 6	L
ac	sharp	9	L
-ac	A	9	G
-acl~-acul (< -l diminutive)	little	9	L
-acle~-acule (< -l diminutive)	little	9	L
acr	height, tip	9	G
ad-	to, toward	3, 6	L
aden	gland	8	G
-ae	[plural]	9	L
aesth~esth	feel	5	G
ag~ig	act, do, drive	5	L
agr	field	9	L
-al~-ial	A	9	L
al	other	10	L
al	wing	11	L
al~ol~ul	nurture, grow	4	L
alb	white	9	L
alg	pain	8	G

APPENDIX 1

Element	Gloss	Chapter	Source
all~allel	other	10	G
alt (< *al* 'grow')	high	5	L
am~im	love	4	L
ambul	walk, go	5	L
an-~a-	not, without	3, 4	G
ana-	up, again, back	3, 6	G
-ance	N	3, 4	L
-and~-end	N [gerundive]	9	L
andr	male, man	5	G
anim	soul, mind, spirit, (nonplant) life	2	L
ann~enn	year	4	L
-ant	A, N [present participle]	3, 9	L
ante-~anti-	before	3	L
anthrop	human	1	G
anti-~ante-	before	3	L
api	bee	11	L
apo-	away from, off	3	G
apt~ept	fit, capable	4	L
arachn	spider	11	G
arch	first, govern	5	G
-arium	place	9	L
-ary	A, N	3	L
aster~astr	star	9	G
-ate	N, A, V	3, 7	L
aud	hear	9	L
aur	ear	8	L
auto~tauto	self	9	G
av	bird	5	L
axill	armpit	8	L
bath~bathy	depth	9	G
bell	war	6	L
bene~bon	good, well	9	L
bi	two	6	L

APPENDIX 1

Element	Gloss	Chapter	Source
bi	life	1	G
bin	two (each)	6	L
bl~bol	throw, extend	4	G
-ble~-able~-ible	A	3, 11	L
bol~bl	throw, extend	4	G
bon~bene	good	9	L
bou~bu	cow	11	G
bov	cow	11	L
brach~brachy	short	9	G
bu~bou	cow	11	G
cac	bad	1	G
cad~cas~cid	fall	5	L
cap~cep~cip~cup	take, contain	4	L
car~carn	flesh	9	L
card	heart	10	G
carn~car	flesh	9	L
cas~cad~cid	fall	5	L
cata-	down, backward	3	G
caud~cod	tail	8	L
ced~cess	go, let go	5	L
cens	judge, assess	6	L
cent	hundred	6	L
cep~cap~cip~cup	take, contain	4	L
cephal	head	6	G
cer~cri~cre	separate	4	L
cervic	neck	8	L
chili	thousand	6	G
chir	hand	11	G
chrom	color	1	G
chron	time	1	G
cid~cad~cas	fall	5	L
cid~cis	cut, kill	4	L
cip~cap~cep~cup	take, contain	4	L

Element	Gloss	Chapter	Source
cis~cid	cut, kill	4	L
clam	call out	11	L
clav	key, locked	11	L
-cl~-cul (< -l diminutive)	little	9	L
cli	lean, lie, bed	9	L, G
clud~clus	close (v)	5	L
co-~con-~com-	with, together	3	L
col	inhabit, grow	11	L
con-~com-~co-	with, together	3	L
contra-~counter-	against, facing	3	L
cord	heart	10	L
corp~corpor	body, flesh	2, 3	L
cosm	universe, adorn, order	1	G
counter-~contra-	against, facing	3	L
crac~crat	govern	6	G
crat~crac	govern	6	G
cre~cri~cer	separate	4	L
cred	believe	9	L
cri	judge, separate	4	G
cri~cre~cer	separate	4	L
cruc	cross, important point	10	L
cryph~cryp	secret, hidden	9	G
cub~cumb	lie down, remain	4	L
-cule~-cle (< -l diminutive)	little	9	L
culp	fault	2	L
cumb~cub	lie down, remain	4	L
cup~cap~cep~cip	take, contain	4	L
cur	care	6	L
curs~curr	run	11	L
cut	skin	8	L
da~do~di	give	9	L
damn~demn	loss, harm	9	L

APPENDIX 1

Element	Gloss	Chapter	Source
de-	reverse, from	3, 7	L
de~div	god, augury	4	L
dec	acceptable	10	L
deca	ten	6	G
decem	ten	6	L
decim~deci-	tenth	6	L
dem	people	6	G
demn~damn	loss, harm	9	L
den	ten (each)	6	L
dendr~dry	tree	11	G
dent	tooth	11	L
dermat~derm	skin	8	G
deuter	second	6	G
di~da~do	give	9	L
di~dy	two	6	G
dia-	through	3	G
dic	say, point	9	L
dich (< *di*)	(split in) two	6	G
dipl	double	6	G
div~de	god, augury	4	L
do	give	9	G
do~da~di	give	9	L
doc	teach	5	L
doc~dog	opinion	5	G
dol	suffer	9	L
duc	to lead	2	L
dy~di	two	6	G
dyn	power	11	G
e-~ex-	out	3, 6, 7	L
ec-	out	3	G
ecto-	outside	3	G
ed~es	eat	10	L
-ell (< -*l* diminutive)	little	9	L
em~hem~haem	blood	8	G

Element	Gloss	Chapter	Source
-eme	[abstract unit]	4	G
en-	in	3	G
-ence	N	3, 4	L
-end~-and	N [gerundive]	9	L
endo-	inside	3	G
enn~ann	year	4	L
ennea	nine	6	G
-ent	A, N [present participle]	3, 9	L
epi-	on, over	3	G
ept~apt	fit, capable	4	L
equ~iqu	even, level	4	L
erg~urg~org	work	4	G
ero	physical love	5	G
err	wander, do wrong	9	L
-esc~-sc	begin	9	L
-esim	-th (ordinal number)	6	L
esth~aesth	feel	5	G
eu-	good	5	G
ev	age	11	L
ex-~e-	out	3, 6, 7	L
extra- (< *ex*-)	outside	3, 7	L
fa	speak	10	L
fac~fec~fic	do, make	4	L
fec~fac~fic	do, make	4	L
fer	carry	10	L
fic~fec~fac	do, make	4	L
fla	blow	6	L
flu~fluc~fluv	flow, river	9	L
formic	ant	11	L
frag~frang~fring	break	4	L
frang~frag~fring	break	4	L
fratr	brother	10	L
fring~frag~frang	break	4	L

APPENDIX 1

Element	Gloss	Chapter	Source
fug	flee	2	L
fund~fus	pour, melt, blend	4	L
fus~fund	pour, melt, blend	4	L
galact	milk	8	G
gam	marry, unite	1	G
gastr	stomach	8	G
ge	earth	10	G
gemin	twin	10	L
gen~gn~na	birth, type, origin	4	L
gen~gon	birth	4	G
ger	old person	10	G
giga	giant, billion	6	G
gloss~glott	tongue, speech	9	G
gn~gen~na	birth, type, origin	4	L
gno	know	9	G
gno~no~gni	know	9	L
gon~gen	birth	4	G
grad~gred~gress	step, go	5	L
graph~gramm	write	10	G
grat	goodwill, thankful, pleased, kind	2	L
gravid (< *grav* 'heavy')	pregnant	8	G
gred~grad~gress	step, go	5	L
greg	social group, gather	2	L
gress~grad~gred	step, go	5	L
gyn~gynec	woman, female	9	G
haem~hem~em	blood	8	G
hecaton	hundred	6	G
heli	sun	5	G
hem~haem~em	blood	8	G
hemi-	half	6	G
hepat	liver	8	G
hepta	seven	6	G

Element	Gloss	Chapter	Source
her~hes	to stick, hold back	9	L
herp~herpet	to creep, reptile	11	G
hes~her	to stick, hold back	9	L
hetero-	other, different	3	G
hexa	six	6	G
hist	body tissue	8	G
hom	human	2	L
homo-	same	3	G
hor	hour	11	G
hydr~hydat	water	9	G
hypo-	under, below, partial	3	G
hyster	womb, neurotic disorder	8	G
-i-	[empty interfix]	3	L
-ia	land, state, medical condition	8	G, L
-ial~-al	A	9	L
iatr	heal	1	G
-ible~-able~-ble	A	3, 11	L
-ic	A, N	3	G, L
ichthy	fish	11	G
-icl~-icul (< -l diminutive)	little	9	L
icosa	twenty	6	G
idi	personal	1	G
ig~ag	act, do, drive	5	L
-il	A	4, 9	L
-ill (< -l diminutive)	little	9	L
im~am	love	4	L
in-	not	3	L
in-	in, into	3	L
infra-	below, after	3	L
inter-	between, among	3	L
intra-	within	3	L
iqu~equ	even, level	4	L

APPENDIX 1

Element	Gloss	Chapter	Source
iso-	equal	3	G
-itis	inflammation	8	G
-ity	N	3	L
-ium~-um	thing [singular]	9	L
-ive~-tive	A, N	3, 4, 6	L
-ize	V	3	G
jun~juven	young	10	L
jus~jur	law, judge	9	L
juven~jun	young	10	L
kilo-	thousand	6	G
-l	[diminutive] little	9	L
lab	lip	8	L
lachrym~lacrim	tear [tir]	8	L
lacrim~lachrym	tear [tir]	8	L
lact	milk	8	L
laryng	voice box	8	G
lat	carry	10	L
leg	law, deputize	2	L
leg~lex~log	speak, study	1	G
leg~lig	gather, read	5	L
lex~leg~log	word, speak	1	G
libr	balance, weigh	2	L
lic	permit, unrestrained	5	L
lig	tie, bind	10	L
lig~leg	gather, read	5	L
lign	wood	10	L
lit~lith	stone	9	L
liter	letter	2	L
lith~lit	stone	9	G
loc	place	6	L
locu~loqu	speak	10	L

Element	Gloss	Chapter	Source
log~leg~lex	speak, study	1	G
loqu~locu	speak	10	L
lu~lv	dissolve	11	L
lumen~lumin~luc	light	6	L
ly	loosen	11	G
-ma	thing [singular]	9	G
macr	large	1	G
magn	great, large	10	L
mal~male	bad	11	L
mamm	breast	8	L
man	hand, handle	6	L
mant~manc	prophesy	11	G
matr	mother	10	L
mega~megal	great, million	9	G
men~mon	think, mind	4	L
-ment	N	9	L
meso-	middle	3	G
meta-	beyond	3	G
metr	mother, uterus	10	G
micr	small	1	G
mille	thousand	6	L
milli-	thousandth	6	L
mis	hate	1	G
misc~mix	mix	9	L
mitt~miss	send	3, 4	L
mne	remember	4	G
mo	move	4	L
mon	one	6	G
mon~men	remind, think	4	L
-mony	N	9	L
morph	shape, form	1	G
mov~mo	move	4	L
mult	many	6	L

APPENDIX 1

Element	Gloss	Chapter	Source
mun	public service, gift	11	L
myc	fungus	10	G
myri	countless, ten thousand	6	G
na~gen~gn	birth, source, tribe	4	L
nano-	billionth	6	G
nar~nas	nose	8	L
nas~nar	nose	8	L
nau	boat	11	G
nav	boat	11	L
-nd~-and~-end	N [gerundive]	9	L
ne	new, recent	5	G
nec~noc~nic~nox	harm	4	L
nec~necr	die	4	G
nephr	kidney	8	G
nic~nec~noc~nox	harm	4	L
nihil~nil	nothing	9	L
no~gno~gni	know	9	L
noc~nec~nic~nox	harm	4	L
noct	night	10	L
nom	law, system	1	G
nomen~nomin	name	10	L
non	ninth	6	L
nov	new	2	L
novem	nine	6	L
noven	nine (each)	6	L
nox~noc~nec~nic	harm	4	L
-nt	A, N [present participle]	3, 9	L
null	nothing	11	L
nyct	night	10	G
-o-	[empty interfix]	3	G
ob-	toward, against	3	L
octa	eight	6	G

Element	Gloss	Chapter	Source
octav	eighth	6	L
octo	eight	6	L
octon	eight (each)	6	L
ocul	eye	9	L
odont	tooth	11	G
oen~en	wine	11	G
-oid (A, N)	resembling	3	G
ol~al	nurture, grow	4	L
-ol (< -l diminutive)	little	9	L
olig	few	6	G
-oma	tumor, growth	8	G
omn	all	2, 6	L
-on	N [singular] thing	9	G
onom~onomat~onym	name	10	G
oo	egg	11	G
op	see	8	G
ophthalm	eye	8	G
org~erg~urg	work	4	G
orn~ornith	bird	11	G
orth	straight, correct	10	G
-ory	A, N	3	L
os~or	mouth, opening	8	L
oss	bone	8	L
oss~os	bone	8	L
oste	bone	8	G
-ous~-ose	A	3	L
ov	egg	11	L
ox~oxy	sharp	11	G
paed~ped	child, teach	10	G
pale~palae	old	10	G
pan-~pant-	all	6	G
par	give birth to	2	L
para-	beside, nearly	3	G

APPENDIX 1

Element	Gloss	Chapter	Source
path	feel, illness	1	G
patr	father, country	10	G, L
pauc	few	6	L
ped	foot	10	L
ped~paed	child, teach	10	G
pen~pun	punish	9	L
pend~pond	hang, weigh	4	L
penta	five	6	G
per-	through, thorough	3	L
peri-	around, near	3	G
pet	seek, go to	2	L
petr	rock	1	G
pha~phe	speak	10	G
phag	eat	11	G
phe~pha	speak	10	G
pher~phor	carry	10	G
phil	liking, tendency	1	G
phleb	vein	8	G
phob	fear	8	G
phon	sound	1	G
phor~pher	carry	10	G
phot~phos	light	5	G
phylac	guard	8	G
phyll	leaf	10	G
phyt	plant	10	G
pithec	ape	11	G
pl~plec~plic	fold, entwine, times	6	L
plac	please	11	L
plac	flat	11	G
ple	full, many	9	L
plec~pl~plic	times, fold, entwine	6	L
plic~pl~plec	times, fold, entwine	6	L
plur	many, more	6	L
pne~pneum	breathe, lung	8	G

Element	Gloss	Chapter	Source
pod~pus	foot	10	G
pol	community	1	G
poly	many	6	G
pom	fruit, apple	10	L
pon~pos	place, put	9	L
pond~pend	hang, weigh	4	L
pos~pon	place, put	9	L
poss~pot	able, powerful	2	L
post-	after, behind	3	L
pot	able, powerful	2	L
prac	act, do	5	G
pre-	before	3	L
pred	preying	10	L
prim	first	6	L
pro-	forward, for	3	L, G
prob	good, test	2	L
prot	first	6	G
pseud	false	1	G
psych	mind	1	G
pter	wing, feather	11	G
pugn (< *pug*)	fist, fight	9	L
pulm~pulmon	lung	8	L
pun~pen	punish	9	L
pus~pod	foot	10	G
pyr	fire	1	G
quadr	four	6	L
quart	fourth	6	L
quatern	four (each)	6	L
quin	five (each)	6	L
quinque	five	6	L
quint	fifth	6	L
re-~red-	again, back	3, 4, 6	L

APPENDIX 1

Element	Gloss	Chapter	Source
reg~rig	rule, straight	5	L
rhin	nose	8	G
rhiz	root	10	G
rig~reg	rule, straight	5	L
rog	ask	11	L
sacr~sanc~secr	holy	4	L
sal~sil	jump	10	L
salv~salu	safe, greet, healthy	10	L
sarc	flesh	8	G
-sc~-esc	begin	9	L
sci (< *sec*)	know, discern	2	L
scind~sciss (< *sec*)	split	2, 11	L
scler	hard	8	G
se-~sed-	apart	3, 6	L
sec	cut, split	2	L
semen~semin	seed	4	L
semi-	half	6	L
sen	old (person)	11	L
sen	six (each)	6	L
sent~sens	feel	5	L
sep	putrid, infected	8	G
septem	seven	6	L
septen	seven (each)	6	L
septim	seventh	6	L
serp	to creep, snake	11	L
sesqui-	one and a half	6	L
sex	six	6	L
sext	sixth	6	L
sil~sal	jump	10	L
-sis	N	3	L
som~somat	body	11	G
somn	sleep	2	L
son	sound	6	L

Element	Gloss	Chapter	Source
soph	wise	11	G
soror	sister	10	L
spec~spic	look, see	4	L
spor	scatter, seed	10	G
sta~ste	stand, state	4	G
sta~ste~sti~st	stand, state	4	L
sti~sta~ste~st	stand, state	4	L
stom~stomat	mouth, opening	8	G
strat	stretch, level, layer	11	L
sub-	under, inferior	3, 6, 7	L
super-	above, excessive	3	L
syn-	with, together	3, 6	G
-t	[perfect participle]	9	L
tac	arrange, order	9	G
tach~tachy	fast	9	G
tag~teg~tig~tang~ting	touch	4	L
tauto~auto	self	9	G
teg~tag~tig~tang~ting	touch	4	L
tel~tele	end, complete	11	G
tele	far	5	G
tempor	time	3	L
ten~tend~tens	stretch, thin	5	L
ten~tin	hold, maintain	4	L
tend~tens~ten	stretch, thin	5	L
tern	three (each)	6	L
terr	earth	9	L
terti	third	6	L
tetra~tessara	four	6	G
the	put, place	10	G
the	god	1	G
thromb	clot	8	G
tig~ting~tag~teg~tang	touch	4	L
-tion~-ion	N	3	L

APPENDIX 1

Element	Gloss	Chapter	Source
-tive~-ive	A, N	2, 3, 6	L
tom~tm	cut	4	G
top	place	1	G
tot	whole, all	6	L
tra-~trans-	across, through	3, 6	L
trans-~tra-	across, through	3, 6	L
tri	three	6	L
tri	three	6	G
trich (< *tri*)	three (parts)	6	G
trit	third	6	G
trop	to turn	11	G
trud~trus	thrust	5	L
-ture~-ure	N	9	L
-ty	N	4, 9	L
-ule (< -*l* diminutive)	little	9	L
-um~-ium	thing [singular]	9	L
un	one	6	L
urg~erg~org	work	4	G
-us	N, A [masculine singular]	9	L
uxor	wife	10	L
vac~van	empty	9	L
val	strong, useful	10	L
van~vac	empty	9	L
vas	vessel, blood vessel, duct	8	L
ven	come	2	L
ven	vein	8	L
ver	true	2	L
ver	turn	9	L
verg (< *ver*)	turn	9	L
verm (< *ver* 'turn')	worm	11	L
vic~vinc	conquer	4	L
viginti	twenty	6	L

Element	Gloss	Chapter	Source
vin	wine	11	L
vinc~vic	conquer	4	L
vit~viv	live	9	L
viv~vit	live	9	L
voc	call, voice	10	L
vom	regurgitate	3	L
vor	eat	4	L
xen	foreign	1	G
xyl	wood	11	G
-y	N	3	G, L
zo	animal	4	G

APPENDIX 2

Glosses to Elements

Gloss	Element	Chapter	Source
A	-able~-ible~-ble	3, 11	L
A	-al~-ial	9	L
A	-il	4, 9	L
A	-ous~-os	3	L
A, N	-ant, -ary, -ent, -ory, -ive	3	L
able, powerful	pot~poss	2	L
above, excessive	super-	3	L
(abstract unit)	-eme	4	G
acceptable	dec	10	L
across, through	trans-~tra-	3, 6	L
act, do	prac	5	G
act, do, drive	ag~ig	5	L
after, behind	post-	3	L
again, back	re-~red-	3, 4, 6	L
again, up, back	ana-	3	G
against, facing	contra-~counter-	3	L
against, toward	ob-	3	L
age	ev	11	L
all	omn	2, 6	L
all	pan-~pant-	6	G
all, whole	tot	6	L
among, between	inter-	3	L
animal	zo	4	G
ant	formic	11	L

Gloss	Element	Chapter	Source
apart	se-~sed-	3, 6	L
ape	pithec	11	G
armpit	axill	8	L
around, near	peri-	3	G
arrange, order	tac	9	G
ask	rog	11	L
augury, god	de~div	4	L
away from, off	apo-	3	G
away from, reverse	de-	3	L
back, again	re-~red-	3, 4, 6	L
back, up, again	ana-	3	G
backward, down	cata-	3	G
bad	mal	11	L
balance, weigh	libr	2	L
bee	api	11	L
before	ante-~anti-	3	L
before	pre-	3	L
beget, give birth to	par	2	L
begin	-sc~-esc	6	L
behind, after	post-	3	L
believe	cred	9	L
below, after	infra-	3	L
below, under, partial	hypo-	3	G
beside, nearly	para-	3	G
between, among	inter-	3	L
beyond	meta-	3	G
billion, giant	giga	6	G
billionth	nano-	6	G
bird	av	5	L
bird	orn~ornith	11	G
birth	gen~gon	4	G
birth, give birth to	par	2	L
birth, type, origin	gen~gn~na	4	L

APPENDIX 2

Gloss	Element	Chapter	Source
blood	hem~haem~em	8	G
blow	fla	6	L
boat	nau	11	G
boat	nav	11	L
body	som~somat	11	G
body, flesh	corp~corpor	2, 3	L
body tissue	hist	8	G
bone	oss	8	L
bone	oste	8	G
break	frag~frang~fring	4	L
breast	mamm	8	L
breathe, lung	pne~pneum	8	G
brother	fratr	10	L
cac	bad	1	G
call, voice	voc	10	L
call out	clam	11	L
care	cur	6	L
carry	fer	10	L
carry	pher~phor	10	G
carry	lat	10	L
child, teach	ped~paed	10	G
city, community	pol	1	G
close$_v$	clud~clus	5	L
clot	thromb	8	G
color	chrom	1	G
come	ven	2	L
common, public service, gift	mun	11	L
community	pol	1	G
complete, end	tel~tele	11	G
conquer	vic~vinc	4	L
correct	orth	10	G
countless, ten thousand	myri	6	G
courage, soul	anim	2	L

Gloss	Element	Chapter	Source
cow	bov	11	L
cow	bu~bou	11	G
creep_v, reptile	herp~herpet	11	G
creep_v, snake	serp	11	L
cross, important point	cruc	10	L
cry out, call	clam	11	L
cut	tom~tm	4	G
cut, kill	cid~cis	4	L
cut, split	sec	2	L
depth	bath~bathy	9	G
dissolve	lu~lv	11	L
do, act	prac	4	G
do, act, drive	ag~ig	5	L
do, make	fac~fec~fic	4	L
double	dipl	6	G
down, backward	cata-	3	G
drive	ag~ig	5	L
ear	aur	8	L
earth	ge	10	G
earth	terr	9	L
eat	ed~es	10	L
eat	phag	11	G
eat	vor	4	L
egg	oo	11	G
egg	ov	11	L
eight	octa	6	G
eight	octo	6	L
eight (each)	octon	6	L
eighth	octav	6	L
empty	vac~van	9	L
end, complete	tel~tele	11	G
equal	iso-	3	G

APPENDIX 2

Gloss	Element	Chapter	Source
even, level	equ~iqu	4	L
excessive, above	super-	3	L
eye	ocul	9	L
eye	ophthalm	8	G
facing, against	contra-~counter-	3	L
fall	cad~cas~cid	5	L
false	pseud	1	G
far	tele	5	G
fast	tach~tachy	9	G
father, country	patr	10	G, L
fault	culp	2	L
fear	phob	8	G
feather, wing	pter	11	G
feel	esth~aesth	5	G
feel	sent~sens	5	L
feel, illness	path	1	G
few	pauc	6	L
few	olig	6	G
field	agr	9	L
fifth	quint	6	L
fight	pug~pung, pugn	9	L
fire	pyr	1	G
first	prim	6	L
first	prot	6	G
first, govern	arch	5	G
fish	ichthy	11	G
fist, fight	pugn	9	L
fit, capable	apt~ept	4	L
five	penta	6	G
five	quinque	6	L
five (each)	quin	6	L
flat	plac	11	G
flee	fug	2	L

Gloss	Element	Chapter	Source
flesh	carn~car	9	L
flesh	sarc	8	G
flow, river	flu~fluc~fluv	9	L
fold, times, tangle, entwine	pl~plec~plic	6	L
foot	ped	10	L
foot	pod~pus	10	G
for	pro-	3	L, G
foreign	xen	1	G
forward, for	pro-	2	L, G
four	quadr	6	L
four	tetra~tessara	6	G
four (each)	quatern	6	L
fourth	quart	6	L
from, away	ab-~abs-, de-	3	L
front (in front of)	pre-	3	L
fruit, apple	pom	10	L
full, many	ple	9	L
fungus	myc	10	G
gather, read	leg~lig	5	L
gather, social group	greg	2	L
gift, public service	mun	11	L
give	do	9	G
give	do~da~di	9	L
gland	aden	8	G
go, let go	ced~cess	5	L
go, step	grad~gred~gress	5	L
go to, seek	pet	2	L
god	the	1	G
god, augury	de~div	4	L
good	bon~bene	9	L
good	eu-	3	G
good, test	prob	2	L
goodwill	grat	2	L
govern	crat~crac	6	G

APPENDIX 2

Gloss	Element	Chapter	Source
govern, first	arch	5	G
great, large	magn	10	L
great, million	mega~megal	9	G
greet	salv~salu	10	L
grow, inhabit	col~cul	11	L
grow, nurture	al~ol	4	L
guard	phylac	8	G
half	hemi-	6	G
half	semi-	6	L
hand	chir	11	G
hand, handle	man	6	L
hang, weigh, pay, consider	pend~pond	4	L
hard	scler	8	G
harm	nec~noc~nic~nox	4	L
harm, loss	damn~demn	9	L
hate	mis	1	G
head	cephal	6	G
heal	iatr	1	G
hear	aud	9	L
heart	card	10	G
heart	cord	10	L
height, tip	acr	9	L
hide, secret	cryph~cryp	9	L
high	alt	5	L
hold, maintain	ten~tin	4	L
holy	sacr~sanc~secr	4	L
hostility, soul	anim	2	L
hour	hor	11	G
human	anthrop	1	G
human	hom	2	L
hundred	cent	6	L
hundred	hecaton	6	G
illness, feel	path	1	G

Gloss	Element	Chapter	Source
in, into	in-	3	L
in, into	en-	3	G
infected, putrid	sep	8	G
inferior, under	sub-	3, 6, 7	L
inflammation	-itis	8	G
inhabit, grow	col~cul	11	L
inside	endo-	3	G
into	in-	3	L
into	en-	3	G
judge, assess	cens	6	L
judge, law	jus~jur	9	L
jump	sal~sil	10	L
key, locked	clav	11	L
kidney	nephr	8	G
kill	cid~cis	4	L
kind, goodwill	grat	2	L
know	gno	9	G
know	gno~no~gni	9	L
know, discern	sci	2	L
land, state, medical condition	-ia	8	G, L
large	macr	1	G
large	magn	10	L
law, deputize	leg	2	L
law, judge	jus	9	L
law, system	nom	1	G
layer, stretch, level	strat	11	L
lead$_v$	duc	2	L
leaf	phyll	10	G
lean, lie, bed	cli	9	L, G
letter	liter	2	L
level, even	equ~iqu	4	L

APPENDIX 2

Gloss	Element	Chapter	Source
lie, lean	cli	9	L, G
lie down, remain	cub~cumb	4	L
life	bi	1	G
life	viv~vit	9	L
life, soul	anim	2	L
light	luc~lumen~lumin	6	L
light	phot~phos	5	G
liking	phil	1	G
lip	lab	8	L
little	-acl~-acul, -cl~-cul, -ell, -icl~-icul, -l, -ule	9	L
live	viv~vit	9	L
live, inhabit, grow	col~cul	11	L
liver	hepat	8	G
look, see	spec~spic	4	L
loosen	ly	11	G
loss, harm	damn~demn	9	L
love	am~im	4	L
love, liking	phil	1	G
love (physical)	ero	5	G
lung	pulm~pulmon	8	L
lung, breathe	pne~pneum	8	G
make, do	fac~fec~fic	4	L
male, man	andr	5	G
many	mult	6	L
many	poly	6	G
many, more	plur	6	L
marry, unite	gam	1	G
medical condition	-ia	8	G, L
melt, pour, blend	fund~fus	4	L
middle	meso-	3	G
milk	galact	8	G
milk	lact	8	L
mind	psych	1	G

Gloss	Element	Chapter	Source
mind, soul	anim	2	L
mix	misc~mix	9	L
mother	matr	10	L
mother, uterus	metr	10	G
mouth	os~or	8	L
mouth, opening	stom~stomat	8	G
move	mov~mo	4	L
N	-ance, -ence, -ity, -tion	3	L
N	-ment, -mony	9	L
N	-sis	3	G
N	-ty	4, 9	L
N	-y	3	G, L
N [gerundive]	-and~-end	9	L
N [singular]	-us	9	L
N [singular], thing	-ma	9	G
N [singular], thing	-um~-ium	9	L
N, A	-ant, -ary, -ent, -ory	3	L
name	nomen~nomin	10	L
name	onom~onomat~onym	10	G
near, around	peri-	3	G
nearly, beside	para-	3	G
neck	cervic	8	L
new	nov	2	L
new	ne	5	G
night	noct	10	L
night	nyct	10	G
nine	ennea	6	G
nine	novem	6	L
nine (each)	noven	6	L
ninth	non	6	L
nose	nas~nar	8	L
nose	rhin	8	G
not	in-	5	L

APPENDIX 2

Gloss	Element	Chapter	Source
not, without	a-~an-	3	G
nothing	nihil~nil	9	L
nothing	null	11	L
nurture, grow	al~ol	4	L
off, away from	apo-	3	G
old	pale~palae	10	G
old person	ger	10	G
old person	sen	11	L
on, over	epi-	3	G
one	mono	6	G
one	un	6	L
one and a half	sesqui-	6	L
opinion	doc~dog	5	G
other	al	10	L
other	all~allel	10	G
other, different	hetero-	3	G
out	ec-	3	G
out	ex-~e-	3, 6, 7	L
outside	ecto-	3	G
outside	extra-	3	L
over, above	super-	3	L
over, on	epi-	3	G
pain	alg	8	G
people	dem	6	G
perceive, feel	esth~aesth	5	G
[perfect participle]	-t	9	L
permit, unrestrained	lic	5	L
personal	idi	1	G
physical love	ero	5	G
pick, read	leg~lig	5	L
place	-arium	9	L
place	loc	6	L

APPENDIX 2

Gloss	Element	Chapter	Source
place	top	1	G
place, put	pon~pos	9	L
plant	phyt	10	G
please	plac	11	L
pleased, goodwill	grat	2	L
[plural]	-a, -ae, -i	9	L
point, say	dic	9	L
pour, melt, blend	fund~fus	4	L
power	dyn	11	G
powerful, able	pot	2	L
pregnant	gravid	8	G
preying	pred	10	L
prophesy	mant~manc	11	G
public service, gift	mun	11	L
punishment	pen~pun	9	L
put, place	pon~pos	9	L
put, place	the	10	G
putrid, infected	sep	8	G
read, gather	leg~lig	5	L
recent, new	ne	5	G
regurgitate	vom	3	L
remember	mne	4	G
reptile	herp~herpet	11	G
resembling	-oid	3	G
reverse, from	de-	3	L
rock	petr	1	G
root	rhiz	10	G
rule, straight	reg~rig	5	L
run	curs~curr	11	L
safe, greet	salv~salu	10	L
same	homo-	3	G
say	dic	9	L

APPENDIX 2

Gloss	Element	Chapter	Source
scatter, seed	spor	10	G
second	deuter	6	G
secret, hidden	cryp~cryph	9	G
see	op	8	G
seed	semen~semin	4	L
seed, scatter	spor	10	G
seek, go to	pet	2	L
self	auto~tauto	9	G
send	mitt~miss	3, 4	L
separate$_v$	cri~cre~cer	4	L
separate$_v$, judge	cri	4	G
seven	hepta	6	G
seven	septem	6	L
seven (each)	septen	6	L
shape, form	morph	1	G
sharp	ac	9	L
sharp	ox~oxy	11	G
short	brach~brachy	9	G
sister	soror	10	L
six	hexa	6	G
six	sex	6	L
six (apiece)	sen	6	L
sixth	sext	6	L
skin	cut	8	L
skin	dermat~derm	8	G
sleep	somn	2	L
small	micr	1	G
snake	serp	11	L
social group	greg	2	L
sound	phon	1	G
sound	son	6	L
source, birth, tribe	nat	2	L
speak	leg~lex~log	1	G
speak	loqu~locu	10	L

Gloss	Element	Chapter	Source
speak	fa	10	L
speak	pha~phe	10	G
speak, call, voice	voc	10	L
speak, say, point	dic	9	L
speech sound	phon	1	G
spider	arachn	11	G
spirit, soul	anim	2	L
stand, state	sta~ste~sti~st~sist	4	L
stand, state	sta~ste	4	G
star	aster~astr	9	G
state, condition, stand	sta~ste~sti~st	4	L
state, condition, stand	sta~ste	4	G
state, land, medical condition	-ia	8	G, L
step, go	grad~gred~gress	5	L
stick$_v$, hold back	hes~her	9	L
stomach	gastr	8	G
stone	lith~lit	9	G
straight, correct	orth	10	G
straight, rule	reg~rig	5	L
stretch, level, layer	strat	11	L
stretch, thin	ten~tend~tens	5	L
strong	val	10	L
study, speak	log	1	G
suffer	dol	9	L
sun	heli	5	G
system, law	nom	1	G
tail	caud~cod	8	L
take, contain	cap~cep~cip~cup	4	L
teach	doc	5	L
teach, child	ped~paed	10	G
tear [tir]	lacrim~lachrym	8	L
ten	deca	6	G
ten	decem	6	L

APPENDIX 2

Gloss	Element	Chapter	Source
ten (each)	den	6	L
ten thousand, countless	myri	6	G
tendency, liking	phil	1	G
tenth	decim	6	L
test, good	prob	2	L
-th (ordinal number)	-esim	6	L
thankful, goodwill	grat	2	L
thin, stretch	ten~tend~tens	5	L
think, mind	men~mon	4	L
third	terti	6	L
third	trit	6	G
thorough, through	per-	3	L
thousand	chili	6	G
thousand	kilo-	6	G
thousand	mille	6	L
thousandth	milli-	6	L
three	tri	6	G, L
three (each)	tern	6	L
three (parts)	trich	6	G
through	dia-	3	G
through, across	trans-~tra-	3, 6	L
through, thorough	per-	3	L
throw, extend	bol~bl	4	G
thrust	trud~trus	5	L
tie	lig	10	L
time	chron	1	G
time	tempor	4	L
times, fold, entwine	pl~plec~plic	6	L
tip, height	acr	9	L
tissue (body)	hist	8	G
to, toward	ad-	3, 6	L
together, with	con-~co-	3	L
together, with	syn-	3, 6	G
tongue, speech	gloss~glott	9	G

Gloss	Element	Chapter	Source
tooth	dent	11	L
tooth	odont	11	G
touch	tag~teg~tig~tang~ting	4	L
toward	ad-	3, 6	L
toward, against	ob-	3	L
tree	dendr~dry	11	G
true	ver	2	L
tumor, growth	-oma	11	G
turn$_v$	trop	11	G
turn$_v$	ver	9	L
twenty	icosa	6	G
twenty	viginti	6	L
twin	gemin	10	L
two	bi~du	6	L
two	di~dy	6	G
two (each)	bin	6	L
two (parts)	dich	6	G
under, below, partial	hypo-	4	G
under, inferior	sub-	3, 6, 7	L
unite	gam	1	G
universe, adorn, order	cosm	1	G
up, again, back	ana-	3	G
uterus	metr	10	G
v	-ize~-ise	3	G
vein	phleb	8	G
vein	ven	8	L
vessel, blood vessel, duct	vas	8	L
voice, call	voc	10	L
voice box	laryng	8	G
walk, go	ambul	5	L
war	bell	6	L

APPENDIX 2

Gloss	Element	Chapter	Source
water	hydr~hydat	9	G
weigh, consider	libr	2	L
weigh, hang, consider	pend~pond	4	L
well, good	bene~bon	9	L
white	alb	9	L
whole, all	tot	6	L
wife	uxor	10	L
wine	en~oen	11	G
wine	vin	11	L
wing	al	11	L
wing	pter	11	G
wise	soph	11	G
with, together	con-~co-	3	L
with, together	syn-	3, 6	G
within	intra-	3	L
without, not	a-~an-	3	G
woman, female	gyn~gynec	9	G
womb, neurotic disorder	hyster	8	G
wood	lign	10	L
wood	xyl	11	G
word	lex	1	G
work	erg~urg~org	4	G
worm	verm	11	L
write	graph~gramm	10	G
year	ann~enn	4	L
young	juven~jun	10	L

GLOSSARY

At the end of many definitions are one or more elements in the word along with glosses.

ablaut An Indo-European morphological pattern whereby roots change their vowel in different contexts (ch. 4, 10). [German *ab* 'away', *laut* 'sound']

acronym An initialism whose letters are read off as spelling a word, as *scuba*. A **reverse acronym** is one where the form of the acronym is the main justification for the longer phrase, as in the *USA PATRIOT* Act (ch. 3). [*acr* 'tip', *onym* 'name']

adapt When a language adapts a borrowed word or element, it modifies it to conform to sounds and structures of other words and elements already in the language. [*apt* 'fit']

adjective (A) A word that modifies (i.e., further specifies or labels) a noun. E.g., *Pat is **tall**; They have an **old wooden** fence; Jess is **wiser** than I am.* [*jac~jec* 'throw, lay']

adverb (ADV) A word that either (1) marks the manner or direction in which a verb is performed, e.g., *Sandy **slowly** walked toward the door; Kim watched **silently**; The clouds floated **away***; or (2) modifies an adjective, e.g., *I became **completely** frantic; That was **rather** nice of them*; or (3) comments on an entire sentence, usually from the speaker's perspective, e.g., ***Surely** Sam won't go; Julie **probably** went.*

affix A morphological component that does not contain a root but is only attached to a base form that has one or more roots. Prefixes, infixes. and suffixes are examples of affixes. The act of attaching an affix to a word is called **affixation** (ch. 3). [*fix* 'attach']

affricate An oral stop produced with a slow release of airflow. Consequently the stop is followed by a fricative at the same place of articulation and with the same voicing as the stop (ch. 5). [*fric* 'rub']

airstream The flow of air through the vocal tract that is used in producing speech sounds (ch. 5).

Alfred the Great King of West Saxons, 871–899 (ch. 2, 8).

allomorph If two morphs are variant forms of the same morpheme, we say that those morphs are allomorphs of each other. This variation is known as **allomorphy** (ch. 4). [*all* 'other']

alternation When different forms with the same function appear in different environments, they alternate with each other and are said to be **alternants**. (ch. 4, 6, 10). [*al* 'other']

alveolar Describes consonants produced by placing the tongue on or near the gums of the upper front alveolar ridge, the raised area behind the upper front teeth. The alveoli are the sockets the teeth are set in. Consonants produced by placing the tongue on or near the gums of the upper front alveolar ridge, the raised area behind the upper front teeth. The **alveoli** are the sockets the teeth are set in. (ch. 5).

analogy When a word is formed by correlating form and function with one or more other words, we say that analogy is involved. E.g., *arachnophobia* mimics the structure of previously existing phobia names. (ch. 3). [*log* 'speak']

ancestor A language X is an ancestor, or parent, of Y if X evolved into Y. E.g., Latin is the ancestor of French. [*ced~cess* 'go']

Angle A member of the group of West Germanic speakers who settled north of the Thames in England.

anglicize To make a sound or word conform more to English language patterns.

Anglo-Saxon A generic name for the West Germanic–speaking tribes that conquered and occupied England in the fifth century.

anticipatory Describes a sound change based on the property of a sound that comes after it in a word: it anticipates the following sound (ch. 6). [*ante-* 'before', *cap~cip* 'take']

apical Sounds made with the tip (apex) of the tongue are called apical (ch. 5). [*apec~apic* 'tip']

approximant A consonant produced with a relatively wide opening between the oral articulators (ch. 5). [*proxim* 'near']

archaeology Linguistic archaeology is an attempt to infer knowledge about a prehistoric language by studying the vocabulary that is shared among its attested descendant languages (ch. 10). [*arch* 'first', *log* 'study']

articulator An organ in the vocal tract, such as the tongue or lips, that forms different speech sounds by manipulating the airflow through the vocal tract. An **upper articulator** is a place in the top part of the mouth, including the upper lip, teeth, palate and soft palate; a **lower articulator** is the lower lip or the tongue. **Articulation** is the production of individual speech sounds (ch. 5). [*art* 'joint']

aspiration When the glottis is held open when pronouncing a consonant, a puff of air known as aspiration can be heard after the consonant. Such consonants are described as being **aspirated** (ch. 5). [*spir* 'breathe']

assimilation If sound X becomes more similar to sound Y, we say that X **assimilates** to Y. If X changes its place of articulation to agree with that of Y, it undergoes **place assimilation**; if it changes its phonation, it is **phonation assimilation**; if it becomes a liquid, it is **liquid assimilation**. If X becomes indistinguishable from Y, the process is a **total assimilation**; otherwise it is **partial assimilation** (ch. 6). [*simil* 'like']

association A mental connection made between two or more concepts that seem to be related in some sense, such as by metaphor or metonymy. [*soci* 'companion']

attested A language is attested if it is presently spoken or if we have found writing in that language. Specific words and word elements are also said to be attested if they have been heard or if they have been found in written texts. [*test* 'witness']

back Describes a sound produced when the tongue is raised toward the velum or uvula (ch. 5).

back-formation Reversing imputed derivational processes to make a simpler word that did not actually exist previously. E.g., by assuming that *back-formation* had been formed by adding *-ation* to a theoretical ˣ*back-form*, we can reverse that process to back-form a new word *back-form*.

backronym A reverse acronym (ch. 3). [blend of *back* and *acronym*]

Balto-Slavic The branch of Indo-European that comprises the Baltic and Slavic languages (ch. 10).

base A lexical component to which affixes are attached. ['bottom']

bilabial A sound produced by bringing the two lips together (ch. 5). [*bi* 'two', *lab* 'lip']

blade The blade of the tongue is its flexible front part (ch. 5).

blend A new word formed by combining parts of other words without regard for their internal morphological structure; e.g., *netiquette* from *net* and *etiquette*; *fignature* from *finger* and *signature* (ch.3).

borrow A language is said to borrow a word or word element when it copies or adapts it from another language. When a language borrows a word, it is under no obligation to pay it back (ch. 2).

bound A bound morph is one that cannot appear as an independent word (ch. 3).

branch A set of related languages smaller than a family. English belongs to the Germanic branch of Indo-European (ch. 2, 10).

breathy voice A type of phonation produced when the vocal cords are vibrated even though they are held relatively far apart (ch. 5).

cardinal numbers These tell how many of an object you are referring to; e.g., *three* (ch. 6). [*cardin* 'hinge'].

case A grammatical category that marks a noun, pronoun, or adjective as fulfilling a certain type of role in a sentence. E.g., *he* is in the nominative case because it can be used as subject of a verb, *him* is in the accusative case because it can be used as an object of a verb, and *his* is in the genitive case because it limits another noun (ch. 2, 8, 9, 10). [*cad~cas* 'fall']

Celtic The branch of Indo-European including Welsh, Irish, and Scots Gaelic, among others (ch. 2, 10).

central A central vowel is pronounced with the tongue raised toward the velum, between the places where front vowels and back vowels are made (ch. 5). [*centr*]

chain shift A series of sound changes where X turns into Y at about the same time that Y turns into Z. The existence of Z that came from Y but not ultimately from X indicates that the change X > Y couldn't have been completed before the change Y > Z began (ch. 10).

classical Classical languages are the language forms used when ancient Latin and Greek literature flourished. The classical Latin period was approximately the three centuries leading to 200 CE; classical Greek was the dialect used in Athens from about 500 to 300 BCE. Modern loans from Latin and Greek are almost always based on the form the word elements had in the classical period of the respective language.

clipping A word shortened without regard to morph boundaries. E.g., *info* is a clipping of *information* (ch. 3).

closed A **closed syllable** is a syllable that ends in a consonant.

cluster A sequence of two or more consonants.

cognate Words and word elements are cognate if they descend from the same word in the common ancestor language (ch. 2, 4, 7, 10). [*con-* 'with', *gen~na* 'birth']

coin To coin a word is to create it.

coloring When a consonant affects the quality of a nearby vowel, the effect is called **vowel coloring**. **[l] Coloring** takes place when an [l] affects the preceding vowel (ch. 6).

common noun A noun that refers to a class of objects and not just to a single individual.

comparative A comparative adjective—also called an adjective in the comparative degree—is one that describes people or things that have more of a certain quality than does another. In English it ends in *-er*, as in *bigger*. [*par* 'equal']

comparative method A technique for discovering what languages are related to each other and what their prehistoric ancestor languages sounded like. The technique relies heavily on the analysis of sound correspondences (ch. 10).

complex A complex word is a word built from two or more morphs (ch. 3). [*plec* 'entwine']

compound word A complex word formed from two or more elements that each contain a root, e.g., *blackbird, photograph, White House* (ch. 3).

connotation Secondary associations of a word, including style, mood, and familiarity (ch. 1, 7). [*not* 'mark']

consonant A speech sound made with significant narrowing or obstruction in the vocal tract (ch. 5). [*son* 'sound']

conversion When a word is used as a different part of speech than it originally was used as, the change is known as conversion or zero derivation. E.g., *butter* is basically a noun, but by conversion it is used as a verb in *Don't butter that toast* (ch. 3). [*ver* 'turn']

coronalization Moving velar sounds forward in the mouth, especially when conditioned by nearby front vowels. E.g., pronouncing Latin *cent*, which originally had [k], with initial [s] instead is a coronalization (ch. 11). [*coron* 'crown']

correspond When sounds in related languages descend from the same sound in a common ancestor language, they are said to correspond to each other, or to form a **recurrent sound correspondence**. Documenting recurrent sound correspondences is a scientific way to prove that languages are related and to reconstruct the common ancestor language (ch. 10). [*spond* 'promise']

degree In English and many other languages, adjectives and adverbs are inflected when they are used in comparison of degree. E.g., *bigger* is the comparative degree of *big*, and *biggest* is the superlative degree.

delete When a rule results in the complete loss of a sound, that sound is said to be deleted, and the phonological process is called **deletion**. In the phrases **vowel deletion**, **[s] deletion**, and **stop deletion**, the qualifier tells what kind of sound is deleted (ch. 6).

denotation The basic meaning of a word (ch. 1, 7). [*not* 'mark']

dental Describes a consonant produced with the tongue against the teeth (ch. 5). [*dent* 'tooth']

derive A **derivational** affix is an affix that turns one lexeme into another; e.g., *un-* or *-less*. A word with a derivational affix is said to be derived from the simpler word. The process of deriving one word from another is called **derivation** (ch. 3, 6, 9). [*de-* 'from', *riv* 'stream']

descend Language A has descended from language B if B evolved into A. A is called a **descendant** of B (ch. 2). [*de-* 'from', *scand~scend* 'climb']

diacritic Marks added to letters to express nuances of pronunciation. [*cri* 'separate']

dialect A form of a language associated with a particular geographical region (ch. 2, 5, 8, 10). [*leg* 'speak']

digraph Two letters used together to represent one sound. [*di* 'two', *graph* 'write']

diminutive Small. A diminutive affix has the basic function of naming something that is smaller than that named by the original word. Often, however, a diminutive form simply expresses affection, familiarity, or some even vaguer notion suggested by smallness. [*min* 'little']

diphthong When two vowels are pronounced in succession in the same syllable, the result is a diphthong (ch. 5). A **diphthongization** is a sound change that turns a simple vowel into a diphthong (ch. 11). [*di* 'two', *phthong* 'sound']

distributive numbers Used in Latin to answer the question "how many each?"; e.g., *terni* 'three each' (ch. 6). [*trib* 'tribe, give']

diverge A language diverges into two or more different languages when changes are localized and do not spread through the entire language community. [*ver~verg* 'turn']

dorsal Sounds made with the back of the tongue are called dorsal (ch. 5). [*dors* 'back']

double letter A letter that appears twice in a row in the same word, especially if the sequence represents a single sound, as in *letter*.

doublet A pair of words in the same language that differ because of different paths of descent. Usually borrowing is involved (ch. 2, 4).

dual A grammatical category used in Proto-Indo-European when referring to objects that were two in number (ch. 10). [*du* 'two']

East Germanic An extinct group of Germanic languages that included Gothic (ch. 2).

element A word element is a morphological constituent that is used to build words.

ellipsis Omitting one or more words from a longer expression (ch. 7). [*lip* 'leave']

ending An inflectional suffix, such as *-ed* or *-s* in English.

environment The environment of a sound is the other sounds that may influence its pronunciation. Normally the most important environment is sounds that occur in fairly close proximity in the same word (ch. 6).

epenthesis Inserting a sound to a word when it has only a phonetic justification, as the *p* in *redemptive* (ch. 6). [*the* 'put']

etymology The history of a word. Etymologists are linguists who study the histories of individual words. [*etym* 'true', *leg~log* 'speak, word']
euphemism Referring to a concept by a new or less straightforward term in order to avoid unpleasant connotation (ch. 7). [*eu-* 'good', *phe* 'speak']
extension An element that is added at the end of a morph. Originally a separate suffix, the element now simply makes a new, **extended**, morph. E.g., *corpor* is an extended allomorph of *corp* (ch.4). [*ten~tens* 'stretch']
external When a change occurs in a language due to sociohistorical forces that are not themselves linguistic, such as migration, one speaks of external causes of language change (ch. 8). [*exter* 'outside']
extinct A language is extinct if it is no longer spoken. [*stingu* 'quench']

family A language together with all the other languages that are related to it constitute a language family. English belongs to the Indo-European family (ch. 2, 10).
folk etymology A morphological reanalysis that leads to a new word. E.g., *pea* by reanalyzing *pease* [piz] as having a plural ending (ch. 3).
Frank A member of the tribes that conquered much of what is today France, lending their name and a substantial amount of their West Germanic vocabulary to the Romance language spoken in that region (ch. 2).
free Describes a morph that can appear as an independent word (ch. 3).
fricative An obstruent consonant produced by forcing air to pass through the mouth through a narrow opening, creating a rasping sound (ch. 5). [*fric* 'rub']
front A front vowel is one made with the body of the tongue raised toward the hard palate (ch. 5).

gender An inflectional category used in Latin or Greek to show agreement between adjectives and nouns, among other things. Each noun had one of three genders—masculine, feminine, or neuter—and any adjective that modified that noun would inflect to match that gender (ch. 10).
generalization Using a word to refer to a broader concept that properly includes its former range of usage. Also called *widening* (ch. 7).
genetically related Languages are genetically related to each other if they descend from a common ancestor (ch. 2). [*gen* 'birth']
genitive A case used especially to show that a noun or pronoun specifies or limits what another noun refers to; e.g., **Mary's** *promotion*. [*gen* 'birth']
Germanic The branch of Indo-European to which English belongs. It consists of East, North, and West Germanic languages (ch. 2, 10).
gerundive A participle in Latin that denotes that something ought to be done; e.g., *agenda* (ch. 9). [*ges~ger* 'do']
glide A sound similar to a vowel, but pronounced very quickly and used in contexts where one would expect a consonant; e.g., [j] and [w] (ch. 5).
gloss A brief definition of a word. ['tongue']
glottis The hole in the larynx through which air can pass, past the vocal cords. Sounds whose primary articulation is at the glottis are called **glottal** sounds (ch. 5). [*glott* 'tongue']

Gothic An East Germanic language that has been extinct for a millennium but whose written records have been key to understanding the development of the Germanic languages (ch. 2).

grade In Indo-European morphology, the ablaut grade indicates what vowel the element had in Proto-Indo-European: *e*, *o*, or zero (ch. 4). [*grad* 'step']

grammatical function The role a word or phrase plays in the larger clause or sentence; e.g., the subject or direct object of a verb (ch. 9, 10, 11).

Great Vowel Shift A change in the pronunciation of the long vowels of English, which happened in the centuries around 1500. Most long vowels were raised, but the high vowels became diphthongs (ch. 2, 3, 10, 11).

Grimm's law A statement of how obstruent consonants in the Germanic languages correspond to consonants in other Indo-European languages (ch. 10).

Hellenic The branch of Indo-European that consists of the Greek language (ch. 10).

high A high vowel is produced when the tongue is raised close to the roof of the mouth (ch. 5).

historical linguistics The branch of linguistics that studies language change.

homeland The homeland of a language family is the region where the common ancestral protolanguage was spoken (ch. 2, 10).

homograph Two words or elements are homographs if they are spelled the same way (ch. 1). [*homo-* 'same', *graph* 'write']

homonymy Words that are unrelated in origin and meaning but have the same form are called **homonyms** and are said to be **homonymous** and exhibit homonymy; e.g., *ring* 'circular band' and *ring* 'bell sound' (ch. 7). [*homo-* 'same', *onym* 'name']

ill-formed Describes a form that would violate the rules of a language's grammar.

Indic A group of languages that contains Sanskrit and its many modern descendants, such as Hindi, Bengali, and Urdu (ch. 10).

indicative Verbs that express simple statements or questions are generally inflected with what is called indicative mood. E.g., *The children are playing* is in the indicative mood (ch. 8). [*in-* 'in', *dic* 'point']

Indo-European The language family to which belong English, French, Latin, Greek, and dozens of other languages (ch. 2, 10).

Indo-Iranian A branch of Indo-European, which contains the Indic and Iranian languages (ch. 10).

infix An affix that is inserted inside a morpheme. Proto-Indo-European and several of its daughter languages have a nasal infix (ch. 5, 10). [*in-* 'in', *fix* 'attach']

inflection A modification of a word to show some grammatical function such as number, degree, tense, person, and case. This modification is often accomplished through **inflectional affixes**, which in English and Latin are almost always suffixes (**inflectional endings**). Words undergoing inflection are said to **inflect** for the grammatical function in question, or to be **inflected** (ch. 2, 3, 4, 9, 10). [*in-* 'in', *flect* 'bend']

inherited A word is inherited from an ancestral language when the word is passed down from speaker to speaker from that language.

initialism A word formed from the initial letters of a phrase, such as *CIA* from *Central Intelligence Agency* (ch. 3). [*in-* 'in', *i* 'go']

innovation A linguistic change. [*in-* 'in', *nov* 'new']

insertion When a sound is added to a word by a phonological process, it is said to be inserted, and the process is called an insertion or epenthesis. In rule names like **Vowel Insertion**, **[d] Insertion**, and **[s] Insertion** the qualifier tells what kind of sound is inserted (ch. 6). [*in-* 'in', *ser* 'join']

interfix An affix that is only attached between two other morphological constituents, as the *i* in *pedicure* (ch. 3). [*inter-* 'between', *fix* 'attach']

internal When the only explanation for language change is in terms of language structure itself, one speaks of internal causes of change (ch. 8). [*inter* 'inside']

International System of Units (SI) A modern, internationally standardized form of the metric system (ch. 6).

irregular Describes a word whose form cannot be predicted from the ordinary rules of the language. [*in-* ~ *ir-* 'not', *reg* 'rule']

Italic The branch of Indo-European to which belong Latin and all the Romance languages (ch. 2, 10).

Kent A member of the group of West Germanic speakers who settled in the southeast of England (ch. 2).

kurgan A grave with a mound. This word is also used to describe the possibly Indo-European culture that used this interment technique approximately six thousand years ago (ch. 10).

labial Describes a speech sound produced at the lips (ch. 5). [*lab* 'lip']

labiodental A consonant produced by bringing the lower lip to the upper teeth (ch. 5). [*lab* 'lip', *dent* 'tooth']

labiovelar A sound produced with the back of the tongue raised toward the soft palate and the lips rounded (ch. 5). [*lab* 'lip', *vel* 'veil']

laminal A sound made with the blade of the tongue (ch. 5). [*lamin* 'blade']

laryngeal lengthening The lengthening of a vowel occasioned by a following laryngeal that was once there but has disappeared (ch. 10).

laryngeals Proto-Indo-European sounds of uncertain phonetic value. Some of them colored adjacent vowels, and all of them lengthened preceding vowels when they were deleted from the end of a syllable (ch. 10). [*laryng* 'larynx']

larynx The Adam's apple, or voice box (ch. 5).

lateral A sound made in such a way that air flows around the sides of the tongue (ch. 5). [*later* 'side']

Latin The Italic language that originated as the language of Rome and environs, then spread throughout Europe with the Roman Empire. The classical language was the basis for an international (or pan-European) scholarly language that was used up to modern times.

Latin Vowel Weakening A set of rules that change short vowels in noninitial syllables (ch. 6).

Latinate Describes a word borrowed from Latin, whether directly or indirectly, with only small amounts of adaptation (ch. 2).
lax Describes vowels produced with slightly less lingual effort than tense vowels (ch. 5).
learned Words borrowed by scholars are known as learned borrowings. Learned borrowings from Latin and Greek agree closely in spelling to the classical Latin and Greek forms (ch. 11).
lexeme A word form with any inflections removed. E.g., *throw, throws, threw, thrown,* and *throwing* are all considered forms of the same lexeme (ch. 4). [*leg~lex* 'speak, word']
lexical Having to do with individual words. More narrowly, a lexical morphological component is one that provides a meaning. A lexical morph or morpheme is a root. [*leg~lex* 'speak, word']
lexicographer A person who writes dictionaries. [*leg~lex* 'speak, word', *graph* 'write']
lingua franca A common language for groups that share no other language.
linguist A scholarly expert on language. [*lingu* 'tongue']
linguistic archaeology Study of history with linguistic data as the primary source of evidence.
liquid An approximant like [r] and [l] (ch. 5).
long Describes a consonant or vowel whose duration lasts longer than other comparable ones (ch. 5).
low Describes a vowel produced when the tongue, and usually the jaw, is farther from the roof of the mouth than for other vowels (ch. 5).
Low German German language varieties spoken in northern Germany (ch. 2).
lower articulators The lower lip, teeth, and gum ridge, and the tongue (ch. 5).
Lower Saxony A state in northwestern Germany. Most of the Germanic settlers of England probably came from in or near this region (ch. 2).

macron The diacritic ¯ placed over a vowel to indicate that it is long. [*macr* 'large']
manner of articulation The manner and degree of manipulation of the airstream when producing a sound (ch. 5).
masculine One of three genders a noun can have in Latin and Greek. The masculine is traditionally considered the default gender, so that adjectives (which inflect to match the gender of the noun they modify) are usually cited in the masculine gender [*mascul* 'male'].
melioration A change in the meaning of a word to have a more positive denotation or connotation (ch. 7). [*melior* 'better']
merger A morphemic merger occurs when word elements that could formerly be analyzed as a sequence of morphs come to be treated as a single morph. E.g., *anim* was originally a root *an* 'breathe' plus a noun suffix, but the two have merged to form a single morph (ch. 4).
metaphor Using a word to refer to something that is similar in some way to the thing the word represents previously or more basically; e.g., *horse* for a sawhorse. The **spatial metaphor** uses morphemes that basically represent spatial relations to represent

more abstract concepts that are felt to be somehow similar to those spatial relations (ch. 7). [*meta-* 'beyond', *pher~phor* 'carry']

metonymy Using a word to represent something that is associated with the thing more basically named by that word. A word that does this is called a **metonym**. In current usage the term also includes what has traditionally been called synecdoche. However, metonymy excludes association based on resemblance, which is called metaphor (ch. 7). [*onym* 'name']

mid A mid vowel is produced when the tongue is neither raised nor lowered from a neutral position (ch. 5).

Middle When languages have a relatively long literary tradition, that tradition is conventionally divided into three periods, of which the second is labeled *middle*. The **Middle English** period was 1100–1500; Middle French, 1300–1500 (ch. 2).

Modern When living languages have a relatively long literary tradition, that tradition is conventionally divided into three periods, of which the current is called *modern*. The **Modern English** and Modern French periods began in 1500 (ch. 2).

monolingual Something that consists of only one language (ch. 6). [*mon* 'one', *lingu* 'tongue']

morph The smallest unit of meaning or function in word construction (ch. 3). ['shape']

morph split A change whereby a morpheme with only one form comes to have additional forms (ch. 4).

morpheme The set of morphs that have the same meaning or function but some differences in pronunciation depending on the other elements in the word. E.g., the plural morpheme *s* comprises the morphs [-s], [-z], and [-əz] (ch. 4).

morphemic merger A change in which a morph sequence comes to be reinterpreted as a single morph (ch. 4).

morphological element A constituent that is used to build words, also called a **word element** or an **element** in the text. A morphological element may be a single morph or a sequence of morphs (ch. 3).

morphology The systematic study of word structure. Complex words are built up from two or more morphological components. Morphological analysis, or parsing, seeks to reveal the structure of words in terms of their components. A **morphologist** is a linguist who studies morphology (ch. 3). [*morph* 'shape', *leg~log* 'speak, study']

narrowing Restriction of a word's meaning to a subset of what it formerly represented. Also called *specialization* (ch. 7).

nasal Describing sounds made with air passing through the nose (ch. 5). [*nas* 'nose']

nasal infix A nasal consonant that is added as an affix inside a root; e.g., *-n-* in *tangible* (ch. 4, 6, 10).

native Describes words and elements that are not borrowed from another language (ch. 2). [*gen~na* 'birth']

neologism A newly created word (ch. 1, 2). [*ne* 'new', *log* 'speak']

new Englishes Varieties of English that arose in regions where English was not the mother tongue (ch. 2).

nominative The case used to mark nouns, pronouns, and adjectives when they are used as subjects of verbs, or cited by themselves out of context. E.g., *he* in English (ch. 8, 9). [*nomen~nomin* 'name']

Norman Normans were French-speaking descendants of Vikings who lived in Normandy. Their successful invasion of England in 1066 is called the **Norman Conquest** (ch. 2).

Norse The ancestor of the North Germanic languages. Viking Norse is the stage spoken by the Vikings who settled in the English Danelaw; Old Norse is the later form of the language that is attested in written texts (ch. 2).

North Germanic A branch of Germanic that includes Norse, Icelandic, Norwegian, Swedish, and Danish (ch. 2).

noun (N) A word that labels an actual or abstract thing that may act as subject or object of a verb. E.g., *That **dog** is barking again*; *Only **Leigh's pride** was injured*; ***Running** is supposed to be good **exercise**.*

number A grammatical category classifying how many objects a noun comprises. In English and many other languages, nouns inflect depending on whether they refer to one item (singular number) or more than one (plural number) (ch. 2, 9).

obstruent A consonant whose production entails substantial obstruction of airflow: an oral stop, affricate, or fricative (ch. 5). [*ob-* 'against', *stru* 'pile up']

Old When languages have a relatively long written history, that tradition is conventionally divided into three periods, of which the first is labeled *old*. The **Old English** period was 700–1100; Old French, 1000–1300; Old Norse, 1100–1350. Many people also lump in earlier, minimally attested forms of the language under the same label (ch. 2).

onomatopoeia The process of forming a word intended to mimic some natural sound; e.g., *creak* (ch. 3). [*onom~onomat* 'name', *poei* 'make']

oral Sounds produced with the nasal cavity sealed off by the velum, so that the air stream passes entirely through the mouth (ch. 5). [*os~or* 'mouth']

ordinal numbers These identify which position a referent holds in a series; e.g., *third*. [*ordin* 'order']

orthography The standard, conventional spelling. [*orth* 'straight, correct', *graph* 'write']

palate The hard palate is the bony part of the roof of your mouth. The soft palate, or velum, is the soft part behind it. When people use the unqualified word *palate*, or the adjective **palatal**, the hard palate is meant (ch. 5). **Palatalization** refers to many different sound changes that bring the tongue closer to the hard palate or beyond; see also *coronalization* (ch. 11).

parent Language X is a parent, or ancestor, of Y if X evolved into Y. E.g., Latin is the parent of French (ch. 2). [*par* 'give birth to']

parse When you parse a word, you analyze it in terms of its component morphemes. E.g., *blackbirds* can be parsed into *blackbird* plus *s*, and *blackbird* itself parses into *black* plus *bird*.

partial assimilation Process whereby one sound acquires some but not all of the properties of another period.

participle A verb that is used as an adjective to modify a noun. E.g., *fall* is used in a **present participle** form in *Watch out for falling rocks*. In Latin loanwords, participles not infrequently can also be nouns. **Present participles** tend to have active meaning, and **perfect participles** have passive meaning or describe a state (ch. 9). [*part* 'part' *cap~cip* 'take']

passive The passive voice indicates that the subject of the passive verb (or the noun modified by a passive participle) is to be construed as the object upon which the action is done. E.g., *The piñata **was struck** by the children* (ch. 3, 9, 11). [*pat, pass* 'suffer']

pejoration A shift in the meaning of a word to have a more negative denotation or connotation (ch. 7). [*pejor* 'worse']

person A grammatical category referring to whether the speaker is referring to self (first person), the addressee (second person), or something or someone else (third person). In English and several other languages, the verb may change its inflection depending on which person the subject of the verb has (ch. 2).

phonation The type of vibration made by the vocal cords when a sound is produced (ch. 5). [*phon* 'sound']

phonetics The sounds of language, or their systematic study (ch. 5). [*phon* 'sound']

phonology The way sounds function in language, or the systematic study of the functioning of sounds (ch. 1, 4, 6). [*phon* 'sound', *log* 'study']

place of articulation Point or area of contact or constriction between two speech organs (ch. 5).

plural A value of the grammatical category of number, used when referring to more than one object; e.g., *books* is the plural of *book* (ch. 4, 9, 11). [*plur* 'many']

polysemy A word or morpheme that has multiple meanings is called **polysemous** and is said to exhibit polysemy (ch. 7). [*poly-* 'many', *sem* 'meaning']

popular Words that are inherited from the ancestor language in the normal way, without interference from scholars who want to maintain or restore classical spelling and pronunciation, are referred to as popular vocabulary. Popular Romance words are often very much different from the classical Latin form; e.g., popular French *chef* as opposed to classical *capit-* 'head'. A somewhat different use of the word *popular* is to refer to a variety of language that is highly colloquial and not strongly influenced by high literary style; e.g., **popular Latin** (ch. 11).

postalveolar Describes a sound produced by raising the blade of the tongue to an intermediate position between the alveolar ridge and the palate (ch. 5). [*post-* 'after', *alveol*]

prefix An affix that is attached before its base (ch. 3). [*pre-* 'before', *fix* 'attach']

Prehistoric English English in its formative period before the development of substantial writing, ca. 400–700 CE (ch. 2).

prescriptive Describes an approach to language that tells people how they ought to speak, rather than describing how they do speak (ch. 8). [*pre-* 'before', *scrib~scrip* 'write']

Proto-X The reconstructed language that is the ancestor of all languages of family or branch *X*. E.g., Proto-Germanic is the ancestor of all Germanic languages, and Proto-Indo-European (PIE) is the ancestor of all the Indo-European languages (ch. 2, 10). [*prot* 'first']

reanalysis Giving a historically incorrect analysis to a linguistic construction, such as taking *uproar* to be a compound of *up* plus *roar* 'make a loud noise' (ch. 3). [*re-* 'again', *ana-* 'thoroughly', *ly* 'loosen']

reconstruction Inferring what a protolanguage sounded like based on evidence from attested languages that descended from it (ch. 2, 10). [*re-* 'back', *stru* 'pile up']

recurrent sound correspondence A pattern in which a sound in one language systematically matches a sound in another language, helping to establish a relationship between the two languages (ch. 10).

recursion Describes a rule taking its own output as input. The rule is called **recursive**. E.g., a prefix can attach to a base, forming a base to which a prefix can be added: *post-post-modern* (ch. 3). [*re-* 'again', *curs* 'run']

regular Describes a form that can be predicted by the rules of the language (ch. 6). [*reg* 'rule']

related Languages are related to each other if they diverged from the same ancestral language (ch. 2, 10). [*lat* 'carry']

repair If certain linguistic rules or historical circumstances would produce a word that violates other rules of the language, the word may be changed to conform to those other rules. Such a change is called a repair (ch. 4).

Rhotacism The change of [s] to [r] (ch. 6). [*rho*, the name of the Greek letter for the sound [r]]

Romance Languages that descended from Latin. They include Italian, French, Spanish, Portuguese, and Romanian, among other languages.

romanize Describes a language normally written in a different script, such as Greek, that is written in Latin letters (ch. 6).

root The smallest meaningful lexical component of a word. A word must have at least one root, but words can also have several, as in *psychopath*, built on the roots *psych* and *path* (ch. 3).

round Describes a speech sound made with the lips at least partially rounded, or pursed. **Rounding** is the state of being rounded (ch. 5).

runes A variant of the Latin alphabet formerly used for carving inscriptions in Germanic languages (ch. 2).

Sanskrit An Indic language that served as the classical language of India (ch. 10).

Saxon A member of the Germanic-speaking peoples who settled in England south of the Thames (ch. 2).

schwa A mid central vowel, [ə] (ch. 5). [Hebrew]

scientific notation A method of representing numbers as a number from 0 to 10 multiplied by a power of 10 expressed as an exponent; e.g., 35,000,000 is 3.5×10^7 (ch. 6). [*sci* 'know', *not* 'mark']

semantics Meaning, or the systematic study of how language expresses meaning. **Semantic change** is change in the meaning of a word (ch. 7). [*sem* 'meaning']

short Describes a speech sound that is not held for the same length of time as a long sound. **Consonant Shortening** is a rule that makes long consonants short (ch. 6).

silent e An *e* found at the end of many English words. It rarely corresponds to an *e* in the classical languages but is introduced in English to indicate how other letters in the word are to be pronounced (ch. 11).
simplex Describes a word or morphological component lacking internal structure and consisting of only one morpheme (ch. 3). [*sim* 'one', *plec* 'fold']
simplification A reduction in complexity. **Cluster Simplification** reduces the number of consonants in a cluster (ch. 6).
singular A value of the grammatical category of number, used when referring to a single object (ch. 3). [*sim* 'one']
sociolinguistics The study of social factors in language variation and change (ch. 1). [*soci* 'companion', *lingu* 'tongue']
sound symbolism The unusual situation in which a sound bears some natural connection to the object it names; e.g., *teeny* (ch. 3). [*syn-~sym-* 'with', *bol* 'throw']
specialization Using a word to represent only a subset of what it formerly applied to. Also called *narrowing* (ch. 7). [*spec* 'look']
split A morph split occurs when a single morph turns into two or more different morphs over time, which usually end up functioning as allomorphs of the same morpheme (ch. 4).
standard A set of linguistic norms accepted by a social group (ch. 8).
stem A lexical base to which an inflectional affix may be attached. E.g., *book-* and *booklet-* are both stems to which the inflectional affix *-s* may be attached (ch. 3).
stop A sound whose production entails the complete stopping of the airflow through the mouth. If the airflow is blocked entirely, an **oral stop** is produced; if air escapes through the nose, a **nasal stop** is produced (ch. 5).
subject The part of the sentence that typically names the doer of the action. In English, it almost always precedes the main verb, with which it agrees in number: *He plays music*; *They play music* (ch. 2). [*jac~jec* 'throw, place']
suffix An affix that is attached after its base. E.g., the derivational affix *-less* and the ending *-ing* are affixes. The act of attaching a suffix is called **suffixation** (ch. 3). [*sub-* 'under', *fix* 'attach']
superfix A morph that operates not by adding more sounds to a word but by changing some more abstract property like stress. E.g., the difference between the noun *contract* and the verb *contract* can be attributed to a superfix (ch. 3). [*super-* 'above', *fix* 'attach']
suppletion The use of different roots in different inflected forms of the same morpheme. E.g., the comparative of *good* is **suppletive** because it is made by adding *-er* to the unrelated root *bett* (ch. 4). [*ple* 'full']
syllabic consonants Consonants that can be used as the core of a syllable, in place of a vowel (ch. 10).
synonymy A relation between words with nearly the same meaning (ch. 1, 7). [*syn-* 'with', *onym* 'name']

tense (1) An inflectional category of verbs that indicates the relative time an event took place, such as the present or the past. (2) Describes a vowel produced with slightly more lingual effort than another; that phonetic property is called **tenseness** (ch. 5).

total assimilation Assimilation of one sound to another, whereby the first becomes indistinguishable from the second (ch. 6).

umlaut A phonological rule that makes back vowels like [u] be pronounced farther front in the mouth, like [i]. Historically, this was caused by a front vowel or glide later in the word (ch. 4). [German *um* 'around', *laut* 'sound']

unattested If a word or element is unattested, we know of no written document that contains it (ch. 2, 11). [*test* 'witness']

ungrammatical Describes a word or phrase that does not conform to the rules of grammar in ordinary speech. E.g., ˣ*killedjoy* would be an ungrammatical type of compound word (ch. 3, 8). [*graph~gramm* 'write']

upper articulators The upper lip, teeth, and gum ridge, the hard and soft palate, and the uvula (ch. 5).

uvula The part of the soft palate that dangles at the back of your mouth. Sounds made there are **uvular** (ch. 5). [*uv* 'grape']

variant One of multiple linguistic elements that can have the same meaning or function.

velar Describes a sound made at the soft palate, or **velum** (ch. 5). [*vel* 'veil']

verb (v) A word that details activity, process, or state of being or becoming in a construction with a subject or object noun. E.g., *Tony **slapped** the wall*; *Jan **wears** running shoes every day*; *On Monday I **learned** how sick she **was**.*

Viking Norse The North Germanic language spoken by the Vikings who conquered and settled in the east of England. In Scandinavia, Viking Norse developed into literary Old Norse and further into Icelandic, Norwegian, Swedish, and Danish (ch. 2).

vocal cords Membranes that are capable of closing the glottis. They can also vibrate many times a second, creating the characteristic buzzing known as voice (ch. 5). [*voc* 'voice']

vocal tract The part of the mouth and nasal cavities above the larynx that is used to produce different speech sounds (ch. 5). [*trah~trac* 'pull']

voice A type of phonation in which the vocal folds are held close together and vibrate rapidly, producing a buzzing sound (ch. 5).

vowel A sound made with air passing through a relatively unobstructed mouth (ch. 5).

vowel coloring Modification of a vowel's sound and pronunciation due to an adjacent sound, typically a following [r] or [l] (ch. 5).

vulgar Vulgar Latin is another word for popular Latin. Vulgar Latin was spoken at the same time as classical Latin, but it had many differences in pronunciation, grammar, and vocabulary (ch. 11). [*vulg* 'common folk']

weakening (Latin Vowel Weakening) A sound change whereby vowels become higher, and therefore less sonorous, in less prominent positions in the word (ch. 6).

Welsh The native language of Wales, descended from the language of the ancient Celts (ch. 2).

West Germanic A branch of Germanic that includes English, Dutch, Frisian, German, and Yiddish (ch. 2).

widening Using a word to refer to a broader concept that properly includes its former range of usage. Also called *generalization* (ch. 7).

word A morphological construction that can be moved about relatively freely and independently within a sentence. The word *word* sometimes is used to refer to lexemes (q.v.) and sometimes to **word forms**. When we speak of word forms we take account of inflections; thus *throw* and *thrown* are considered two separate word forms (ch. 3).

word element A morphological constituent that is used to build words. This book uses this term in a way intended to be virtually synonymous with the term **morpheme** (ch. 1, 3).

zero When no audible or visible element appears where one is logically expected by analogy with other forms, one may speak of a zero element. E.g., one may speak of forming the plural of *sheep* by adding a zero plural ending, or of converting the noun *butter* to a verb by zero derivation. Often represented by the symbol ∅ (ch. 3).

FURTHER READING AND RESEARCH TOOLS

COMPLEX MORPHOLOGY AND VOCABULARY

The following dictionaries of morphemes may be useful for finding more about word elements in the text as well as for elements not in the text.

Borror, Donald J. *Dictionary of Word Roots and Combining Forms, Compiled from the Greek, Latin and Other Languages, with Special Reference to Biological and Scientific Terms.* Palo Alto, CA: Mayfield, 1960.

Quinion, Michael. "Affixes: The Building Blocks of English." Last updated 2020. http://www.affixes.org/.

Shipley, Joseph Twadell. *The Origins of English Words: A Discursive Dictionary of Indo-European Roots.* Baltimore, MD: Johns Hopkins University Press, 2001.

Urdang, Laurence, and Alexander Humez. *Prefixes and Other Word-Initial Elements of English.* Farmington Hills, MI: Gale / Cengage Learning, 1984.

Urdang, Laurence, Alexander Humez, and Howard G. Zettler. *Suffixes and Other Word-Final Elements of English.* Farmington Hills, MI: Gale / Cengage Learning, 1982.

These dictionaries define loanwords that have come into English:

Mawson, C. O. Sylvester. 3rd ed., rev. and ed. by Eugene Ehrlich. *The Harper Dictionary of Foreign Terms.* 3rd ed. New York: Harper & Row, 1987.

Speake, Jennifer, and Mark LaFlaur. *The Oxford Essential Dictionary of Foreign Terms in English.* Oxford: Oxford University Press, 1999. https://www.oxfordreference.com/, 2002.

ETYMOLOGICAL DICTIONARIES

The most comprehensive of all historical treatments of English is the renowned *Oxford English Dictionary*. Now in its second edition and available from Oxford Univesity Press in print, online, and on CD-ROM, it is without doubt the single most valuable source available on English etymology. The printed version of the dictionary exists in both its original twenty-volume format and a photographically reduced one-volume edition—sold with a good magnifying glass! The printed books have been supplemented by a three-volume Additions series with material from the electronic sources. Other recommended etymological dictionaries include the following:

The American Heritage Dictionary of the English Language. 5th ed. Boston: Houghton Mifflin, 2012. https://www.ahdictionary.com/. This dictionary differs from competitors by offering Indo-European etymologies in definitions plus an appendix of Indo-European roots including words derived from them.

Harper, Douglas. "Online Etymology Dictionary." Last modified 2020. https://www.etymonline.com/. This online-only dictionary draws from the major etymological dictionaries of modern English.

SOURCES ON RELEVANT AREAS OF LINGUISTICS

The student may want to refer to the following introductory works for additional information and reading in the various subdisciplines of linguistics discussed in this book.

General Linguistics

Crystal, David. *The Cambridge Encyclopedia of Language.* 3rd ed. Cambridge: Cambridge University Press, 2010.

Finegan, Edward. *Language: Its Structure and Use.* 7th ed. Belmont, CA: Wadsworth, 2014.

Fromkin, Victoria, Robert Rodman, and Nina Hyams. *An Introduction to Language.* 11th ed. Belmont, CA: Wadsworth, 2018.

History of English

Baugh, Albert C., and Thomas Cable. *A History of the English Language.* 6th ed. Abingdon-on-Thames: Routledge, 2012.

Bragg, Melvyn. *The Adventure of English: The Biography of a Language.* New York: Arcade, 2004. This is a companion volume to an eight-part TV series available on DVD.

Millward, C. M., and Mary Hayes. *A Biography of the English Language.* 3rd ed. Boston: Cengage Learning, 2011.

Phonetics

Ladefoged, Peter, and Keith Johnson. *A Course in Phonetics.* 7th ed. Boston: Cengage Learning, 2014. (Includes a CD-ROM.)

Usage and World Englishes

Eschholz, Paul A., Alfred E. Rosa, and Virginia Clark. *Language Awareness.* 13th ed. New York: St. Martin's Press, 2019.

Jenkins, Jennifer. *Global Englishes: A Resource Book for Students.* Abingdon-on-Thames: Routledge, 2014.

Sociolinguistics and Dialectology

Hughes, Arthur, Peter Trudgill, and Dominic Watt. *English Accents and Dialects: An Introduction to Social and Regional Varieties of English in the British Isles.* Abingdon-on-Thames: Routledge, 2013.

Wardhaugh, Ronald. *An Introduction to Sociolinguistics.* 6th ed. Hoboken, NJ: Wiley-Blackwell, 2009.

Wolfram, Walt, and Natali Schilling. *American English: Dialects and Variation.* Hoboken, NJ: Wiley-Blackwell, 2015.

Language and Culture

Bonvillain, Nancy. *Language, Culture, and Communication: The Meaning of Messages.* 8th ed. Lanham, MD: Rowman & Littlefield, 2019.

Language Change, Historical Linguistics, and Language Classification

Campbell, Lyle. *Historical Linguistics.* 4th ed. Edinburgh: Edinburgh University Press, c2021.

Changes from Latin to French to English

Pope, M. K. *From Latin to Modern French.* Rev. ed. Manchester: Manchester University Press, 1961.

Spelling

Cummings, D. W. *American English Spelling.* Baltimore, MD: Johns Hopkins University Press, 1988.

INDEX

For the benefit of digital users, indexed terms that span two pages (e.g., 52–53) may, on occasion, appear on only one of those pages.

abbreviation, 68
  creative, 172
ablaut, 101–2, 243
acronym, 68–70, 74
active voice, 222
acute accent, 238*t*
Adam's apple, 117, 118*f*, 122–24
adaptability, 3–5
adjective
  conversion, 61
  formed by suffixation, 51–52, 53–55, 58, 220–21
affix, 50–55, 58, 63, 72, 78
affricate, 119, 120
Africa, 20, 34
airstream, 117, 122–23
Alfred the Great, 28–29, 32, 194
allomorph, 93–95
  extended, 99–101
  phonology, 95–98
allomorphy, 91–113, 137–51, 243, 245
alveolar articulation, 120
alveolar ridge, 118*f*, 119, 120
American Indian languages, 34
Americanism, 194–95, 199–200
analogy, 72–76
ancestor, 20–21, 22, 28, 29, 235–36
Angle, 27
Anglian dialect, 32

Anglo-Saxon, 25–26, 27
anticipatory assimilation, 138–40
apical articulation, 118*f*
approximant, 119, 121, 124*t*
  Latin, 138, 259–60
  Proto-Indo-European, 241*t*, 242
archaeology, 243–44
arrow, 141
art, 213
articulator, 117, 118*f*, 118–19, 120–22
aspiration, 123–24, 141, 239, 245, 246
assimilation, 115–16, 117, 138–44
  total, 141, 142–44
association, 171, 175–80
asterisk, 239
attested language forms, 20–21
Australia, 34

Babel, 75, 235
back-formation, 72–74
back vowel, 126–27
backronym, 74
base, 51, 53, 54–55, 67, 78–79, 219
bilabial articulation, 121, 138–41
blade of tongue, 118*f*, 120
blend, 65–68, 73–74, 79
borrowing, 5–6, 8–10, 24, 70–71, 77, 92, 96–98, 103–5, 151–52, 220, 257–73
  and Latin and Greek inflections, 214–18

borrowing (*cont.*)
   and Latin verbal forms, 221–23
   and meaning change, 174–75
   Middle English, 30–31
   Modern English, 33, 34–37
   Old English, 29
   prehistoric English, 27
   and usage, 199
bound morph, 51
branches of Indo-European, 22–26, 236–37
breathy phonation, 123–24
   Proto-Indo-European, 238*t*, 239, 241*t*, 245, 246
Britain, 25, 26–27
Britannia, 25

case, 22, 200–1, 214–15, 242–43
Celtic languages, 22, 23*f*, 25, 26–27, 236
central vowel, 126*t*, 127
chain shift, 240
change, 5–6, 10, 11, 20–21, 26–37, 47–48, 235–36, 244–46, 257–73
   [e]>[o], 101–2, 243
   external source, 194
   from variation, 194–96
   internal source, 194
   [k]>[tʃ]>[ʃ], 8–9, 9*t*
   of meaning, 37, 55–56, 167–91, 258
   of pronunciation, 259–60
   of spelling, 258–59
   phonological, 138–51, 217, 222–23
   punctuation of compounds, 60–61
   sound, 8–10, 23–24, 33, 115–16
   source, 194–95
   vowels before [i], 96
Chaucer, 31–32
Chinese, 34
Christianity, 27
circle diacritic, 242
clarity, 200, 201, 203–4
clipping, 63–65, 66–67, 69
Cluster Simplification, 145–46, 151, 217, 222–23
cognate word, 29, 36*f*, 236*t*

coining words, 57–76, 151–52
colonies, 34, 195–96
coloring, 149–50, 242, 245
comparative degree, 220–21
comparative method, 21
complex word, 45–89
compound word, 35–37, 58–78
connotation, 3–4, 194–95
consonant, 117–24, 124*t*, 238*t*, 239–40, 241*t*
   assimilation, 138–44, 217
   deletion, 145–47
   insertion, 116, 147–48
   length, 138
   phonation, 122–24, 141–42, 217, 222–23, 239
conversion, 61–63
coronalization, 264
correspondence, 9–10, 236*t*, 237–41, 238*t*, 243, 246, 247*t*
corruption, 5, 10, 199
creativity, 172
culture terms, 24, 30, 35–36, 243–44

[d] Insertion, 147
deletion, 33, 101, 144–47, 156–57, 221–22, 263
denotation, 3–4, 56, 204
dental articulation, 118*f*, 121, 124*t*, 150–51
   Proto-Indo-European, 240, 241*t*, 245
derivation, 35–36, 36*f*, 53–55, 57–76, 151–52, 219–23, 261–62
   adjective, 55, 220–21
   noun, 219, 220*t*
   verb, 221–23
descent, 9–10, 20–21, 22, 30–31, 35*f*, 36*f*, 235–36, 244–46, 262–63
dialect, 121, 125–26, 127, 194, 195–96, 199–200
dictionary, 1, 4–5, 10, 48–50, 196–97
diminutive, 55, 219
diphthong, 127–28, 258–59, 260, 264
distributive number, 153–54
divergence, 20–21, 104, 194–95, 235, 236–37

INDEX

dorsal articulation, 118*f*
double letter, 144
doublet, 29, 103–5
dual number, 242–43

e-grade, 101–2
East Germanic, 23*f*, 24
element, 45–46, 49, 50–56
ellipsis, 172
end of word, 146–47
ending, 22, 91, 96, 214
    Latin and Greek, 214–18, 216*t*, 223, 242–43, 260–61
    Middle English, 31
    Old English, 28
England, 19, 25–27, 29, 30, 32, 195–97
English
    history, 19–37
    relatives, 22–26
    vital statistics, 1
epenthesis, 156–57
etymology, 47–50, 75–78
euphemism, 182, 203–4
extension, 99–101
extinction, 24, 237

false friends, 13
family of languages, 20–21, 22, 235–38, 243
folk etymology, 75–76
formal style, 3–4, 6, 193–94, 201–3
France, 25, 30, 32, 260
Franks, 25
French, 257–73
    borrowing from, 5–6, 8–9, 9*t*, 33, 34, 35*f*, 103–4, 257–73
    borrowing into Middle English, 30–32
    history, 20–21, 22, 23*f*, 236, 257–73
    Norman, 30
    popular, 262–64
fricative, 118–19, 120–21, 124*t*
    Grimm's law, 239
    Proto-Indo-European, 241, 241*t*
front vowel, 126, 126*t*, 245, 259–60
function, 50–55, 91–94
    grammatical, 51, 54–55

gender, 242–43
generalization, 181
genetic relatedness. *See* relatedness between words
Germanic languages, 22–27, 23*f*, 35*f*, 236, 237–40
gerundive, 223
globalization, 19
glottis, 118*f*, 121, 122–23, 124*t*
Golden horns of Gallehus, 24
Gothic, 24
grade, 101
grammatical function, 51, 54–55
Great Vowel Shift, 33*t*, 33, 71, 240, 260
Greek, 22, 23*f*, 236, 238*t*, 245, 247*t*
    borrowing from, 13, 34–36, 39
    doublets, 104–5
    morphology, 59–60, 78, 213–33
    numeral, 151–56
    pronunciation, 123, 138
Greek Final Stop Deletion, 146
Grimm's law, 23–24, 71, 237–40, 238*t*

height, 125–26, 126*t*, 127–28, 138
Hellenic branch, 22, 23*f*, 236
high vowel, 125–26, 126*t*, 127–28, 138
historical linguistics, 11, 235–36
history, 8–10, 19–44
homonym, 170–71
Hundred Years' War, 32
hyphen, 45–47, 58, 60–61, 214, 221–22

Indo-European, 21–26, 48, 235–54
Indo-Iranian languages, 236
infinitive, 200
infix, 101, 141, 243
inflection
    Latin and Greek, 214–18, 260–61
    Middle English, 31
    Old English, 28
    Proto-Germanic, 22
    Proto-Indo-European, 21, 242–43
informal style, 193
inherited vocabulary, 8–9, 36–37, 261
initialism, 68–70

innovation. *See* change
insertion, 147–48
International System of Units, 154–55
Ireland, 26, 27–28
Italic languages, 22, 23f, 236

jaw, 121, 125–26, 128
Jones, William, 235–36

Kent, 27
kurgan, 244

[l]-Coloring, 150
labial articulation, 118f, 120, 121–22, 124t
    Greek, 245
    Latin, 138–41
    Proto-Indo-European, 241t
labiodental articulation, 121, 141
labiovelar articulation, 121–22
laminal articulation, 118f
laryngeal, 241, 242, 245, 246
larynx, 117, 118f, 122–23
Latin, 23f, 236, 238t, 245–46, 257–73
    borrowing from, 8, 9–10, 9t, 25, 257–62
    borrowing into French, 30–31
    borrowing into Germanic, 24
    borrowing into Middle English, 30–31, 32
    borrowing into Prehistoric English, 27
    doublets, 104
    morphology, 213–33
    numeral, 151–54, 153t
    pronunciation, 137–38
Latin Vowel Weakening, 97–98, 149, 246
    Latin [a] Weakening, 149
    Latin [e] Weakening, 149, 217
Latinate vocabulary, 30–31, 34, 35f, 152
lax vowel, 126t, 127
learned borrowing, 257–62
legal language, 3–4, 203
lengthening, 242, 245, 260
lexeme, 98
lexical element, 58
line, 141
lingua franca, 195–96

lip, 118f, 119, 120, 121–22, 126–27, 238t
Liquid Assimilation, 142
literal meaning, 54, 177, 179, 181
long scale, 154
long sound, 33, 138, 141, 151, 242, 245
low vowel, 126t, 127, 128, 138
lower articulator, 120, 121

macron, 242
manner of articulation, 118–19, 124t, 239
meaning, 3–4, 37, 46, 47–48, 50–57, 167–91, 203–4, 258
melioration, 181–82
metaphor, 56, 175–77, 178t, 179–80, 183
metonymy, 175, 178–80, 183–84
metric system, 154–56, 155t
mid vowel, 126t, 127, 128, 138
Middle English, 29–32, 35f
Midlands, 32
Modern English, 23f, 33–37, 35f, 36f
morph, 91–113
morpheme, 45–58, 77, 91–113
morphology, 3, 11, 45–89, 213–33, 242–43
movable type, 33

narrowing, 180–81
nasal air flow, 119
nasal infix, 101, 141, 221, 243
nasal stop, 118f, 119, 124t
    Latin and Greek, 138–41
    Proto-Indo-European, 241t, 242, 245
native vocabulary, 5–6, 29, 36–37, 97, 246
negation, 53, 56, 115–16, 178t
neologism, 35–36, 57–60
new Englishes, 195–96
nominative case, 200–1, 214–18, 216t
Norman conquest, 29–30
Normandy, 30, 32
Norse, 23f, 24–25, 29, 30
North Germanic languages, 23f, 24–25, 27, 236
North Sea, 25–26
noun
    compound, 58–59
    conversion, 61–63

INDEX 335

formed by suffixation, 54–55, 219
inflection, 28, 214–18
number, 214
stress, 62–63
numeral morpheme, 151–56

o-grade, 101–2
object of verb, 28
obstruent, 119, 124, 124t, 138, 141–42, 259–60
    Proto-Indo-European, 237–38, 238t, 241t
Old English, 23f, 27–29, 35f, 194
Old Norse, 23f, 24–25
onomatopoeia, 70–71
oral articulation, 118–22, 124t
ordinal number, 153–54
origin of language, 20–21

palatal articulation, 121, 124t, 126, 264
palate, 118f, 120, 121–22, 125–26
parent, 20–21
parenthesis, 95
parsing, 7, 46, 47–48, 57, 94–95, 100–1, 144, 171
part of speech, 53, 54–55, 58, 61–63, 168–69
participle, 101, 221–23
passive voice, 53, 222, 261
past tense, 98, 101
pejoration, 181–82
pejorative meaning, 64, 181–82
perfect participle, 222–23
phonation, 122–24
Phonation Assimilation, 141–42, 150, 217, 222–23
phonetics, 115–36
phonological repair, 95–96
phonology, 95–98
pitch, 242
place assimilation, 138–41
place of articulation, 117, 120–22, 138–41
plural, 75, 96, 214–18, 223, 242–43
    allomorphy, 91–93
polysemy, 167–91
postalveolar articulation, 120, 121, 124t, 264
precision, 3–5

prefix, 45–52, 80, 94–95, 97
    allomorphy, 138–41, 142–46, 147–48, 152–53
    meaning, 169, 177, 178t, 183–84
    numeric, 154–56
Prehistoric English, 26–27, 35f, 96
prehistory, 21, 235–54
prescriptivism, 199–203
present participle, 221–22
productivity, 5
pronunciation, 70–72, 91, 93, 115–36. *See also* allomorphy; phonetics
Proto-Indo-European (PIE), 21–22, 48, 235–54
    consonant, 238t, 241, 241t
    grammar, 242–43
    Greek reflexes, 238t, 245
    Latin reflexes, 238t, 245–46
    vowel, 242
protolanguage, 22
punctuation, 60–61, 67, 197
purism, 199–203

Rask, Rasmus, 237–38
reanalysis, 75–76
reconstruction, 21, 238t, 239–44, 241t
regularity, 47–48, 105
relatedness between words,
    derivational, 57–60
    etymological, 8–10, 9t, 29, 47–48, 103–5, 263
    semantic, 47–48, 54–57, 58–59, 170–71, 175–84
Renaissance, 33, 34–35
reverse acronym, 69–70, 74
Rhotacism, 148, 245
Roman Empire, 24, 25, 26–27, 30–31
Romance languages, 22, 30–31, 198–99, 236
romanization, 138
root, 45–51, 58, 152
    aid to spelling, 11
    constituent in compounds, 59–60
    etymological conformity with, 151–52
    Latin and Greek, 219–23
    meaning, 54–56
    same or different, 171
    and word analysis, 49–50

rounding, 121–22, 126–27, 138, 238*t*
rule, 92–93, 138–51
rune, 24

[s] Deletion, 145, 146
[s] Insertion, 147–48
Sanskrit, 235–36, 236*t*
Saxon, 25–26, 27, 28–29, 32
Scandinavian languages, 24–25, 27, 236
schwa, 127
semantics, 11, 54, 55
   change, 167–91
   Latin and Greek affix, 219
   See also meaning
Shakespeare, 28, 33, 167, 175, 198
short scale, 154
side of tongue, 119
singular number, 75, 214, 215–17, 260–61
slash, 141
sociolinguistics, 11
sound. *See* phonetics
sound symbolism, 71–72
space in compound words, 60–61
specialization, 180–81, 183–84
spelling
   clues from word analysis, 11, 57
   French loanwords, 264
   Greek, 13
   inconsistency, 197
   Latin, 137–38, 258–59
   Middle English, 32
   Old English, 28
spelling rule, 145, 216
square bracket, 52, 58
standard, 28–29, 33, 194, 196–99
stem, 214
   Latin, 217, 221–23, 261–62
stop, 118, 119, 120, 123, 124*t*, 150
   breathy, 123–24
   Greek, 146
   Proto-Indo-European, 238*t*, 239–40, 241*t*, 245, 246, 247*t*
stress, 62–63, 97–98, 125, 127, 261, 263
structure, 11, 51–52, 66–68, 72–73, 75
style, 3–4, 172, 193–94

subject of verb, 28, 214–15
suffix
   adjectival, 58, 220–21, 221*t*, 261–62
   allomorphy, 144, 146, 150–51
   derivational, 53, 80, 219–23
   inflectional, 21, 28, 31, 214–18, 216*t*
   meaning, 53–54, 168–69, 168*t*
superfix, 63
suppletion, 98–99
syllabic consonant, 242, 245, 246
syllable, 63, 97–98, 150, 242, 246
   in clipping, 67, 69
   deletion, 261
   distinct from word element, 45
   Latin Vowel Weakening, 149
   and root, 219
symbol, 56–57. *See also* sound symbolism

[t]+[t] to [ss], 150–51
technology, 28–29, 34, 35–36, 167, 213
tense, 22, 98, 101, 221, 243
tense vowel, 126*t*, 127, 128
tip of tongue, 118*f*, 120, 121
tongue, 118*f*
   position for consonants, 118, 119, 120, 121–22
   position for vowels, 125–27, 128
tooth, 118*f*, 118, 119, 121
total assimilation, 141, 142, 143–44
Total Assimilation of *ad*-, 143

umlaut, 96
upper articulator, 120–22
usage, 10, 193–212
uvula, 117, 118*f*

variation
   meanings, 53–56, 167–91
   creative, 172
   dialect and individual, 10–11, 116, 193–212
   punctuation, 60–61
   source, 194–96
   vowel, 125–26, 128
   See also allomorphy

velar, 118*f*, 120, 121–22, 124*t*
   Latin, 138, 141, 143
   Proto-Indo-European, 238*t*, 241*t*, 245
Velar Softening, 163–64, 217, 259–60, 264
verb
   compound, 58–59, 73–74
   conversion, 61–63
   Latin, 221–23
   stress, 62–63
vibration, 122–23
Viking Norse, 23*f*, 24–25, 29, 30
vocabulary,
   Proto-Indo-European, 243–44
   size, 1–5, 10, 172–73
vocal cord, 117, 118*f*, 122–24
vocal tract, 117, 118*f*, 122–23
voicing, 122–24, 124*t*
   Grimm's law, 239
   obstruent, 141–42
   vowel, 125
   See also aspiration; breathy phonation

vowel, 126*t*
   allomorphy, 96, 101–2, 149–50
   deletion, 144–45, 263
   diphthongization, 264
   Great Vowel Shift, 33*t*, 33, 71, 240, 260
   Latin, 138
   phonetics, 125–28
   Proto-Indo-European, 242, 243, 245, 246
   weakening. *See* Latin Vowel Weakening
Vowel Deletion, 144–45

Welsh, 22, 23*f*, 25, 26, 236
West Germanic languages, 23*f*, 24–26, 236
West Saxon, 28–29
widening, 180–81
Winchester, 28–29, 32
writing, 20, 21, 61, 116, 197–98, 203, 204

zero, 101, 144
zero derivation (conversion), 61–63